Riots and Victims

Riots and Victims

Violence and the Construction of
Communal Identity Among
Bengali Muslims, 1905–1947

Patricia A. Gossman

Westview Press
A Member of the Perseus Books Group

Copyright © 1999 by Westview Press, A Member of the Perseus Books Group

Published in 1999 in the United States of America by Westview Press, 5500 Central Avenue, Boulder, Colorado 80301-2877, and in the United Kingdom by Westview Press, 12 Hid's Copse Road, Cumnor Hill, Oxford OX2 9JJ

Library of Congress Cataloging-in-Publication Data
Gossman, Patricia A.
  Riots and victims / Patricia A. Gossman.
    p. cm.
  Includes bibliographical references and index.
  ISBN 0-8133-3625-2
  1. Communalism—India—Bengal.   2. Muslims—India—Bengal.
  3. India—History—20th century.   4. Violence—India—Bengal.
  5. Riots—India—Bengal.   I. Title.
  DS480.45.G675   1999
  303.6'0954'14—dc21   98-50487
                                                                                              CIP

The paper used in this publication meets the requirements of the American National Standard for Permanence of Paper for Printed Library Materials Z39.48-1984.

10   9   8   7   6   5   4   3   2   1

For Joost

Contents

Preface   ix

I   Constructions of Ethnicity
      and Communal Identity   1

II   Creating a Political Community:
      The First Partition of Bengal   19

      The "Backwardness" Factor and
        the Legacy of Religious Reform, 21
      The Agrarian Context, 29
      The 1905 Partition, 34
      The Annulment, 40

III The Function of Violence: Renegotiating
      the Status Order 1918–1926   49

      Renegotiating the Status Order, 51
      The Plasticity of Identity Symbols, 52
      The Rise of Pan-Islamic Concerns, 55
      The Calcutta 'Riot' of 1918, 56
      The Legacy of Non-cooperation and
        Khilafat and the Hindu-Muslim Pact, 63
      The Praja Movement, 66
      The Swarajists and the Hindu-Muslim Pact, 70
      The Search for a 'Muslim' Party, 71
      The Communal Violence of 1926:
        Symbols, Elections, and Violence, 73
      The Calcutta Riots of April–July 1926, 75
      The Pabna Riots of July 1926, 86
      Conclusion, 90

IV   The Politics of Violence:
      Patterns of Organization 1926–1941   102

      The Representation of Violence and Victimization, 103

The Choreography of Violence in Public Spaces, 104
The Dacca 'Riot' of September 1926, 106
The Shivaji Disturbance, 114
The Independence Day 'Riot' of 1930, 115
The Dacca Riot of May 22–30, 1930, 117
The 1941 Dacca 'Riot,' 125
Conclusion, 129

V   The Muslim League's Struggle for Bengal   136

The Search for a Muslim Party (reprise), 137
Capturing the Symbols of Agrarian Reform, 140
The 1936–37 Election Campaign, 141
The KPP-Muslim League Ministry, 143
Capturing the Symbols of Victimization, 147
Muslim League Commissions of Inquiry, 148
The Fight for Control of the
   Bengal Provincial Muslim League, 152

Conclusion   160

Symbols, Elections, and Violence: A 1990 Parallel, 160
Was Bengal Unique? 164
The Logic of Violence, 165

Glossary of Selected Items   173
Bibliography   177
Index   183

Preface

The decade-long itinerary of this study began as an investigation into the construction of a separatist Bengali Muslim political identity. The decision to look more closely at the function of violence in shaping that identity was in part a natural consequence of my coming to terms with what had originally been a rather unwieldy research topic. More important, my decision to focus specifically on violence grew out of my experience monitoring human rights developments in South Asia in my position as principal South Asia researcher for the human rights organization, Human Rights Watch. In the ten years since I began my field work, "communal" violence has become an issue of more than academic interest to South Asianists and South Asians. It has become an issue of urgent concern for all countries of the region.

When I arrived in India in December 1984, Delhi was still reeling from the carnage that had followed the assassination of Prime Minister Indira Gandhi by her Sikh bodyguards on October 31, 1984. Some three thousand Sikhs were killed in an orchestrated pogrom for three days in early November. Despite credible evidence of official connivance and police participation in the violence, no officials or police were ever prosecuted. In the years that have followed, the targets of attack have been Muslim, and police and politicians have again been identified as instigating the violence or participating in attacks.

Yet the myth that even these incidents represent spontaneous eruptions, ignited by historic animosities between religious communities, persists. The politicians who exploit these incidents have frequently cited similar incidents from pre-partition India to bolster their claim that the hatreds that divide communities are immutable and permanent. My frustration with their success in doing so prompted me to look closer at incidents of "communal" violence from the pre-partition period for evidence of planning and clear political motivation behind these "riots." While such an analysis is part of human rights documentation, it has seldom been applied to historical incidents of communal violence.

I have used examples from pre-partition Bengal to show that incidents of "communal" violence are politically-motivated; that incidents of violence are more often than not deliberate and planned; and that the representation of violence itself becomes a symbol which helps freeze popular constructions of identity. In their roles as targets of attack, or recruiters of the perpetrators, and as creators of the myths in their roles as regular witnesses before government commissions of inquiry, the representatives of Bengali Muslim organizations and their Hindu counterparts used violence to redefine relations between the two communities. As reports of aggression and victimization were remembered, embellished and publicly commemorated, violence became ritualized. Because Bengali Muslim leaders were able to create out of the violence symbols that cut across class and religious divisions, they succeeded where peasant leaders and others had failed in identifying Bengali Muslims' sense of themselves as a threatened community, and linking that identity with the movement for a separate state of Pakistan.

A note on terminology: because I contest most colonial applications of the words "riot" and "communal," those words are frequently found within quotation marks. Congress stands for the Congress Party; the League for the Muslim League (ML), and KPP for the Krishak Praja Party. Because all of the records I consulted use the colonial spelling "Dacca" for the capital city of what is now Bangladesh, I have done the same, rather than the generally preferred spelling "Dhaka," which is a more accurate transliteration.

The fact that my research required visits to national archives of three different countries says something about the contested history of this period. I began my work at the India Office Library in London. My time in India was spent at the National Archives and the Nehru Memorial Museum and Library in New Delhi, and the West Bengal State Archives and National Library in Calcutta. In Bangladesh, I examined records at the National Archives of Bangladesh and at district records offices in Dhaka and Chittagong. The collections at Bangla Akademi and the University of Dhaka proved invaluable. Although in my original research plan I had not intended to include any work in Pakistan, I soon discovered that many of the important Bengal Muslim League records were housed in the Archives of the Freedom Movement and the Qaid-e Azam Academy in Karachi. I owe a debt of gratitude to the staff at all of these institutions for their efforts in helping locate files and reports which were often difficult to trace. I am particularly grateful to the staff at the Archives of the Freedom Movement and Qaid-e Azam Academy in Karachi who allowed me to make the most of my limited time there.

None of this travel would have been possible without the generous support I received from the American Institute of India Studies for my research in India, a United States Department of Education Fulbright grant for research in Bangladesh, and a Social Science Research Council grant for research in London. I am also grateful for the support I received from the Committee on Southern Asian Studies at the University of Chicago throughout my tenure there.

In the ten years since I began this project, I have benefited from the support and advice of countless people, most of whom I will be unable to thank here. I would like to single out my advisor, Susanne Hoeber Rudolph, and the other members of my committee, Edward C. Dimock Jr. and Clint Seely. I am particularly grateful to them and other members of the Department of South Asian Languages and Civilizations at the University of Chicago for not losing faith in me as my career as a doctoral candidate dragged on into ten years. I would also like to express my gratitude to the late Professor Fazlur Rahman, who helped me think critically about Islam and identity in the early stages of my research. I am very grateful to the staff of the American Institute of Indian Studies in Calcutta and Delhi for helping me gain access to the research materials I needed in the official archives. Barun De, Partha Chatterjee and others at the Centre for Studies in Social Sciences in Calcutta were generous in providing encouragement and advice. In Bangladesh, a number of people provided invaluable help in everything from locating documents to photocopying them and helping me ship them home. I would like to single out Rafiuddin Ahmed, whose work in this area was an inspiration to me, my research assistant, Ms. Huque, and Mike Boardman, who was a great friend throughout my stay. The staff at the American Cultural Centre were always enormously helpful in getting me access to official records.

In 1994–95, I would not have been able to find the time to complete my research and writing had not my employers at Human Rights Watch generously allowed me to take leave. I am particularly grateful to my colleagues who covered for me in my absence. I would also like to thank Katherine Prior who helped insure that my time off was productive by locating a number of crucial official documents for me in London. Shajahan K. Miah very generously helped me with some translations. Farhad Karim kindly loaned me most of his library on communal violence. A special thanks to those who reviewed my early drafts, particularly Lisa Hajjar and Paula Newberg. And a very special thanks to Diana Tai-Feng Cheng who helped avert a catastrophe when a software upgrade changed the formatting on all my footnotes.

Finally, I would like to thank my best editor and greatest support. It is no exaggeration to say that I could not have finished without the steady encouragement and critical eye of my husband, Joost. Our son, Arent, conceived years later but released to the world months sooner, provided an inspiration all his own.

1

Constructions of Ethnicity and Communal Identity

The history of violence has been treated in the historiography of modern India as an aberration and absence: a distorted form, an exceptional moment, not the 'real' history of India at all. . . . The history of violence is, therefore, almost always about context—about everything that happens around violence. The violence itself is taken as 'known.' Its contours and character are simply assumed: its form needs no investigation.[1]

The cataclysmic events that took place in the town of Ayodhya in the north Indian state of Uttar Pradesh in December 1992[2] compelled many to question the assumptions behind popular explanations of "communalism" in subcontinental politics. South Asianists have not been alone in this exercise. In recent years, theories about ethnicity and nationalism have come under new scrutiny by Western and non-Western social scientists and historians. The impetus for this concern to revisit established theories has come in part from contemporary events, including ethnic genocide in the former Yugoslavia and Rwanda, conflicts over state and ethnic identity in the former Soviet Union, and the growing influence of openly communal political organizations in South Asia. Long before these events, the "primordialist" analysis of ethnic identity was under attack by theorists who argued that ethnic identity was a political construction.[3] One of the most serious challenges to Western theories on nationalism has come from South Asian scholars and those of other post-colonial societies.[4]

At the same time, little has happened to change popular perceptions of communal violence. Western journalists, for example, frequently characterize Hindu-Muslim conflict in India as the product of deeply-rooted historical antagonisms, dating from the Muslim conquest of the subcontinent in the 16th century and exacerbated by the partition of colonial British India into the independent states of India and Pakistan in 1947. Much of the commentary on incidents of conflict over religious sites and symbols in India, including the violence of 1990 and 1992–1993, falls into the same pattern by describing these episodes as regrettable but inevitable given the historical differences between Hindus and Muslims. Following the destruction of the Babri Masjid at Ayodhya, newspapers in the United States and Europe typically depicted the ensuing violence as an example of India's "ancient hatreds." Such views are also endorsed by political groups which espouse the idea of India as a Hindu state.

Although this portrayal has been especially common in the Western press, political leaders and some intellectuals have adopted the same stereotypes. In "The Coming Anarchy," essayist Robert D. Kaplan warns of a future in which a minority will enter a "post-historical" realm where the environment has been mastered and ethnic animosities quelled by bourgeois prosperity, "while the majority will be doomed to a marginal existence on a rundown, crowded planet of skinhead Cossacks and *juju* warriors, influenced by the worst refuse of Western pop culture and ancient tribal hatreds."[5] J. Milton Yinger's 1994 monograph on ethnicity is another case in point. While purporting to "provide analytic tools" for understanding ethnicity, Yinger presents a cursory overview of ethnic conflicts around the world and concludes that, "India's tragic outbreak of religious violence is not surprising . . . India is indeed riven by ancient differences and animosities. But this may, sadly, be more expressive of the human condition in this period than of anything peculiarly Indian."[6] Yinger's work belongs to a genre which has tended to treat communal violence as endemic, flaring up in response to other changes, political or economic, which force social groups into new allegiances or old animosities. Violence, in this view, becomes simply an inevitable by-product of political mobilization.

Much the same kind of thinking is characteristic of press reports and commentary about contemporary "ethnic" conflicts in Europe, Africa, and the former Soviet Union. When the genocidal massacre of Tutsis by pro-government militias in Rwanda began in April 1994, the press routinely characterized it as another example of "tribal slaughter" in Africa.[7] The belief that the potential for such violence lies just below the surface of post-colonial states was confirmed for many by the fact that it followed in the wake of the apparent assassination of the country's president.[8] As Gyanendra Pandey notes, one of the crucial functions such an analysis performs is to legitimize the state—even a dictatorial state—as the only force capable of drawing order out of chaos.[9]

In the past twenty years, a number of writers on nationalism and ethnicity have challenged this view by analyzing the constructed nature of ethnic identity, its variability, and the role leaders play in using symbols to consolidate group identity.[10] Other observers have closely examined the critical role played by popular protest, and have made use of previously untapped sources to document changes in popular perceptions of identity and the motives and interests of those participating in mass movements. Among these, the subaltern school, a collective of scholars of the social sciences and humanities, has raised fundamental questions about the entire historiography of the nationalist movement in colonial India, and in colonial societies generally.

The study of popular culture has taken us another step further from the stereotype of the rioting crowd to look at the function of public ceremony and collective ritual in legitimizing authority and shaping political identities.[11] Finally, academics and civil libertarians who have investigated contemporary incidents of communal violence have documented the role that the state, particularly the police, and other political players, have played in fomenting and organizing outbreaks of communal violence and in participating in them, providing further evidence that such incidents are used to create solidarities and cleavages within and between social groups.[12]

The common thread linking these new studies is the perception that communal identity is not "fixed" but is a political construction, and that collective violence is not the behavior of a frenzied crowd acting out of centuries-old animosities, but a planned political act, a tool of political mobilization used to change popular perceptions of group identification. The process of identity formation is also variable, as competing groups within the same "community" attempt to define the issues and symbols that will unite members who may respond to many different claims on their loyalty. The membership of ethnic or religious communities, too often assumed to be monolithic in character, has divisions which complicate any effort to forge political consensus around any particular symbol.[13] Before the late nineteenth century, Muslims did not, for the most part, understand themselves as part of a larger, North Indian Muslim identity. Nor did they understand themselves as a solidarity—Bengali Muslims—in conflict with their neighbors—Bengali Hindus.[14] Because Bengali Muslim political leaders between 1905 and 1947 were able successfully to create out of the violence symbols that cut across class and religious divisions, they succeeded where peasant leaders and others had failed in creating a unified Bengali Muslim identity and ultimately fusing that identity with the movement for a separate state of Pakistan.

The historiography of communal violence and Muslim identity in South Asia has generally focused on the Muslims of north India.[15] In fact, the Muslims of India never constituted a homogenous community but reflected the regional and linguistic varieties of South Asian Islam. Particularly sharp differences obtained between the Muslims of Uttar Pradesh (U.P.) and other northern provinces, who retained some of the benefits of their previous status as a ruling class, and their co-religionists in Bengal. Unlike the U.P. Muslims, the Bengalis were notably underrepresented in government service, education and other professions, and their numerical strength lay in the *mofussil*, the rural districts where Bengali Muslims made up almost the entire class of tenant farmers and landless laborers.[16] At the same time, patterns of social stratification among Bengali Muslims argue against the construction even of a monolithic Bengali Muslim political culture. The structure of land ownership and cultivation precluded any one single pattern of mobilization among Bengali peasants.

Before Bengal's Muslims could learn to see themselves as part of an all-India Muslim community, they had to have a reason for understanding their political interests as being linked to their identity as Muslims. How and why they came to identify with a common political identity requires a closer study of the various actors that shaped it, and the discursive process in which these actors articulated this identity in contest with each other: the colonial state, the Muslim political parties, the intermediary (initially non-political) organizations and the emerging Bengali Muslim press. But these actors can only tell us so much about changing popular perceptions and mass mobilization. As the subalterns point out, the historiography of the subcontinent[17] has been dominated by the idea that the development of a nationalist consciousness is an achievement of elites, including large landowners, upper-level bureaucrats, and other dominant groups which gradually learned to adapt themselves to the institutions of the colonial state and led the masses from subjugation into freedom.[18] If historians dealt with mass activism in any substantive way, it was as a "law and order problem" or as evidence of the charisma of elite leaders and their ability to attract mass support.[19]

What these accounts leave out is not only changes occurring at the popular level, but the part played by intermediary structures of authority. As David Gilmartin has demonstrated, such intermediaries, particularly the local saints, or *pirs*, played a critical role as links between elite politics and peasant mobilization among Muslims in rural Punjab.[20] In Bengal, religious reformers and peasant leaders who, for different reasons, were hoping to instill in the Bengali Muslims a more developed consciousness of Muslim identity were foremost among those leaders who saw the 1905 partition of the province as a watershed. The partition's repeal in 1911 provided equally fruitful opportunities for these middle level leaders to exploit the loss of the Muslim-majority province of East Bengal as a betrayal of the Muslims by the colonial administration. The years between 1905 and 1911 were marked by violent agitations, as religious reformers joined ranks with peasant organizers to challenge both "anti-Islamic" practices and Hindu dominance in land-holding and money-lending. At the same time, as religious reformers tried to counter colonial encroachments into areas of religious jurisdiction, they competed with each other and with other leaders for positions of authority within the community. Much of that competition took place around symbols that were used to forge new solidarities among Bengali Muslims.[21]

Rival political leaders select symbols out of a variety of available alternatives, and stand to gain or lose by their choice. Which symbol is given priority makes a difference. For example, in Bengal, the struggles over the appropriateness of Bengali as first a "Muslim" language and later a "national" language reflect something of this tension. For non-Bengali Muslim religious reformers at the turn of the century, as for non-Bengali leaders in the Pakistan movement, the Bengali language was deemed suspect because it represented part of a culture shared by Bengali-speaking Hindus. Attempts by West Pakistani leaders to impose a political unity on the diverse cultures that comprised independent Pakistan led, in the case of east Pakistan, to protests over the sanctity of Bengali as an integral part of Bengali Muslim identity, and contributed to the civil war that brought about the independence of Bangladesh.[22] In pre-partition Bengal, other disagreements over the correct interpretation or the appropriateness of Islamic symbols reveal cleavages within the Bengali Muslim community over the role of religious leadership in defining a world view.

The process by which Bengali Muslims, who otherwise had little in common with their Urdu-speaking co-religionists in north India, came to see their common interest with the movement for a separate state of Pakistan did not follow a direct or predictable pattern. Indeed, many of the "communal" disturbances of the 1920s and 1930s reflected divisions within the Muslim leadership much more than they did divisions between Hindus and Muslims. In the pattern that emerges from these incidents, Muslim leaders seeking to unseat those recognized by the British as the "natural" and legitimate spokesmen for the Muslim community used public protest to assert their own claims to be considered legitimate representatives. Incidents that arose out of disputes over custom, in particular, reflected conflicting claims among Bengali Muslim parties over who had a right to interpret tradition.

Even the Muslim League—the party that spearheaded the movement for a separate state of Pakistan that had been founded in Bengal—splintered into rival factions in the province, each claiming to represent the interests of Bengali Muslims but promoting very different policies. Provincial Muslim league politics in the period before partition provides a good example of the importance of a group's political organization not merely representing the interests of, but becoming identical with, the community.[23] Because the Muslim League always insisted on being recognized as the sole representative of Muslim political interests,[24] in Bengal it had to struggle not only to restrain its members from joining with the Congress party[25] or any other groups but also to deal with divisions within its own organization which threatened to split the party into two rival Muslim

Leagues. The factions' competing newspapers reflected the sharp divide over fundamental issues, including land reform, secularism, and the partition of the province.

It is clear that the discourse on ethnicity and nationalism has shifted considerably from the debate over whether ethnic identity is "primordial" or given, or whether it is a social and political construction. Historical differences are not in themselves sufficient to compel social groups to construct separate and unitary political communities or nation-states on the basis of religious or ethnic identity. One of the most articulate spokespersons for the view that elites construct and use cultural symbols to create political solidarities has been Paul Brass, whose work has elaborated the variabilities of ethnic identities and examined how elites manipulate symbols to mobilize members of an ethnic group for specific political objectives. Brass argues that political elites and institutions translate revived loyalties and symbols into political self-consciousness and mold that into a coherent identity capable of making demands on the state.[26] The subalternists, while agreeing that ethnic identity is created, not given, would go further to argue that the idea of primordial identities is itself a colonial construction.[27] In colonial discourse, sectarian conflict is described as arising out of age-old hatreds, "primitive" loyalties—in short, irrational or fanatical behavior peculiarly characteristic of the inhabitants of countries colonized by the West. But no leader is completely free to manipulate symbols for political advantage; a community's history imposes limits on the ways political leaders and other elite groups use symbols to unite a community behind political action.[28]

More important, historical conjunctures in a community's recent past structure political choices about allegiances and identities. By the time major communal riots erupted in Bengal in the 1930s and 1940s, the province had already experienced a fundamentalist Islamic reform movement and Mahatma Gandhi's first mass civil disobedience campaign, both of which at different times mobilized rural Muslims and brought them into conflict with their Hindu landlords. Other events in early twentieth-century Bengal, such as the Khilafat Movement in 1919–1924 and the conflict between tenants and cultivators over the Land Reform Act in 1932 altered the debate over a Muslim identity in the context of mass politics in mid-twentieth-century Bengal. In both cases, Muslim leaders were successful in identifying the interests of the Hindu elite as inimical to the interests of the Bengali Muslim peasant.

Ethnicity, of course, is as much a construction as communalism, determined by political choice not historical accident. In Bengal, examples of this included efforts from the turn of the century up until partition and after to get Bengali Muslims to either change or "Islamize" their language, which was denigrated as corrupted by Hindu (i.e. Sanskrit-derived) words; reform their religion, believed to be similarly corrupted by Hindu or at least non-Muslim practices; and shun non-Muslim political organizations, particularly the Congress.[29]

The argument that political actors plan and carry out acts of communal violence challenges certain assumptions common to colonialist, nationalist, and subaltern "constructions" of communal violence. These constructions generally fail to adequately account for the role of the state and other institutions of civil society in promoting and perpetrating communal violence. Though they differ in their conclusions about the motivations behind communal violence, all three also share a common flaw in attributing either irrationality or, in the case of the subalternists, an idealized class consciousness to those who participate in acts of violence. In addition, the subalternists, who tend to romanticize all initiatives from below, generally fail to recognize that these initiatives are not necessarily unifying. They may also be divisive.

This is not to say that no incident of "subaltern" violence is spontaneous, or that there is not an element of spontaneity in crowd violence. Many of the incidents that most concern the subalterns involve peasant uprisings and other acts of popular resistance against colonial exploitation which may well have been largely directed and controlled internally and would certainly have involved some spontaneous acts of violence against agents of the state. It is true that incidents of "communal" violence often include individual acts of violence motivated by personal or economic considerations. But for most incidents of violence characterized as "communal," violence is used a tool for political mobilization. The formal institutions of the state, particularly the police and other agencies operating at the local level, play a critical role in instigating and participating in acts of violence, or in siding with one or another political group involved in the confrontation. In doing so these agencies create opportunities and reasons for groups to forge separate political agendas on the basis of their perceived role in the violence and their differing relationship to the state.

Although few writers have focused on this aspect of communal violence, the mechanisms by which violence acquires its own symbolic and ritualized place in political mobilization is also constitutive of the process of identity formation. Communalism as a political tool may be defined as the use of violence to forge and strengthen group solidarities. By creating or building on existing feelings of vulnerability, violence is a relatively efficient tool for delegitimizing one group of leaders in favor of another and ensuring electoral victories for certain leaders—those who claim to protect the community and represent its interests. In a charged political atmosphere, contending parties trade accusations of "communalism" and represent incidents of violence to suit their purposes.[30]

The "communal" riots that marked the pre-partition period in Bengal were not the inevitable result of constitutional changes that redefined the balance of power between Hindus and Muslims. The incidents that sparked critical outbreaks of violence were chosen and used by leaders on both sides with an aim toward distinguishing themselves from their rivals as the only ones capable of protecting their community at a time of grave threat. To carry this off, they had to construct their own community as being aggrieved and endangered, the other community as being predatory, and the established leadership as being either complicit or incapable of countering the threat.

The motivations for particular "riots" vary: in Calcutta in 1918, the protests that culminated in a riot were aimed at the British authorities and, by extension, those who collaborated with them. Those who organized the protests were successful in turning a small incident into an issue around which they could rally communal support. The ensuing violence was in effect an act of resistance to state power, a response to the authorities' refusal to permit the protesters from holding their demonstration. While the authorities characterized the incident as "communal," what is more important is the lesson it taught community leaders about the efficacy of taking political action to the streets. By 1926 those same leaders were used to using public protests to spark street violence that would in turn bolster their candidates in local elections. Restrictions imposed by the colonial authorities were repeatedly the target of the protests, as Hindu and Muslim leaders made opposing claims to public space. The violence that followed was designed to demonstrate that they could make that space unsafe for the other community.

Other incidents of violence in 1926 represent a power struggle between different kinds of Muslim leaders: local religious leaders attempted to assert their own authority over Bengali Muslim society by imposing new rules designed both to make Bengali Muslims more *Muslim* and to challenge the established leadership on the grounds that it had not done enough to promote Bengali Muslim interests. Still, the use of religious symbols and loyalties also exposed fissures in the Bengali Muslim "community." While such symbols were useful when used in conjunction with economic grievances to mobilize Muslim peasants against the Hindu land-holding elite in Bengal, they created problems for the Bengali Muslim leadership in its efforts to combine forces with other Indian Muslim leaders who had the support of Muslim landlords.

Violence is an effective tool for political mobilization because it cuts across other divisions and generates solidarity against threatened aggression. I have used examples from pre-partition Bengal to show that incidents of "communal" violence are politically motivated; that incidents of violence are more often than not deliberate and planned; and that the representation of violence itself becomes a symbol which helps freeze popular constructions of identity. In their roles as targets of attack, or recruiters of the perpetrators, and as creators of the myths in their roles as regular witnesses before government commissions of inquiry, the representatives of Bengali Muslim organizations and their Hindu counterparts used violence to redefine relations between the two communities. As reports of aggression and victimization were remembered, embellished and publicly commemorated, violence became an instrument for marking and consolidating group identity.

One important example of this phenomenon in colonial India was the "communal riot report," which generally explained violent outbreaks in terms of "historic" antagonisms which only the British presence could contain. While these reports were the principal historical documents about the riots, the major political parties in India also constructed their own versions of such narratives to explain riots in terms favorable to their own interests and to portray their constituency as victimized. Both kinds of reporting on violence illustrate the way groups perceived the role of the state and the role of competing interests in civil society as perpetrators of the violence and as the forces responsible for granting legitimacy to the claims, and by extension the identities, of those affected by it. Here, Ali Asghar Engineer's description of the state's law and order institutions as including not only the police, but also the "political leaders, bureaucracy and administrative machinery" is apt.[31] In looking at Muslim mobilization in pre-partition Bengal, it is critical to examine the part played not only by the colonial state, but also by elements of civil society, especially the nascent Congress and Muslim League bureaucracies, all of which staked a claim on the loyalty of the Bengali Muslims and played a part in either rationalizing or perpetrating violence. The motives for using violence as a political tool vary. In the incidents in Bengal examined here, political groups resorted to violence to discredit an opponent's perceived accommodationist position, to prejudice election results or the outcome of other official events, or to destabilize the local government by demonstrating that it could not maintain law and order or protect the "minority" community.

What determined a "minority" varied tremendously, depending on whether the speaker was referring to the national, provincial, or local context. The ability of community leaders to persuade their group members and the administration that they constituted a threatened minority was an important factor in the representation of violence in Bengal. In east Bengal, Hindus were in the minority in all but a few districts, although they constituted the majority nationally; in west Bengal, Muslims were the minority, yet, depending on how the "communities" were defined, either group could be made to feel threatened.[32] Political leaders manipulated volatile symbols and created new ones out of each new incident of violence not only as part of a strategy calculated to polarize the Hindu and Muslim communities but also to elicit popular support for whichever political party claimed to represent the interests of the newly vulnerable group.

Similar motivations and strategies lie behind contemporary incidents of communal violence as well, as state and would-be state actors in contemporary South Asia foment communal divisions to further their own agendas. As Engineer's overview of post-independence communal violence makes clear, political parties and organizations, as well as factions within such groups, have continued to exploit communal violence as a tool of political mobilization and a means of redefining political identities. Communal "riots" have been used to bring down state governments, and to demonstrate the unassailability of the dominant political group, be it the Congress party in the 1984 Sikh massacre in Delhi, or upper-caste landlords in violence against Dalits[33] in Gujarat, Bihar and Andhra Pradesh. As Engineer observes, "a riot is generally supposed to be a spontaneous outburst of violence between the two communities. However, it is rarely so. In [the] pre-independence period some major riots belonged to this category. Most of the riots then and almost all the riots now are meticulously planned and executed."[34]

Indeed, the word "riot" for most episodes of communal violence is a misnomer because what these incidents have in common is that they were not the acts of unruly mobs. As George Rudé and E. J. Hobsbawm have shown, the behavior of those participating in popular disturbances is, in many cases, not only disciplined but even routinized.[35]

Few of the incidents that racked Bengal during the pre-partition period represented spontaneous protests against the established order, carried out by the disenfranchised. Rather, the pattern that emerges from these incidents is that they were more calculated than impulsive, as emerging leaders appropriated public space to assert the rights of communities they claimed to represent. Their choice of public space, such as public streets for procession routes, to advertise their separateness was significant, for as Sandria Freitag has observed, "public arena activities legitimated actions that, because they were based on popular culture and shared indigenous values, exerted a tremendous appeal."[36] Each major incident achieved mythic status, living on first in press accounts, then in official inquiries established to determine culpability and award compensation, and finally in the next violent outbreak, in which previously identified targets took on new symbolic significance. This re-enactment was a matter of political design.

Recent studies have distinguished several different categories of violence that emerge in South Asian historiography. In colonialist discourse, violence almost always refers to the behavior of insurgents and seldom to the behavior of the state. The former is illegitimate, the latter, a necessary use of force for the greater good. While recognizing the potential for using popular protest, official nationalist discourse, like its colonialist counterparts, saw most popular violence as inspired by religious fervor or other irrational forces. More important, popular violence posed a threat to a unified resistance to colonial rule, and was therefore denied or suppressed.[37] For the colonialist, outbreaks of violence had to be crushed and proper controls implemented to make sure that it would not break out again. For the nationalist, such impulses should be channeled when useful, and eradicated through education and development when not. In most accounts, violence

> attains the status of an unfortunate fall-out of the onward march of history: an effect of recognizable, 'rational' causes, generally related to the enforcement of state policy, standardization, increased exploitation, dislocation or, somewhat less surely, the clash of 'modern' and 'pre-modern' cultures. . . . The will and reason of the mass of the actors count for little in the historical account of popular violence.[38]

Contrary to what some subalternists would argue, to maintain that most incidents of communal violence are planned and manipulated is not to say that only elites control the popular construction of identity. Because the principal subject of the subalternists' study has been anti-imperialist protest, many acts of popular violence which do not have this as their objective fall outside the scope of their analysis. This includes much of the violence of the 1920–1947 period. The exception is Gyanendra Pandey, whose work on the construction of communalism and whose later essay, "The Prose of Otherness," exposes the failure of both colonialist and nationalist writers to address the violence which in his words not only characterized but constituted partition.[39] Pandey defines communalism as "a form of colonialist knowledge," used to describe a kind of inborn, "primitive" behavior, characterized by religious bigotry and irrationality, which the British believed was endemic to India.[40] Nationalist writers differed from their colonialist counterparts in seeing communalism as largely a product of colonialism itself and of the political and economic disparities created by the colonial state. They nevertheless shared the colonialist view that communalism was a symptom of "backwardness" that could be cured through education and economic development. For nationalist leaders, communalism "was nationalism gone awry."[41]

As the subalternists carefully point out, nationalists borrowed much from the colonialist structures they claimed to reject, including a deep ambivalence about the potential for "fanaticism" among the very masses the nationalist leaders were attempting to mobilize. At the same time, nationalist leaders sought "evidence" in history to bolster their own claims to represent the "real" India, that is an India where an "'enlightened leadership" would bring its "backward peoples" into a truly modern state and realize the dream of India's "historic" unity.[42] Pandey argues that nationalist leaders consigned violence to the sphere of unreason because they could not accommodate it in their view of the rational march toward progress of the modern nation-state.[43]

It is useful to distinguish between two kinds of violence that had a part in the politics of the colonial period: (a) insurgent violence of the kind exemplified in peasant uprisings and worker revolts, and (b)"communal" violence, which was generally marked by attacks on religious symbols and institutions. Politicians from both communities were aware that both kinds of violence created opportunities for mass mobilization. Indigenous elites made efforts to integrate subaltern politics and use them for other purposes. Ranajit Guha notes that, "such effort, when linked to struggles which had more or less clearly defined anti-imperialist objectives and were consistently waged, produced some splendid results." He rather simplistically blames any resulting violence—"nasty reversions in the form of sectarian strife"—on efforts by elites to mobilize subaltern support for issues that lacked a clear anti-imperialist focus.[44] Jawaharlal Nehru and others who found Gandhi's mass appeal fundamentally incomprehensible and somewhat frightening recognized the utility of such techniques, even while they feared the potential for mass violence.[45] In many instances of violence in the latter decades of the nationalist movement, the distinction between clearly "anti-imperialist" objectives and those that were perhaps more mixed becomes more ambiguous. Nevertheless, elites who were not at all inclined to support subaltern objectives on issues like land reform recognized the necessity of engaging mass participation in meetings and campaigns.

This ambivalence among nationalist leaders and colonial authorities about the potential for violence in a mass movement had implications for the recording of incidents of violence by both colonial rulers and their nationalist counterparts. The descriptions fall into a few types. Most commonly, nationalist leaders like Nehru, and the British officials deputed to write reports on the incidents, typically described the participants as a mob, subject to religious passions and superstitions and prone to mindless violence. Responsibility for the violence was also frequently assigned to "outside agitators." Many of the reports on communal disturbances point to recently arrived immigrants and criminal elements as being the principal perpetrators. Even though there was little doubt that such groups did play a part, the reporting tended to remove primary responsibility from locals to the "other."[46] The same kind of reporting is evident in contemporary India. In January 1993, when over 1,000 people, mostly Muslims, were killed in communal "riots" in Bombay, early press reports focused on criminal and "lumpen" elements involved in the violence, and not on the role of the police, many of whom were believed to be sympathetic to the mobs. Leaders of the Shiv Sena, a political party that espouses the cause of *Hindutva*, or Hindu rule, in India, also instigated and participated in acts of violence.

In fact, as many contemporary accounts of communal disturbances in India show, criminal gangs continue to play a part in such outbreaks, usually as recruits of political parties or other patrons.[47] They represent one element in the design of such incidents. Contemporary incidents of mass violence have shown that there are those who plan the killings, those who carry out the orders, and those who join in out of fear or personal vengeance. Participants may include party leaders, civil servants and other political figures who employ the criminals, and other party members or other persons of sufficient wealth or rank to have access to weapons, vehicles, and printing presses or cyclostyles for reproducing handbills and other propaganda. The way in which the police and other state authorities act to encourage or quell the violence also varies. In her introduction to a volume of essays on communal violence in South Asia, Veena Das notes the power of police to declare selective curfews, or time them in such a way that a certain group is affected more than another.[48] Others have examined the construction of identity as arising in arenas of public culture and community action. Violent collective action, like other public ceremonies, functions to unite a community.[49] Freitag discusses outbreaks of violence as "windows" through which we can view the relationships of local communities to each other at points of change. While most "riots" occurred at gatherings of people assembled for other purposes—public ceremonies, especially processions, prayers, and protests—they demonstrate that violence was considered "as one of a range of legitimate options of group action."[50] Those who saw it as such included individuals at every level of participation, including nationalist leaders who elsewhere expressed abhorrence for "the rioting crowd."

The variety of other actors and motives in incidents of collective or communal violence makes any simple elite-mass dichotomy irrelevant. As Das notes,

There is no contradiction between the fact that, on the one hand, mob violence may be highly organized and crowds provided with such instruments as voters' lists or combustible powder, and on the other that crowds draw upon repositories of unconscious images. . . . [J]ust as we study the organization and networks through which crowds are recruited, so must we document the organizing images, including rumours, that crowds use to define themselves and their victims.[51]

Political leaders who attempt to define the issues and symbols that will unite a community may also find their efforts constrained by the fact that different claims on members' loyalty may make it difficult to create political consensus around any particular symbol.

What is significant here is the function of violence in this process and not merely the context in which it has occurred. For Bengali Muslims, violence was used along with other symbols to create solidarities and cleavages within the community and between it and other groups. The "communal" conflict intensified as rival leaders sought to establish themselves as spokesmen and representatives for their community and made use of public events and arenas to evoke the sufferings of the Muslims, their victimization at the hands of Hindu militants, and the failure of the colonial authorities, the Congress, or rival Muslim leaders to protect them. Political leaders manipulated volatile symbols and created new ones out of each new incident of violence not only as part of a strategy calculated to polarize the Hindu and Muslim communities but also to elicit popular support for whichever political party claimed to represent this newly self-conscious Bengali Muslim community.

Notes

1. Gyanendra Pandey, "In Defence of the Fragment: Writing About Hindu-Muslim Riots in India Today," *Representations*, 37, Winter 1992, p. 27.

2. On December 6, 1992, Hindu zealots razed the Babri Masjid, a sixteenth-century mosque in Ayodhya, on the grounds that it had been built over a temple at the site of the birth of the Hindu god Ram. Thousands were killed in the violence which followed, the majority of them Muslims.

3. Paul R. Brass has been one of the most articulate spokespersons for this argument. See especially *Ethnicity and Nationalism: Theory and Comparison* (New Delhi: Sage Publications, 1991).

4. I am thinking primarily of the subaltern school, a collective of scholars many of whose works are collected in the eight-part series of *Subaltern Studies*, published by Oxford University Press. Volumes I–VI are edited by Ranajit Guha; volume VII by Partha Chatterjee and Gyanendra Pandey; and volume VIII by David Arnold and David Hardiman. Partha Chatterjee argues that Western writers on nationalism have presumed the universal applicability of their theories. Moreover, nationalist leaders attempting to free themselves of colonial domination have often adopted the same power relationships and discourse on nationalism they set out to reject. Thus, the states they have created perpetuate the same systems of domination and exploitation. For this reason, some subalternists argue that Indian nationalism is itself a colonial construct, and have attempted to locate a basis for claiming an authentic Indian identity predating colonial rule. Partha

Chatterjee, *Nationalist Thought and the Colonial World: A Derivative Discourse?* (London: Zed Books, 1986).

5. Robert D. Kaplan, "The Coming Anarchy," *Atlantic Monthly*, vol. 273, no. 2 (February 1994), p. 62.

6. J. Milton Yinger, *Ethnicity: Source of Strength? Source of Conflict?* (Albany, NY: State University of New York Press, 1994), pp. 283–284.

7. On April 11, 1994, the *New York Times* reported that the deaths of the presidents of Rwanda and Burundi had "ignited one more round of tribal bloodletting that has plagued this part of Africa for centuries." William E. Schmidt, "Foreigners Evacuated from Battle," *New York Times*, April 11, 1994. In addition to the Tutsis, a number of Hutus known to be critical of the government were also killed.

8. Press reports which described the initial wave of killings as "madness unleashed" are reminiscent of colonial accounts of communal violence in India, in which those participating in the violence were assumed to be operating out of mindless "frenzy." As Alison DesForges has written, "generic analyses of violence in Africa" are limited to "anarchy and/or tribal conflict." These "overlook the organized killings that opened the way to what has become chaos." The assassination of President Habyarimana "provided extremists within the ruling group with the long-sought pretext for wiping out their opponents." Preparations for these killings had been made long before the President's death. Alison DesForges, "The Method in Rwanda's Madness: Politics, Not Tribalism is the Root of the Bloodletting," *Washington Post*, April 17, 1994.

9. Gyanendra Pandey, *The Construction of Communalism in Colonial North India* (Delhi: Oxford University Press, 1990), p. 253.

10. Freitag has used the term "construct" to convey "the active and aware participation of those involved in defining elements of identity." Sandria Freitag, *Collective Action and Community: Public Arenas and the Emergence of Communalism in North India* (Berkeley: University of California Press, 1989), p. 5. See also Brass, 1991.

11. See in particular Freitag, 1989.

12. See *Communal Riots in Post-Independence India*, Asghar Ali Engineer, ed. (New Delhi: Sangam Books, 1984). See also the reports of India's civil liberty organizations, notably the People's Union for Civil Liberties and People's Union for Democratic Rights.

13. See in particular Sandria Freitag, 1989, and Rafiuddin Ahmed, *The Bengal Muslims 1871–1906: A Quest for Identity* (Delhi: Oxford University Press, 1981). Francis Robinson, in *Separatism Among Indian Muslims: The Politics of the United Provinces' Muslims 1860–1923* (Cambridge: Cambridge University Press, 1974), argues that although there certainly have been divisions among Muslims in India, they have a primordial identification with religious symbols and that organizing on the basis of this fixed identity is a given.

14. The British generally used the term "Bengali" to refer only to the Hindu population of Bengal. Bengali Muslims were usually referred to simply as Musulmans, Mussulmans or Muhammadans, as were Muslims throughout India. W.W. Hunter's famous work on the Muslims of Bengal was entitled *The Indian Musulmans*. With the expansion of the Muslim press in Bengal (particularly the Bengali press), and the growth of Muslim political parties in the province, the preferred term became "Bengal Muslims," although its use was also inconsistent.

15. Rafiuddin Ahmed's work was one of the few to deal specifically with Bengali Muslims. See R. Ahmed, op. cit. Partha Chatterjee's, *Bengal 1920–1947: The Land Question* (Calcutta: K. P. Bagchi, 1984) and Sugata Bose's *Agrarian Bengal: Economy, Social Structure and Politics, 1919–1947* (Cambridge: Cambridge University Press, 1986) represent important studies of the links between agrarian changes and political developments in Bengal generally. See also Dipesh Chakravarty's "Communal Riots and Labour: Bengal's Jute Mill-Hands in the 1890's," *Past and Present*, no. 91, May 1981. Suranjan Das' *Communal Riots in Bengal 1905–1947* (Delhi: Oxford University Press, 1991) describes many of the more important disturbances in Bengal. For other works on Bengali politics, see Sumit Sarkar, *The Swadeshi Movement in Bengal 1903–1908* (New Delhi: People's Publishing House, 1973), J. H. Broomfield, *Elite Conflict in a Plural Society: Twentieth Century Bengal* (Berkeley, CA: University of California Press, 1968), Leonard A. Gordon, *Bengal: The Nationalist Movement 1876–1940* (New York: Columbia University Press, 1974), and Rajat Kanta Ray, *Social Conflict and Political Unrest in Bengal 1875–1927* (Delhi: Oxford University Press, 1984). For studies of north Indian Muslims, in addition to Paul Brass and Francis Robinson, see Freitag, 1989, David Lelyveld, *Aligarh's First Generation: Muslim Solidarity in British India* (Princeton: Princeton University Press, 1978), and David Gilmartin, *Empire and Islam* (Berkeley: University of California Press, 1988). George Mathew has discussed Muslims in South India in "Politicization of Religion: Conversion to Islam in Tamil Nadu," parts 1, 2, *Economic and Political Weekly*, June 19 and 26, 1982.

16. For British colonial constructions of Muslim identity, W.W. Hunter's 1871 work, *The Indian Musulmans: Are they Bound in Conscience to Rebel Against the Queen?* (Calcutta: Government of Bengal, 1871), is invaluable. See also Peter Hardy, *The Muslims of British India* (Cambridge: Cambridge University Press, 1972).

17. The subalternist school evolved in a community of scholars studying South Asia, but it is reasonable to assume that the subalternist perspective would apply equally well to other regions that underwent a period of colonial domination, including Africa and the Middle East.

18. Ranajit Guha, "Historiography of Colonial India," in Ranajit Guha and Gayatri Chakravorty Spivak, eds., *Selected Subaltern Studies* (Oxford: Oxford University Press, 1988), pp. 37–38.

19. Guha, 1988, p. 39. See also E. J. Hobsbawm, *Primitive Rebels: Studies in Archaic Forms of Social Movement in the 19th and 20th Centuries* (New York: Manchester University Press, 1967), and George Rudé, *The Crowd in History* (New York: Wiley, 1959).

20. David Gilmartin, *Empire and Islam* (Berkeley: University of California Press, 1988).

21. As Brass notes, "the process of nationality-formation is one in which objective differences between ethnic groups acquire increasingly subjective and symbolic significance, are translated into a consciousness of, and a desire for, group solidarity, and become the basis for successful political demands." Brass, 1991, p. 22.

22. For more on the language movement in East Pakistan, see Rounaq Jahan, *Pakistan: Failure in National Integration* (New York: Columbia University Press,

1971), and Patricia A. Gossman, "Poets and Politics: Some Reflections on the Language Movement in East Pakistan," in Ray Langsten, ed., *Research on Bengal: Proceedings of the 1981 Bengal Studies Conference* (East Lansing, MI: Asian Studies Center, Michigan State University, 1983), pp. 19–26.

23. Brass, 1991, p. 48. As Brass notes, "the important goal for nationalist movements in this regard is exclusivity, the drive to become the sole political representative of the community so that the community may act cohesively and unitedly. This is especially important if the group is a minority, for a cohesive minority may be able to achieve its goals against a larger, but more fragmented group, whereas organizational division in a minority ethnic group may be fatal to its interests." Ibid., p. 49.

24. Ibid.

25. The Indian National Congress was founded in 1885 as a vehicle for representing Indian interests to the British colonial government. Originally loyalist in its stance, it soon became the voice for India's independence movement. The 1905 partition of Bengal was an important factor in spurring the Congress to reject its loyalist position.

26. See Paul Brass, *Language, Religion and Politics in North India* (Oxford University Press, 1974).

27. While it is true that British historiography has held that Muslim and Hindu identities were primordial and natural, that view did not originate with the British. Pre-colonial historians and administrators had made a similar case for "natural" distinctions based on religion or ethnicity.

28. Both Paul Brass and Francis Robinson have discussed the significance and use of primordial symbols in identity formation among Muslims of colonial India. See Brass, 1974, and Robinson, 1974.

29. Other examples can be found in the conflicts in Punjab and Kashmir in the 1980s and 1990s. In Punjab in 1990, militant Sikh groups attempted to impose a "code of conduct," stipulating appropriate dress and behavior for Sikhs in the state. Together with liquor, cinemas, and other symbols of "Western" culture, dowry and elaborate wedding parties were banned, and militant groups frequently scrutinized marriage ceremonies to enforce their dictates. Those found guilty of violating the code could be punished with heavy fines, or in some cases, death. In the early 1990s, similar efforts by some Muslim militants in Kashmir focused on compelling women to wear the *burqa*, a cape-like garment covering the entire body. The campaign proved less successful, in part because the practice was successfully identified by other leaders in Kashmir, including those associated with rival and more popular militant organizations, as being alien to Kashmiri culture. On the other hand, a ban on liquor sales, prohibited by all the groups, was enforced throughout the Kashmir valley for several years.

30. For more on the selective representation of violence, see Paul R. Brass, *Theft of an Idol: Text and Context in the Representation of Collective Violence* (Princeton, NJ: Princeton University Press, 1997).

31. Asghar Ali Engineer, "Communal Violence and Role of Police," *Economic and Political Weekly*, vol. 29, no. 15, April 9, 1994, p. 835.

32. Today in India, Hindu nationalist parties look to regional geo-political configurations to claim a threatened minority status for Hindus because India is

"surrounded" by Muslim majority countries. Much the same strategy has been used by Sinhalese chauvinist groups in Sri Lanka, who have claimed that the Tamil inhabitants of Sri Lanka are part of a Tamil majority that includes the Indian state of Tamil Nadu, and by Jews in Israel who see themselves as a Jewish island in an Arab sea.

33. Dalit, meaning the oppressed, has become widely used to identify low-caste ("untouchable") and tribal groups in India.

34. Engineer, 1994.

35. See Hobsbawm, 1967, and Rudé, 1959.

36. Freitag, 1989, p. 292.

37. Some subalternists, notably Pandey, Chatterjee, and Shahid Amin, criticize official nationalist discourse on this point. See Pandey 1990, 1994; Chatterjee, 1986; Shahid Amin, "Gandhi as Mahatma: Gorakhpur District, Eastern U.P., 1921–2," in *Subaltern Studies III: Writings on South Asian History and Culture*, Ranajit Guha, ed. (Delhi: Oxford University Press, 1984), pp. 1–61.

38. Gyanendra Pandey, "The Prose of Otherness," *Subaltern Studies VIII: Essays in Honour of Ranajit Guha* (Delhi: Oxford University Press, 1994), pp. 191–203.

39. Pandey, 1990 and 1994.

40. Pandey, 1990, pp. 6, 10.

41. Ibid., pp. 12, 14.

42. Pandey, 1990, p. 253.

43. Ibid.

44. Guha, 1988, p. 42.

45. This is the point Partha Chatterjee makes with respect to Gandhi's skills at popular mobilization. Chatterjee, 1986, pp. 150–157. See also Broomfield, p. 159.

46. Pandey, 1994, pp. 199, 212–213.

47. Engineer, 1994.

48. Veena Das, "Introduction," *Mirrors of Violence: Communities, Riots and Survivors in South Asia*, Veena Das, ed. (Delhi: Oxford University Press, 1992), p. 23.

49. Freitag, 1989, p. 280.

50. Ibid., p. 95.

51. Veena Das, p. 28.

2

Creating a Political Community: The First Partition of Bengal

The first major outbreak of "communal" violence in Bengal was precipitated by an act of boundary drawing, when the colonial administration, for reasons both political and administrative, partitioned the province of Bengal into two smaller Hindu- and Muslim-majority provinces in 1905. The redrawing of the boundary provided the catalyst for political organizers to mobilize the majority communities on both sides of the new border around religious and economic symbols. Religious reformers and peasant leaders who, for different reasons, were hoping to instill in the Bengali Muslim a more developed consciousness of his or her Muslim identity were foremost among those leaders who saw 1905 as a watershed. The partition's repeal in 1911 provided equally fruitful opportunities for these middle level leaders to exploit the betrayal of the Muslims by the colonial administration. The years between 1905 and 1911 were marked by violent agitations, as religious reformers joined ranks with peasant organizers to challenge both "anti-Islamic" practices and Hindu dominance in landholding and money-lending.

Before the 1905 partition, Bengal had been one of the largest provinces in British India, too large to be administered effectively, according to local officials. It was also the seat of the colonial government, and for that reason was at the center of nationalist agitations. The partition created the new province of Eastern Bengal and Assam, while for administrative purposes the rest of Bengal, including Calcutta, remained joined to Bihar and parts of present-day Orissa.[1] This act of boundary drawing provided the occasion for a number of actors—political elites, religious reformers and British administrators—to re-formulate Bengali Muslim political identity. In undivided Bengal, Muslims had been a minority; Eastern Bengal and Assam was predominantly Muslim. In a single act, the creation of the new province vaulted Muslim leaders into positions of power. Religious reformers who were hoping to instill in the Bengali

Muslim a more developed consciousness of identity were foremost among those leaders who saw 1905 as a watershed. The changes also created opportunities for new political leaders to emerge and claim themselves as the natural representatives of the Bengali Muslims.

Opposition to the partition and support for it followed religious lines. Economic divisions were particularly sharp in the eastern province, where the Hindu minority made up almost the entire landlord class. Before long, an anti-partition campaign that involved the boycott of British goods and the promotion of indigenous (*swadeshi*) products, engendered its own counter-protests. Itinerant Muslim preachers who had already gained considerable influence in the province in their efforts to reform Bengali Muslim practices mounted a campaign to portray the *swadeshi* movement as anti-Muslim, and linked it with other exploitative practices that affected Muslim tenants and cultivators. In doing so, they provided Muslim leaders with the clinching symbol they needed to forge a link between their political interests and the religious identity of the majority in eastern Bengal. In a pattern that came to characterize political mobilization of the Muslim population in Bengal, Muslim elites formed a temporary, and ultimately untenable alliance with Muslim religious leaders in the rural areas—the *mofussil*—in order to frame their appeals in terms of the interests of the Bengali Muslim peasants. The "backward" and impoverished Bengali Muslim peasantry thus became a symbol for two unlikely sets of leaders: the urban, educated elites who saw it as an instrument that would help persuade the colonial authorities to promote "Muslim" interests, and popular religious leaders who believed that this underclass was the key to spreading their own reform message.

The prominent role assumed by religious leaders in encouraging tenant resistance to *zamindari* oppression has been generally taken for granted in most histories of this period.[2] However, the sufferings of the Bengali Muslim peasant and the growth of religious reform movements in the area had been well understood for at least thirty years prior to the 1905 partition. Why they came together at this time has as much to do with the bureaucratic changes wrought by the partition and the nationalist response to them as with the explicit roles played by leaders who arose to take advantage of the political environment that had been created by the new boundaries. There were four elements that converged at the time of the creation of the new province in eastern Bengal in 1905: the existence of a popular religious leadership which had already found fertile ground among the better-off peasants; increased economic pressure on the poorest cultivators at a time when there was growing recognition of tenants' rights generally; the presence of an educated Muslim elite who, while having virtually no contact with the mass of Bengali Muslims in the new province, voiced their support for the move in terms of the educational and political needs of this disadvantaged group; and the backlash from Bengali nationalists, primarily Hindu, whose *swadeshi* tactics were seen and exploited at both the elite and popular levels of Muslim leadership as evidence of the anti-Muslim intentions of the Hindu nationalists.

While there was no explicit alliance between the educated *ashraf*[3] Muslims who supported partition as a way to secure government patronage for themselves and the *maulvis* (the traditionally educated Muslim clerics) who did not so much support partition as oppose the anti-partition activists, they effectively worked along parallel lines, reinforcing each other's efforts. Both could frame the protests of the anti-partition activists as both anti-peasant and anti-Muslim.

Before turning to the partition itself, it is important to get a sense first of the meaning of the 'Muslim community' in the years that preceded it.

The "Backwardness" Factor and the Legacy of Religious Reform

One of the most important reasons the colonial administration came to the conclusion that Bengali Muslims were a distinct community and needed special consideration was the perception that Muslims were disaffected with British rule because they had suffered disproportionately from it. Before the census of 1871, the colonial administration had not even been aware of the size of the Bengali Muslim population.[4] However, the primary reason for British concern about their Muslim subjects was because of what they feared was a potential for rebellion among them. Two religious reform movements—the Fara'idi and the Tariqah-I-Muhammadiya—which arose in the mid-nineteenth century in Bengal posed a challenge to British authority in India. As discussed below, these movements had considerable impact among Muslim peasants in eastern Bengal where the movements' leaders worked to create a consciousness among Bengali Muslims of their part in a larger Muslim world community. Until then, such a consciousness had not played a significant part in the development of Bengali Islam.

When Islam arrived in Bengal,[5] first by way of the Turks in 1201 A.D., and later by the Mughals, it was absorbed by a culture criss-crossed by the varieties of religious beliefs and practices that had persisted there. These beliefs, which included those espoused by Tantric Buddhist and Vaisnava sects,[6] marked Bengal as a place beyond the pale, a land so ritually impure, that in medieval times Hindus were reportedly obliged to undergo purificatory rites upon returning from it.[7] In some cases, Bengal was used as a place of punishment for recalcitrant Mughal generals.[8] The Muslim penetration of Bengal followed two patterns. One was represented by the scholars, who saw themselves as guardians of the culture and who wrote religious texts, maintained *madrasahs*, and did their utmost to influence the local administration along Islamic lines.[9] The other belonged to the sufis, generally credited with reaching furthest into the rural hinterlands and converting predominantly low-caste Hindus to the faith, the majority of whose descendants made up the Muslim population in east Bengal in the twentieth century.

In much of north India, as in Bengal, the spread of Islam is credited to the teachings of great sufi saints. David Gilmartin credits the increase in conversion in rural Punjab to the presence of saints' *khanqahs*, or centers for teaching and prayer, which operated as outposts of the saint's authority and drew in local tribes. A close relationship developed between these outposts and the political institutions of the Mughal state, bringing the newly converted tribes under the hegemony of the Muslim power in Delhi.[10] In Bengal, the situation was somewhat different. The "frontier"[11] conditions obtaining in Bengal, and rural east Bengal in particular, worked against the establishment of a strong relationship between the centers of Muslim power in Gaur, Dacca, and, later, Murshidabad, and the local Muslim population. The Bengali Muslim peasant community operated within ideas of community and authority that were more or less self-contained, out of sight of the institutions of state power and the Islamic culture of north India. The institution of the sufi saints, or *pirs*, however, was of great importance. *Pirs*—living and dead—represented an extremely powerful social force throughout Bengal, providing mediation to higher spiritual authorities, or boons to the local faithful.[12]

In the Mughal period, the sufis, scholars, and the ruling class in Bengal were all of non-Bengali origin, drawn from the ranks of Muslims emigrating from beyond the western borders of India, or later, from Delhi and the northern centers of Mughal culture. Thus from the outset, a cleavage developed between those Bengali Muslims who could claim foreign descent and the local converts, between those claiming closer blood ties to the Prophet and greater proximity to the sacred places of Islam, and the local converts whose religious practices retained elements arising from the culture in which they found themselves. That this distinction mattered a great deal to *ashraf* Muslims is apparent from an article published in 1895, complaining about the fact that the officiating commissioner of the Burdwan district had described the Muslims of the area as "mostly cultivators, labourers and traders."

The author grumbled that "Mr. Dutt should have been aware of a respectable landowning class [in Burdwan] . . . and that the large Muslim population [there] [is] due to a large settlement of Mohammedans from Northern India rather than to forcible conversion of the people to Islam."[13]

For very different reasons, the discrepancy between these two worlds concerned Haji Shariatullah (1781–1840), a resident of Faridpur who had made the pilgrimage to Mecca and had been inspired by Arabian Wahhabism.[14] Upon his return he founded a reform movement based on the *farz*, or obligatory duties of Islam, from which the movement acquired the name Fara'idi. Shariatullah wanted to purge Bengali Islam of un-Islamic practices, particularly sufi practices, *pirism*, the veneration of Hindu deities and the celebration of Hindu festivals.[15] His followers preached against the "pantheon of confused beliefs which had accumulated: semi-divine deities from multi-religious and cultural contacts, superstition, animism, demotic syncretism, *bhakti* movements, sufi tolerance, ontological monism, poetic license and several other sources, Indian as well as foreign, but all of them alien to fundamental Islam."[16]

Similar reform movements had tremendous impact throughout north India in the second half of the nineteenth century. As David Gilmartin observes, in Punjab:

> During the late 19th and 20th centuries, these ulema developed through public debate, popular preaching and the extensive dissemination of religious literature in Urdu, a new conception of the Islamic community in India which depended not on any sort of links to political authority but on the widespread teaching of the fundamentals of orthodox Islamic belief and practice.[17]

The Fara'idis also declared Bengal *dar-ul-harb* (zone of war), and prohibited Friday prayers as being unlawful in a land lacking a Muslim ruler. However, these efforts put them in direct confrontation with the entrenched leadership of the village *pirs* and mullahs who in fact represented the only authority for the kind of Islam practiced by the majority of Bengal's rural Muslims.[18]

As in Punjab, the reformists took it on themselves to be "the custodians of the conscience of the community."[19] They did not, however, succeed in usurping the position of the *pirs*. In both Punjab and Bengal, *pir*-worship continued. Although they could not, on their own, make Muslims more conscious of their identities as Muslims, the reformers represented instead another voice, another kind of authority for the changing structure of the Muslim community. In fact, both kinds of authority—that of the *pirs* and that of the reformers—found a place in Muslim politics. And in their search for leaders to represent this community, the colonial administration supported yet a third group—the Western educated and urban elites who had little contact with the 'ulama, and still less with the mass of Muslims of rural Bengal.

Shariatullah's son and successor, Dudu Miyan, went further than his father, linking the missionary objectives of the Fara'idi movement to an economic campaign against Hindu landlords. He preached against illegal taxes, arguing that the money might be spent on Hindu practices.[20] Earlier, Titu Mir had worked with Muslim peasants in western Bengal to resist illegal taxes that supported Hindu festivals. He organized his followers to lead attacks on Hindu temples and was killed in a conflict with British troops after one such incident in 1831. These were the first serious rebellions linking Muslim identity to resistance against oppression by Hindu landlords—a theme which came to dominate the symbols of agrarian politics one hundred years later. What was particularly remarkable about the Fara'idis, however, was their extensive organization throughout rural East Bengal. Under Dudu Miyan, membership in the movement was organized under local leaders called *khalifa*s who collected dues, officiated at popular courts of arbitration, and instructed the members on the tenets of the movement.[21] The movement continued to live on in the imagination of British administrators who were inclined to consider all the trouble-making itinerant *maulvis* of later generations and different political causes Fara'idis or "Wahhabis." Later reformers followed the pattern set by the Fara'idis—linking spiritual reform to resistance against oppressive tenancy regulations and illegal taxes.

More worrisome to British administrators, however, was the *jihad* movement of Sayyid Ahmad Barelwi (1786–1831). He launched his reformist Tariqah-I-Muhammadiya movement after returning from the *hajj*, the sacred pilgrimage to Mecca, in 1821, in order to rid Indian Islam of practices that he believed compromised fundamental Islamic tenets.[22] In 1826 he declared jihad against the Sikh ruler of Punjab, Ranjit Singh. After Sayyid Ahmad was killed in 1831, his followers continued to funnel recruits and money, principally from Bengal, to the rebels' base in Sittana, near Peshawar, from where they launched attacks not only on the Sikh forces but on the British. These continued after the British seized Punjab following the defeat of Ranjit Singh's forces in the second Sikh war of 1848–49. The movement was finally crushed after the British captured its top leaders, including a large number of Bengalis, many of whom were tried and convicted of "waging war against the Queen" in the "Wahhabi" trials held between 1864 and 1871.

The fear that the jihad campaign was part of a larger Muslim conspiracy against British rule prompted the Viceroy to commission W. W. Hunter, a civil servant, to research the conditions of the Indian Muslims to determine whether they were "bound by their religion to rebel against the Queen." Although most of Hunter's study concerns what he calls "the rebel camp on our frontier," it was his inquiry into the "grievances of the Muhammadans"[23] which had the greatest impact. Quoting the officer in charge of the prosecution at the Wahhabi trials, Hunter blamed "the great hold which Wahhabi doctrines have on the mass of the Muhammedan peasantry" on "our neglect of their education."[24] His concern was to insure that educated Muslims did not feel an obligation to oppose British rule, and to counter those advocating rebellion by establishing Muslim schools throughout Bengal, and especially in the "fanatical eastern Districts" where

> Fifty cheap schools, with low-paid Musulman teachers . . . would in a single generation change the popular tone of Eastern Bengal. . . . We would thus enlist on our side the very class which is at present most persistently bitter against us. . . . We should thus at length have the Muhammadan youth educated upon our own plan. Without interfering in any way with their religion . . . we should render that religion perhaps less sincere, but certainly less fanatical.[25]

The government was soon convinced to act on Hunter's recommendations in order to foster a Muslim leadership capable of counterbalancing what it saw as the forces of treason within the Muslim population.

Although the focus of Hunter's study was the Bengal Muslims, the conclusions he drew were then generalized for Indian Muslims everywhere.[26] As Pandey observes, from the time that Hunter's book was published, "the belief had gained ground that the Indian Muslim community as a whole had fallen behind the Hindus in education, recruitment to government service, advancement in 'modern' industries and other economic activities, and, consequently, in social and political position as well as in a more general self-confidence."[27] Paul Brass examines the Hunter thesis as it has been used by the Muslim leadership, particularly in the United Provinces (U.P.), to "cultivate a sense of common grievance capable of appealing to the sentiment of the entire community." He notes that "Hunter's arguments, generalized for the whole of India, soon became integrated, with embellishments, into the mind of Muslim elites, who used them to appeal to British policy makers and later to the Muslim masses."[28]

Scholars of Muslim separatism in India, most of whom have focused on the mobilization of Muslims in the U.P.,[29] have noted that sharp differences obtained between U.P. Muslims and their Bengali co-religionists. Francis Robinson, for example, has argued that between 1860 and 1923, Muslims from Punjab and Bengal "contributed little to specifically Muslim politics, their politicians preferring to use other platforms."[30] While his assertion is debatable, there is no question that Bengali Muslims for the most part had little in common with U.P. Muslims. For one thing, by 1911, Bengali Muslims outnumbered U.P. Muslims, with the former making up 53 percent of their province's population to the U.P. Muslims' 14 percent. But while 28 percent of U.P. Muslims lived in towns, only 4 percent of Bengali Muslims did.[31] But these statistics were true of Bengali Hindus as well. Poor Bengali Muslims were not worse off than their Hindu counterparts. The lack of Muslims in higher education in Bengal was a direct consequence of the "preponderance of the poorer classes in the Muslim population,"[32] particularly tenant cultivators and landless laborers.

After the publication of Hunter's report in 1871, education became the battleground for competing claims on Muslim identity. The British authorities, persuaded that English education would foster a loyal leadership capable of checking what they saw as the fanaticism of the lower classes, launched a concerted effort to attract Bengali Muslims to English schools. Contrary to the usual policy of not supporting denominational schools, the government offered scholarships, added Persian, Urdu, and Arabic to the school curricula, and brought traditional *madrasahs* under the supervision of the education department.[33] These last continued to be the more popular among Muslims hoping to improve their status in the community by giving their sons a religious education.

At the same time that British administrators became aware of the need to promote English education among the Muslims, religious reformers were continuing the work of the Fara'idis and others to rid Bengali Islam of unacceptable un-Islamic accretions. The effects of their work among lower-class Muslims became apparent in the years between the census of 1871 and 1901. Although changes in census-taking, including new categories in the kinds of questions asked, make side by side comparisons between the censuses misleading, there is compelling evidence that Bengali Muslims began to identify themselves more and more by the "Muslim" categories of Syed, Sheikh, Pathan, and Mughal. In 1872, only 1.52 percent (somewhat less than 270,000) of the Bengali Muslim population had so identified themselves, but by the 1901 census, those identifying themselves as Sheikhs jumped from 232,189 to 19,527,221.[34] The trend was not restricted to Bengal. In Bihar, between 1901 and 1911, Muslims began identifying themselves as Pathans, Khans, and Sheikhs.[35] At the same time, Muslim journals and newspapers in Bengal increasingly adopted Persian or Arabic names, and made a point of expanding their coverage of events from the larger Islamic world.[36]

Perhaps more important than the activities of itinerant Fara'idi preachers, however, was the colonial government's own effort to classify the Muslim population.

The late nineteenth and early twentieth centuries saw a mushrooming of caste associations and caste movements, of claims to new (higher, purer) status and demands for new names to be registered in the administrative record. Without doubt, this process was considerably accentuated by the Census Commissioner's decision in 1901 to classify 'castes' and 'communities' all over the country in accordance with their ritual purity and standing in local society.[37]

The fact that the 1901 census included these names as "caste" categories for Muslims[38] appeared to confer legitimacy to the changes. According to Rafiuddin Ahmed, in 1901 Muslim *jolahas* (weavers) petitioned the government to permit them to list themselves as "Sheikhs." The government refused, but allowed them to list themselves by other names, including *momin* (faithful).[39] By 1911, the Census Commissioner allowed the change to "Sheikh." Because the authorities would not record "caste-names" unless they were represented in sufficient number in the area or were linked to groups known for "criminal" behavior or other special characteristics,[40] the *jolahas* had to mobilize their own community for the sake of the benefits of registering under a more "respectable" name.[41] Leaders among the *jolaha* clearly saw that the colonial authorities could be persuaded to confer some recognition that the Muslim elite would not.

The formation of the Central National Muhammadan Association and other such elite groups gave the Muslim urban community, which was largely non-Bengali and made up of Muslims from U.P. and elsewhere in north India who resided in Calcutta, a voice, but one with little contact with Muslims in rural East Bengal. The Muslim Education Committee, an organization founded in 1895 to push for greater government support for Muslim education, was made up of wealthy Muslim landlords and merchants.[42] The upper class Muslims in these organizations continued to push for separate facilities in higher education for their own benefit, although they often did so in terms of the needs of the "backward" Muslim community. In fact, members of the educated elite had little interest in mass education. Up until 1872, the Calcutta Madrasah admitted only those students who could produce a *sharafatnama*, a certificate of "respectability."[43] In 1869, Syed Amir Ali, a member of Bengal's *ashraf* Muslim society and founder of the National Muhammadan Association, spoke out against opening *madrasah* education for "the children of those classes who have taken to husbandry or the low professions" because it was against the natural order of things.[44] There was little to link the mass of Bengali Muslims with the kind of leadership represented by these organizations "whose immediate object was to obtain for themselves a larger share in government jobs and higher education."[45]

Other would-be leaders of the Muslims took up the cause of the "backward" Muslims and voiced their demands on the colonial state in terms of redressing this imbalance between Muslims and Hindus even though, outside Bengal, there were not always great discrepancies between the two.[46] From the outset, concern over the "backwardness" of the Muslims was framed in terms of the relative "advancement" of the Hindus. Hunter explained that his primary concern was to determine why Muslims had "held aloof from [the British] system, and the changes in which the more flexible Hindus have cheerfully acquiesced."[47] He concluded that, with education, "the rising generation of Muhammadans would tread the steps which have conducted the Hindus, not long ago the most bigoted nation on earth, into their present state of easy tolerance."[48] The Muslim press adopted the same language to express regret over the fallen state of the Bengali Muslims. The *Moslem Chronicle*, a newspaper which claimed to represent educated Muslims, bemoaned the fact that "so much ignorance prevails in the rural districts . . . several heathen customs have crept into the society." It recommended that the traditional system of education be revived and *maulvis* funded to preach in the "benighted places" and that government officers tour the areas to persuade villagers to establish schools.[49]

The new provisions for expanding educational opportunities for Muslims provided some groups with a springboard for entering local politics. Seeing that they now had an opportunity to gain some advantage from the government, however, most of the Bengali Muslim elite held aloof from the early activities of the Congress and the Bengal Provincial Conference, whose membership was almost entirely Hindu and which were engaged in agitations against the government on a range of issues, including representation on local councils and protests against press restrictions. Muslims were advised that "until we achieve a position equal to our Hindu neighbors, it must be suicidal to our best interests to join with them."[50] Those Muslims who did were either lacking in "real and substantial education" or had "forgotten their nationality."[51] The Malda Muhammadan Association passed a resolution at its meeting on December 15, 1895, urging that more Muslims be appointed to the district boards—an issue that had become increasingly important following passage of the Indian Councils Act of 1892. The act provided for the first time for representatives to the legislative council to be elected from the district boards, local boards, and municipalities. The elite Muslim associations, who knew that Muslims had virtually no chance of competing against Hindu candidates, had opposed the bill.[52]

The *Moslem Chronicle* urged Bengali Muslims to do as Muslims elsewhere were doing, and establish associations—*anjumans*—to promote not only the interests of the community, but to take up issues that the newspaper deemed were of interest to Muslims generally, including international events. It held up as an example the activities of the Muhammadans of Madras, who had submitted a resolution to the government demanding that officials refrain from using "indecent language" against the Turkish Sultan, after Britain and the sultanate severed relations following a serious of violent attacks on Armenians in Turkey. Two weeks later, the Midnapore Moslem Literary Society in Bengal did the same.[53] The Bengali Anjuman-I-Ashaati Islam of Noakhali proclaimed its goal to fund missionaries to preach in areas where Islam was less practiced, paying special attention to the "lower strata of the Muslim community" who were said to be "suffering from moral degradation." In this effort it sought help from Muslims "in more enlightened parts of our country."[54] The Anjuman-I-Islamia of Sylhet in northeastern Bengal also vowed to appoint a preacher who could lecture on Islam all over the district in order to give Muslim youth religious training before they went to English schools.[55] Associations such as these became significant links between politics in the urban centers and the *mofussil*. As Rafiuddin Ahmed observes, the *anjumans* represented a new phenomenon in rural Bengal, one that was capable of organizing the local community, usually around religious discussions or the visit of a traveling *maulvi*, but increasingly around landlord-tenant disputes as tensions rose over land issues in the years before partition.[56]

The Agrarian Context

At the time of the Permanent Settlement of 1793, which fixed "in perpetuity" the revenue due to the state from the *zamindars* and defined their proprietary rights, a surplus of land in Bengal led to fierce competition among landlords to secure cultivators to work the land.[57] Particularly following the famine of 1770, which killed one third of the population, landlords were eager to offer land to cultivators at reduced rents for fear of losing tenants to rival landlords offering lower rents. Over the next fifty years, the situation was reversed. Between 1770 and 1819, the population in the province increased rapidly, leaving land in short supply. Landlords were for the first time in a position to raise rents, something the Permanent Settlement had not foreseen,[58] and which ultimately led to the impoverishment of many tenants who were reduced to sharecropping or landlessness as a result. The Permanent Settlement had not fixed the amount of rent to be extracted from the tenants, called *raiyats*, nor did it define the rights of all tenants. In 1822, the government made some attempt to define these rights in order to determine revenue,[59] but it was not until a century later that thorough settlement operations produced a detailed account of land surveys and records of rights for the districts of Bengal.[60]

The first Tenancy Act (X) of 1859 defined the various classes of *raiyats*.[61] The most important feature of the Act of 1859 was the creation of "occupancy *raiyats*,"[62] those who could prove occupancy in every field of their holdings for twelve consecutive years. The act stipulated that rents for occupancy *raiyats* could only be enhanced on specific grounds, that occupancy *raiyats* could only be ejected by judicial order or decree;

and their crops could only be distrained for the arrears of one year's rent. With this move, the act established definitions that were "to shape and constrain agrarian change in Bengal for the next hundred years."[63] While the absence of adequate village records placed a great burden on *raiyats*,[64] the twelve year requirement provided landlords with the opportunity to deny those rights by interrupting the term or by breaking up the *raiyat's* holdings.

> When it is born in mind how frequently the twelve years proscription is interrupted by a mere shifting of the fields, sometimes by eviction within the term, in other cases by the grant of terminable leases for short periods with the option of renewal, it will become apparent how difficult it is in general for the *raiyat* to acquire a right of occupancy, or to prove it when it is questioned.[65]

At the same time, the act for the first time provided landlords the legal means to enhance rents, and did not stipulate how long the enhanced rents could apply, thus failing to prevent landlords from instituting annual enhancements.[66]

In 1862, the Indian Legislative Council noted that

> the Government of the country never took any practical steps to act up to its earlier reservations of the rights of the cultivators. Indeed, such interference as it did exercise was in the direction of the right of the landlord to enhance rents (Regulation V of 1812), and by the Sale Laws of 1845 to declare his power of eviction of all but the settled resident cultivators. It was only when, some 25 years ago, the oppression of the landlords threatened an agrarian revolution that the Government stepped in by legislative enactment to arrest the natural increase of rent in Bengal, and the result was the land law of 1859.[67]

The agrarian disturbances of the late nineteenth century centered on rent disputes and other claims arising out of the land reform efforts. The tenant uprising in Pabna in the 1870s was provoked by the dispute over enhancement and occupancy rights. These disturbances are particularly noteworthy in that they were organized by the Pabna Agrarian League—a union which had been established to create a reserve fund to meet expenses in litigation against landlords, on the rise since the Act of 1859.[68] The league's efforts were not against the government of Bengal or the payment of rent, but against what it perceived as illegal attempts to take away rights granted by the act.[69]

In 1879 the government established a commission whose findings provided the basis for the Bengal Tenancy Act of 1885, enacted to correct deficiencies in the 1859 Act. The Bengal Tenancy Act of 1885 gave the *raiyat* occupancy right not only in lands held consecutively for twelve years, but in any land held in the village; the *raiyat* had merely to show that he had held some land continually within the village boundaries for twelve years. He then became a "settled *raiyat*" with occupancy rights in all the land he already possessed and would acquire those rights in any new land he took into cultivation.[70] The act also provided, however, for easier enhancements in rent—a provision new to land laws in Bengal.[71] It permitted landlords to raise rents when the price of staple food crops increased, regardless of the actual crops grown on the land.[72] While strengthening the position of the occupancy *raiyat*, the act did not alter the basic landlord-tenant relationship. However, the Act of 1885 made no provision for sharecroppers, known as *bargadars*, a class that increased after 1885, paralleling a significant increase in the richer sector of the peasantry who either sublet their land to under-*raiyats*, or hired laborers to work the land, or let out some of the land and cultivated the rest themselves.[73]

Eastern Bengal saw this increase among well-off cultivators to a greater extent than did west Bengal. The rising price of jute in the late nineteenth century, combined with generally greater fertility in the deltaic regions of the east led to greater prosperity in that half of the province.[74] Rajat Ray argues that the single greatest beneficiary of the Act was the *jotedar*, a well-off cultivator with substantial holdings in which he had the right of occupancy.[75] Partha Chatterjee also discusses the rise of this comparatively rich peasant class in eastern Bengal. According to him, substantial *raiyats* consolidated their hold over cultivation by operating as the major money-lenders throughout the province.[76] In this role they have been compared to *kulaks*, "who managed to enlarge their holdings by renting land, often adding with the farming a little trading and a persistent money-lending; they developed their cultivation through the employment of low-paid wage labour."[77]

The money-lenders had an expanding clientele. The increase in land transfers, and consequently, the increase in landless laborers and sharecroppers in the first half of the twentieth century is attributable directly to rising agricultural debt, particularly in the depression years of the early 1920s. Transferability did not become an issue until after the 1859 Rent Act, when plentiful land began to disappear and competition for it increased.[78] The issue had been discussed when the 1885 Act was being framed, and the Land Revenue Commission at that time was persuaded to leave the question of transfer to be decided by local custom. However, transfers, which had numbered only slightly more than 25,000 in 1881–82, rose to 250,000 in 1913 and 314,000 in 1923.[79] During this same period, the numbers of the landless increased dramatically.[80] The transferability of land and the rights of sharecroppers continued as controversial issues in the debate that preceded passage of the 1928 Bengal Tenancy Act, as the peasant class splintered along competing lines of interest.

Partha Chatterjee has argued, however, that even in areas where such fragmentation of the peasantry occurred, the *jotedars* were still perceived as part of the community, part of the "we" among Muslim cultivators which excluded only the Hindu *zamindars*.[81] As such, they played a crucial role as a rising political force in determining the issues and demands that would define Bengali Muslim identity. It was not the improved financial picture alone that led these better-off cultivators toward a more chauvinistic position on their Muslim identity. A new awareness of status seems to have played a part in their educating their sons and in the leadership role they played in founding *anjumans* in their communities. Supported by this emerging class of better-off cultivators, the *anjuman*'s role as the community's Rotary Club soon expanded into rural politics. In many instances, the *anjumans* became the organization behind tenant resistance to oppressive rents and taxes imposed by the predominantly Hindu *zamindars*.[82] In 1906, the newspaper *Bande Mataram* reported that the *maulvis* and Muslim *jotedars* together were urging tenants to resist paying rents and *abwabs*, the hated illegal taxes.[83] In discussing the rise of this *jotedar* class, Sumit Sarkar cites a petition filed by the Mymensingh Raiyat's Association in west Bengal protesting the illegal enhancement of rent and the imposition of a variety of taxes. Sarkar notes that "the petition with its unusually sophisticated tone . . . obviously emanated from the better-off *jotedar* section of the *raiyats*, who were benefitting from the high prices of primary products and the roaring trade in jute."[84] He goes on to observe that "such men, however, were probably all the more susceptible to revivalist propaganda": "The *raiyats* being well off do not mind paying cesses [taxes] for most purposes, but object to pay for Kali *pujas* and other kinds of idolatry. The *zamindars* too object to their killing cows."[85] As was the case with the name changes during the census, these Muslims perceived that their support of religious causes could boost their own status in the community.

The right of *korbani*, or cow sacrifice, and its counterpart, cow protection, became such causes for, respectively, many upwardly mobile Muslim and Hindu communities in the late nineteenth century. While violence around the issue never assumed the same dimensions in Bengal that it did in Bihar and the United Provinces,[86] it did spark a number of serious incidents in the 1890s. The Cow Protection movement peaked in the U.P. and Bihar between 1888 and 1893, although individual incidents continued well into the 1900s. The issue first arose in Punjab, as a result of the activities of the Hindu revivalist Arya Samaj. It spread to the U.P., Bihar, and the Central Provinces, in large part in response to the Allahabad

High Court's decision that cow killing could not be prohibited merely on the grounds that the cow is an object of religious worship.[87] Detailed coverage of incidents in Bihar and the U.P. in Bengal's Muslim press helped encourage Hindu groups to establish Cow Protection Societies in Bengal. As in other areas of north India, much of the support for cow protection in Bengal came from the *zamindars*. As Pandey makes clear, cow protection was not a purely "Hindu" phenomenon; specific caste associations and communities embraced it as a way to boost their own social status.[88] In 1895, the commissioner in Rajshahi Division was reported to have observed that most of the Hindu *zamindars* were trying to prevent their tenants from killing cows.[89] Bengali Muslim newspapers published the names of some of the landlords who prohibited cow sacrifice and who abused tenants who performed it.[90] Similarly, those organizing tenants around the cause of *korbani* tended to be *zamindars* or *jotedars*. *Mihir O Sudhakar*, a Calcutta-based newspaper owned by Nawab Ali Chaudhuri,[91] took up the Muslim cause, frequently publishing reports of clashes over cow sacrifice. The most serious involved landlords and tenants in the *mofussil*. As was the case elsewhere, efforts by the British to determine what had been "customary" in various districts of Bengal only inflamed the situation, as both sides argued that custom was on their side and took their battle to either slaughter cows or protect them into the public arena.

The "communal" issue of cow killing quickly became linked, in the landlord-tenant relationship, to the tenants' resistance to paying increased rent and illegal taxes—which was itself framed in "communal" terms. By the 1890s, other disputes which were principally agrarian in nature were frequently portrayed—in the press, in official reports and in popular accounts—as having a communal tone. In many cases, "communal" issues were deliberately injected into the dispute. In 1897, a land dispute between Jatindramohan Tagore and a Muslim tenant ended in a bloody confrontation with the police after rumors circulated that a structure on the land was a mosque which the Tagores intended to demolish. The court had ruled that the land belonged to Tagore, but because all involved—including the institutions of the state—were accused by Muslim leaders and the Muslim press of being biased in favor of the Hindus, protests by local Muslims continued until the police opened fire, killing several. According to a report in the *Moslem Chronicle*, the police did not give the "usual" cry of "*Maharani Ki-Jaya*" (victory to the queen) but instead shouted "*Kali-Ma-Ki-Jaya*" (victory to mother Kali—the Hindu goddess).[92] As these clashes erupted more frequently after partition, reports of bias among the police became common.[93]

The partition also coincided with the completion of survey and settlement reports in a number of districts in both halves of Bengal. These settlement reports were carried out in districts throughout Bengal in order to create a record of land rights, rents, and categories of tenure out of the maze of agrarian relations that existed in late nineteenth and early twentieth-century Bengal. A number of surveys were conducted in the years before and after partition. As with other record-keeping exercises performed by the colonial authorities, the settlement officers frequently discovered that the very subject of their study had changed as a result of their attempt to record it.[94] In a letter to the secretary of the board of revenue, S.L. Maddox, the officiating director of the department of land records and agriculture, wrote that there had been an increase in rent suits in all the districts where the surveys had been completed. Armed with records, the tenants felt they could resist illegal increases by landlords. The landlords, on the other hand, were unhappy with the rental records and tried to coerce tenants to drop the suits.[95] After *raiyats* in the subdivision of Madhipura refused to pay rents any higher than those recorded in the settlement survey, a *zamindar* named Janeswar Singh used his servants to intimidate the tenants and extract the increased payments. The subdivisional officer noted that "the open revolt against the landlord's illegal demands" dated from the time the tenants received the *khatians* (settlement papers) "when they presumably realized that there was some finality about settlement proceedings and that they were not absolutely at the landlord's mercy."[96]

The 1905 Partition

Before 1905, the administration of Bengal included most of Bihar and Orissa, Cooch Behar, Sylhet, Hill Tipperah, and the twenty-eight districts of western and eastern Bengal. British administrators had long considered it too large to be governed effectively, and from the mid-nineteenth century, began considering plans to reorganize the provinces. Assam was placed under the authority of a lieutenant commissioner in 1874, but its removal still left an area too large for a single administration. In 1904, the Bengal government, under Lord Curzon, decided to partition Bengal, joining the eastern districts to Assam, and leaving western Bengal with Chota Nagpur, Orissa, and Bihar. Between 1874 and 1904, what had been purely administrative reasons for partition took on an increasingly political hue. With the founding of the Indian National Congress in 1885, Bengal had become a center of nationalist agitation. By partitioning Bengal, Curzon believed he could neutralize the Hindu nationalism among the *bhadrolok*[97] elites while at the same time creating more efficient administrative units.[98]

The announcement of the new boundaries in February 1904 sparked protests throughout the province, like a "match . . . which set fire to a large quantity of combustible material."[99] Those opposed included the

Bengali Muslim elite who resented being cut off from the colonial capital, Calcutta. The *Moslem Chronicle* opposed it as did much of the Muslim press. Muslim leaders were chiefly concerned about being further disadvantaged by being cut off from educational opportunities in the west. There was opposition in particular to having east Bengal attached to Assam in the new province, because Assam was, if anything, more "backward" still. Nawab Syed Ameer Hossain, the honorary secretary of the Central National Muhammadan Association, argued that the association, which had its branches all over Bengal, was not in favor of any boundary change. In a letter to the chief secretary of the government of Bengal dated February 17, 1904, Hossain complained,

> [T]he change proposed is undoubtedly a backward move. The people of the Chittagong Division, of Dacca and Mymensingh, have hitherto looked to Calcutta for inspiration and guidance. The best colleges and the best madrassas are in Calcutta, and students from those quarters are flowing here in daily increasing numbers . . . Besides, the administration of Bengal is carried on on more enlightened principles than that of Assam . . . [100]

Both Hindu and Muslim landlords in Calcutta and other towns in western Bengal complained that they would be separated from their property in the east. A prominent member of the Hindu *bhadrolok*, Babu Sita Nath Roy, raised concerns that the Bengali language would suffer, particularly in the east where it would be thrown in with that of the "backward race inhabiting Assam."[101] In 1904, few petitioners raised concerns about the potential for tension between Hindus and Muslims over the change.[102]

In the months that followed the announcement, British administrators went to great lengths to sell the change to east Bengalis. Curzon told Muslim leaders that they would now "enjoy a unity which they have not enjoyed since the days of the old Mussalman viceroys and kings."[103] They quickly enlisted the support of Nawab Salimulla of Dacca, the descendent of the nawabs who had ruled Bengal in the declining years of the Mughal empire, and who was regarded by the British as a "natural" leader of the Bengal Muslims even though Salimulla was not himself Bengali. The day after partition came into effect, the *Moslem Chronicle* reversed its earlier stand, wishing the new province well and publishing a manifesto from the Muhammadan Literary Society of Calcutta which urged all Muslims to support the government.[104] Within a week of partition, Nawab Salimulla had formed the Mohammedan Provincial Union to "unite the Mohammedans of the new province of Eastern Bengal and Assam" and to "represent to government the views and aspirations of Muslims."[105] In December, the Muslim League was founded and Nawab Salimulla made President. He immediately declared it to be an organization that not only promoted Muslim interests but could "controvert the growing influence of the so-called Indian National Congress, which has a tendency to misinterpret and subvert the British Rule in India."[106]

Not all Muslims supported the government on the issue, however. The nationalist newspaper *Mussulman* opposed the Nawab's stand against Congress and argued that the work of Congress was "beneficial to both communities."[107] Even more than a year after partition took effect, the newspaper published a "Mahomedan Protest" signed by "a thousand" Muslim *jotedars*, *zamindars*, and traders from Faridpur who complained that the separation from Calcutta was "a heavy blow to their future advancement and progress." They argued that the partition would cause residents great expense and that the money spent on establishing the new province could be better spent on improving education and sanitation. In his presidential address to the Tipperah District Conference, A. Rasul spoke against partition, citing meetings "all over the provinces" in support of a united Bengal.[108]

The strongest opposition to partition came from the more radical of Bengal's Hindu nationalists, who quickly launched a campaign against it which included the boycott of British manufacturers and goods and the promotion of *swadeshi*, or locally-made, alternatives.[109] Office-holders were withdrawn from British institutions, workers went on strike at British factories and students left British-run schools to enroll in *swadeshi* classrooms. In the final years of the agitation, a number of the Hindu leaders, frustrated with their failure to force the British to change policy, formed underground societies which engaged in violent attacks on British property. Although most Muslim leaders aligned themselves with the Nawab of Dacca in opposing the *swadeshi* movement and supporting partition, a number of prominent Muslims were active supporters of the *swadeshi* movement. Munshi Kazam Ali, a schoolteacher, and Maulvi Abdul Chatar, a barrister, along with their Hindu and Muslim colleagues, organized *swadeshi* meetings in Chittagong at which they claimed that because foreign sugar was purified by using the bones of cows and other animals, both Hindus and Muslims should boycott it. However, support was apparently limited to the small professional classes and students.[110]

In the *mofussil*, the *swadeshi* boycotts hit Muslim shopkeepers and peasants hardest. As S. Sarkar notes, in many of the court cases arising out of disputes during the *swadeshi* agitations, Hindu "*zamindari* officials and Muslim vendors faced each other as accused and plaintiff."[111] The Hindu newspaper *Charu Mihir* blamed the British for encouraging Muslim tenants to file complaints against their landlords. The editors acknowledged that in some cases, Muslim laborers who had formerly carried wood to cremation grounds and husked rice found that their Hindu landlords would file false charges against them.[112] In a case in which tenants refused to cultivate the land, however, *Charu Mihir* complained that British policy had led to the circulation of rumors in the *mofussil* that officials would not register a *kabuliyat* (rent record) if the rent was deemed excessive. The newspaper argued that the existence of the rumors "indicate[d] the feeling which the authorities have created in the minds of Mussulmans towards Hindus."[113] At the same time, pro-partition Muslim newspapers complained that Hindu police officers refused to register charges against *zamindars* accused of abuses by their Muslim tenants.[114] The Muhammadan Vigilance Committee was established in 1906 with the express purpose of establishing contact with local *anjumans* to prevent Muslim cultivators from being abused by Hindu landlords.[115]

Characteristic of all phases of the *swadeshi* campaign was the revival of militant Hindu symbols to mobilize support. The movement was marked by the use of *Sakta* symbolism, signifying the power of the goddess and often invoking the goddess Kali wearing a garland of skulls. *"Bande Mataram"* (Hail to the Mother) became the slogan and song of the campaign, derived from Bankim Chandra Chatterjee's novel, *Anandamath*, in which politicized *sunnyasis*[116] have taken up the cause of service to the motherland. The *sunnyasis* sing, "We do not want sovereignty/we only want to kill these Mussalmans/root and branch/because they have become the enemies/of god."[117]

In many incidents the line between the state and "communal" group became blurred, as officials and police became identified solely on the basis of their religion. Following a series of anti-partition meetings in Comilla, the Nawab visited the town on March 4, 1907, to make a speech in support of the new provincial arrangement. Before he arrived, the *Bengalee*, a Hindu nationalist paper, announced the visit with the headline, "Nawab Salimulla on the War Path."[118] In his speech, the Nawab criticized the Hindus for having "never been friendly to us in the real sense of the word. They have all along been trying to bring us into discredit before the government and the public."

He also entreated the Muslims not to be rash as "this spark of nationalism . . . was never meant to be wasted in this senseless fashion."[119] According to a government communique, a brick was thrown at the Nawab's procession and "brooms held up in derision." Some looting also reportedly occurred. All remained calm until the next evening when the Nawab's private secretary, "a Parsi, was beaten by Hindu youths." The next evening, supporters of the Nawab took out an unlicensed procession, shouting "Allah-o-Akbar," when they were fired upon and a Muslim man was killed.[120] The processionists then assaulted a number of Hindus. A Hindu constable, who was out of uniform at the time, fired the shots. He was tried and convicted of murder, but on appeal, the Calcutta High Court acquitted him on grounds of self-defense.[121] Government reports on the incident placed the blame almost exclusively on Hindu *swadeshi* activists, and ascribed the motivation not only to the relatively minor incidents that occurred on the day of the Nawab's speech, but apparently also to the shooting the next day. The fact that the constable was a representative of the state mattered less than that he was Hindu.

In the town of Chitpur, Brajendra Babu, the superintendent of police, and Babu K. Lal Das, the municipal commissioner, both Hindus, together with a local Muslim leader, Maulvi Ahmed Ali, reportedly urged local Muslims to join in *swadeshi* agitations. When they refused, Babu Brajendra threatened retaliation. As Muslims were washing cows in the river in preparation for the celebration of 'Id,[122] the superintendent ordered his constables, who were all Hindus, to beat the "poor and backward" Muslims. According to *Mihir O Sudhakar*, the superintendant insulted the Muslims further by saying that they were preparing to sacrifice pigs. He then prohibited any cow sacrifice. In another incident in Chitpur, a Muslim tenant complained that he was arrested for sacrificing a cow and made to pay a fine, even though cow sacrifice had been permitted in the village.[123] As in other parts of Bengal, cow sacrifice had become an issue in Chitpur ten years earlier when local Hindus objected to cow sacrifice at a particular mosque. At that time, the government intervened, ruling that, as cow sacrifice had been permitted for more than twenty years, it could continue. Some Hindus then retaliated by blowing conch shells and ringing bells in front of mosques during prayer times.[124] The tit-for-tat provocation and claims to customary rights, whether for *korbani* or procession routes, became the pattern for communal disturbances in Bengal for the next several decades.

The Hindu press lodged similar complaints against Muslim officials and British authorities it accused of pro-Muslim sympathies. In May 1907, the *Bengalee* accused the government of weakness in dealing with disturbances in east Bengal and denounced local Muslim police officials entering temples with shoes on and, with the assistance of "Mahomedan rowdies," looting the *zamindar*'s office. "We shall say nothing of the high-handed and lawless acts of Mr. Clarke and of the Police Superintendent. . . . But we ask . . . why were the mob allowed to co-operate with the police in these searches? They had attacked the Hindus, looted their shops and had desecrated their sacred images and yet the local authorities embraced them . . . [125]

The newspaper also blamed the *maulvis* for distributing the inflammatory "Red Pamphlet" which urged Muslims to have nothing to do with Hindus. On May 5, the *Bengalee* published the pamphlet in full. However, its timing in relation to the disturbances in Comilla and other areas in March and April is controversial. The pamphlet did not circulate in several of the areas where violence broke out, and the tour of one *maulvi* who preached against taxes to support Hindu festivals was linked to his own campaign to get elected to the local board. He succeeded.[126]

As the protests spread, government concern about the *swadeshi* activists was compounded by a growing uneasiness about a "new consciousness" among Bengali Muslims. Like the Hindu press, British administrators believed the agents of this change were the "itinerant mullahs" whose activities in "stirring up communal passions" was duly recorded in official communiques. As anti-*swadeshi* protests continued, these "mullahs" quickly came to be seen as one of the most powerful instruments for mobilizing rural Muslims to violence and to communal politics."The character of the Muhammadan masses is full of inconsistencies . . . The uneducated Muhammadans are easily excited and when their blood is hot take to breaking heads for the most trivial causes. They follow each other like sheep, and the preachings of outside mullahs and *maulvies* are at the bottom of most of the discontent that exists."[127] The language echoed Hunter's concerns that the Muslim masses, easily "excitable" and easily led, could be lured into rebellion. The Hindu press also adopted this line.

Indeed, virtually every scholar who has described the part the *maulvis* played in the disturbances of the *swadeshi* period as instrumental has seen the religious figures as the British largely did—as part of the fanatical character of the Muslims of eastern Bengal. S. Sarkar argues that the *madrasah*-educated religious leaders, flush with a new sense of their own Muslim identity, were able to elicit a strong response from the tenants because they encouraged them to resist the very figures they already hated: the *zamindar* and the *mahajan* (money lender). While the choice of targets—Hindu *zamindars* and money lenders—seem obvious objects of protest, Muslim money lenders, principally *jotedars*, were not targeted. Unfortunately, Sarkar falls back on explaining "communalism" among Muslim peasants as attributable to the community's "greater cohesion and fanaticism."[128] For support he quotes Lieutenant-General Fraser, who, in a letter to Lord Minto, the Viceroy, observed that "ignorant and uneducated Mahomedans follow their leaders more readily than Hindus."[129] In fact, the explanation may be the reverse: the religious reform movements had had their greatest impact among Bengali Muslims who saw a *madrasah* education and adherence to a more orthodox lifestyle as a way to enhance their own status.

An important measure of the influence of the *maulvis* and *anjumans* in popularizing religious reform and resistance among Muslim cultivators are the *puthis*, a class of popular literature and other ephemera generally devoted to giving advice about how to be a better Muslim and how to conduct relations with non-Muslims.[130] In Abed Ali Miah's *"Polli-dosa,"* for example, Muslims are admonished against going without beards and told to avoid Christian and Jewish, as well as Hindu, practices.[131] Some of the *puthis* were more explicitly political in advocating positions on rent and land tenure, money-lending and other issues. A consistent theme was the link between the general depressed condition of the Bengali Muslims—socially, economically, politically—and the degenerate state of Islam in Bengal. The partition years saw a marked increase in the printing of this literature which was widely distributed in an apparent effort to generate enthusiasm for these efforts. Sumit Sarkar has analyzed one of these *puthis* at length, the poem *Krishak-Bilap* (Lament of the Peasant). The poem is primarily an attack on figures of authority in rural society who have brought misery to the peasant—the *zamindars*, the police, the *mahajan*. The poem describes these figures as Congress party members, and urges Muslims to remember their own community and to seek assistance through the study of Islam and reject all mixing with other religions. The poem advises them to form *anjumans* and rally behind the Muslim League.[132]

Although the *maulvis* who encouraged these protests would not generally be understood as the kind of "elites" who are capable of manipulating symbols to mobilize members of an ethnic group for specific political objectives, that is precisely what they did. But as elites, they had little in common with the majority of Western-educated *ashraf* supporters of the Muslim League. Better educated than the peasants they preached to, the *maulvis* represented instead structures of authority who functioned more at the popular level.[133] They also had their own organizations—the *anjumans*—which could insure that the message they preached reached throughout the local community. As one newspaper observed, the *anjuman* not only promoted stricter adherence to orthodox Islam, it "enabled the individual rayat to adopt a more independent attitude towards the petty oppressions of the local *zamindars*."[134]

What made the *mullahs* so dangerous was that they could link the economic interests of the poor peasants with appeals for religious reform. In doing so, they did, perhaps, build on the symbols evoked by their Fara'idi predecessors. But their success in mobilizing tenants in east Bengal to resist enhanced rents and other abuses by the *zamindars* depended as well on bureaucratic changes that had made tenants more aware of their rights. And it was related to the fact that the Hindu revivalist symbolism of the *swadeshi* activists had vindicated the argument that the mullahs, as well as the Muslim urban elite, had been making all along—that Muslims stood to lose in any politics dominated by the Bengali Hindu elite.

The Annulment

The decision to reverse the partition, and reconstitute the province to join western and eastern Bengal,[135] was announced on December 12, 1911. Simultaneously, the government announced the decision to move the capital of British India from Calcutta to Delhi. The move was prompted more by administrative changes in the provincial government than by the *swadeshi* agitation,[136] but both anti- and pro-partition forces saw it as a capitulation to the extremists. The Muslim press was incensed, accusing the authorities of betrayal.

Having lost their province, the Muslim leaders who had counted on government patronage during the partition years found themselves at a loss. The reunification of the province left them without a clear political direction. Although the Muslim League, the party that ultimately called for—and won—a separate state for Muslims, had been founded in Bengal, its early history was characterized by bitter factionalism and frequent schisms. During the *swadeshi* agitation, Muslims were split over the partition question, with the Muslim League supporting it, and the Bengal Mohammadan Association organizing boycotts to protest it. After reunification of the province in 1911, the Bengal Provincial Muslim League (BPML) found itself without a platform and without a way to appeal for support even among Muslim elites. In April, 1913, the president of the District Muslim League in Rangpur complained that "it is an undeniable fact that Bengal, unlike other Presidencies and Provinces is backward in matter of Establishment of branches of All India Moslem League."[137] True to the class character of the League at the time, which was dominated by a Western-educated non-Bengali elite, he requested that "an Urdu and English knowing competent speaker" be sent "who will with his winning manners and convincing speeches be able to convert the dissenters and the half-minded to our views."[138] At the same time, prominent Muslim leaders began using the new Muslim press to capture the interest of urban Muslims on the Balkans and other "pan-Islamic" issues.

The 1905 partition of Bengal was cataclysmic, not because it confirmed, as some historians have suggested,[139] the divide and rule intentions of India's rulers, nor because it in itself engendered a Muslim leadership bent on a separatist agenda. The act of drawing new boundaries provided the framework in which Bengali Muslims could begin to think differently about themselves. The change in the administrative status of the territory in which they found themselves mattered little to most Bengalis, whether Hindu or Muslim. What did matter was that Bengali Muslims saw themselves as being threatened by those who attacked partition. If they did not have the immediate experience of being the target of *swadeshi* attack or *zamindar* abuse, widely circulated *puthi* tracts and, for those who had access to it, the Bengali Muslim press provided sufficient evidence to convince them that their interests lay on the other side.

The partition also engendered new thinking about the Bengali Muslim "leadership." The British, seeking allies, identified *ashraf* Muslims, particularly those associated with the Nawab of Dacca, as "natural leaders,"[140] and turned to them as representatives of the interests of a population with which they had, at best, limited contact. Other leaders who emerged at this time were the *maulvis*, whose experience in tenant resistance had given them a new base of support. Coming out of the same experience, peasant organizers soon emerged as a critical link for both Hindu and Muslim nationalist leaders as they discovered the importance of mass politics for the Non-cooperation and Khilafat campaigns of 1919–1924.

Notes

1. Until 1905, the administration of Bengal included most of Bihar and Orissa, as well as present-day West Bengal and Bangladesh. When the province was partitioned in 1905, Chota Nagpur was transferred to the Central Provinces. In 1912, East Bengal was again joined to West Bengal; Bihar, Orissa, and Chota Nagpur became a separate province, and Assam reverted to a Chief Commissionership. In 1931, the provinces were established along their present boundaries, with East Bengal and West Bengal together making up the Province of Bengal. For the purposes of the census, Bengal included the districts of present-day West Bengal and Bangladesh, with the addition of Tipperah, Hill Tipperah, and Cooch Behar.

2. See S. Sarkar, 1973, pp. 443–464; Suranjan Das, passim; John R. McLane, "The 1905 Partition and the New Communalism," in Alexander Lipski, ed., *Bengal: East and West* (East Lansing, MI: Asian Studies Center, Michigan State University, 1969), pp. 48–49. Under the Mughals, *zamindars* were assigned tracts of land which they administered and on which they collected taxes for the imperial power; there was no private ownership of land. The British created a permanent landlord class out of the *zamindars*.

3. The elite, i.e. those Muslims who could claim a non-Bengali ancestry. The *ashraf* did not consider themselves to be Bengalis. See Eaton, pp. 99–102. The term Bengali was generally used only for Hindus until sometime in the early twentieth century.

4. Rafiuddin Ahmed, p. 113.

5. For a detailed account of the advent of Islam in Bengal, see Richard M. Eaton, *The Rise of Islam and the Bengal Frontier* (Berkeley: University of California Press, 1993).

6. For more on the history of these practices, see Shashibhusan Das Gupta, *Obscure Religious Cults*. 2nd. ed. (Calcutta: K.L. Mukhopadhyaya, 1962).

7. Edward C. Dimock, Jr., "Hinduism and Islam in Medieval Bengal," in *Aspects of Bengali History and Society*, Rachel Van M. Baumer, ed. (Hawaii: University of Hawaii Press, 1975), p. 8.

8. Ibid. See also Jadunath Sarkar, *History of Aurangzeb* (London, 1920), vol. IV: pp. 51, 374.

9. Abdul Karim, *A Social History of the Muslims of Bengal, Down to A.D. 1538* (Dhaka, 1959), p. 206.

10. Gilmartin, p. 55.

11. See Peter Bertocci, "Models of Solidarity, Structures of Power: The Politics of Community in Rural Bangladesh," in Myron Aronoff, ed., *Political Anthropology Yearbook I: Ideology and Interest: The Dialectics of Politics* (New Brunswick, N.J.: Transaction Books, 1980).

12. Gilmartin, pp. 76–77.

13. *Moslem Chronicle*, January 17, 1895, p. 20.

14. The term "Wahhabi" comes from the movement founded by Ibn-'Abd-al-Wahhab, in Arabia in the early nineteenth century. Ibn-'Abd-al-Wahhab preached against Sufism and tribal customs which he believed had corrupted Islam. See Marshall G. S. Hodgson, *The Venture of Islam: Conscience and History in a World Civilization: The Gunpowder Empires and Modern Times*, vol. 3 (Chicago: The University of Chicago Press, 1974), pp. 160–161. The term "Wahhabism" was used loosely by British officials to refer to Islamic reform movements, whether or not they actually advocated Wahhabi reforms.

15. R. Ahmed, pp. 58–59.

16. Aziz Ahmad, *Studies in Islamic Culture in the Indian Environment* (Oxford: Oxford University Press, 1969), p. 211. The *bhakti* movement was a religious reform movement that stressed a personal devotional relationship to a deity.

17. Gilmartin, p. 75.

18. The village mullah functioned not only as a religious authority but as a guide for day-to-day social matters, acting sometimes as arbiter and as the last voice for the village council, wielding the authority to impose social sanction as well as fines. It was generally understood that the ordinary people would listen only to the mullah—a belief which further fueled the reformists' attacks on the mullah for closing his eyes to the prevalence of Hindu customs among the faithful. See R. Ahmed (passim).

19. W. C. Smith, "The 'Ulama in Indian Politics," in C. H. Philips, ed., *Patron and Society in India* (London: George Allen and Unwin, 1963), pp. 42–43.

20. Hardy, p. 56.

21. Barbara Metcalf, *Islamic Revival in British India: Deoband, 1860–1900* (Princeton: Princeton University Press, 1982), pp. 68–70; see also Muin-ud-din Ahmed Khan, *History of the Fara'idi Movement in Bengal, 1818–1906*. Karachi: Pakistan Historical Society, 1965; and Gilmartin, 1988.

22. Metcalf, pp. 56–57.

23. Hunter, p. 3.

24. Ibid., p. 133.

25. Ibid., pp. 190–194.

26. Hunter himself cautioned his readers against doing just that. Ibid., p. 141.

27. Pandey, 1990, p. 228.

28. Brass, 1974, p. 141.

29. An important exception is Gilmartin, who has focused on the role Punjabi Muslims played in the Pakistan movement. See Gilmartin, 1988.

30. Robinson, p. 6.

31. *Census of India, 1911*, vol. I (Delhi: Government of India), pp. 30–52.

32. R. Ahmed, p. 140.

33. Ibid., p. 140. However, the central government and the government of Bengal were in disagreement as to the best approach, with the provincial government

supporting the integration of more Muslims into existing schools, and the central government supporting *madrasah* education. See Shila Sen, *Muslim Politics in Bengal, 1937–47* (Delhi: Impex: India, [pref. 1976]), p. 11.

34. Total population increase among Muslims went from 17,609,135 to 21,500,000. *Census of India, 1901.* Rafiuddin Ahmed has analyzed this trend among Bengali Muslims as a sign of upward mobility among the lower classes as much as an indicator of a new interest in a "Muslim" identity. As he observes, "*Ashrafization* would confer a double benefit—social status as well as an Islamic identity." R. Ahmed, p. 116.

35. *Census of India, 1911*, vol. v, Bengal, Bihar and Orissa, and Sikkim, pt. I (Calcutta, 1913), pp. 440, 446. See also Pandey, 1990, pp. 83–84.

36. Anisuzzaman, ed., *Muslim Banglar Samayik Patra, 1831–1930* (Dacca, 1968), pp. 24–35, cited in Shila Sen, p. 25.

37. Pandey, 1990, p. 83. Low-caste Hindus also petitioned for recognition of their caste as belonging in a higher status classification.

38. Colonial authorities commonly used the term "caste" to distinguish among various occupations and other social distinctions among Muslims. Of course, the tendency among Muslims to identify themselves according to "castes" has been well-documented. See Imtiaz Ahmed, ed., *Caste and Social Stratification Among the Muslims* (Delhi: Manohar Book Service, 1973).

39. R. Ahmed, p. 116. According to Pandey, *jolahas* in Bihar changed their names to *Ansari* in addition to *Momin*. Pandey, 1990, p. 88.

40. Pandey, 1990, p. 68.

41. Pandey points out that in the 1930s, they had formed the Jamiat-ul-Ansar-ul-Hind, the All-India Momin Conference, to represent the interests of weavers. The term *jolaha* virtually disappeared. Pandey, 1990, p. 89, fn. 56.

42. *Moslem Chronicle*, August 15, 1895, p. 351.

43. Sen, p. 8.

44. Report of the Committee formed to Enquire into the Condition of Madrassas in 1869. Selection from the Records of the Government of India, Home Department, n. CCV, pt. II, p. 43, cited in ibid.

45. R. Ahmed, p. 36.

46. As Paul Brass has noted, U.P. Muslims had not fallen behind Hindus significantly in the areas of urbanization or literacy in English, and were overrepresented in government service, law, medicine, and teaching. See Brass, 1974, pp. 153–156. As late as 1937, Jinnah used the "backwardness" argument to bolster the Muslim League's claim that the Muslims needed special consideration which they had not received under either the British or the Congress. Jinnah's speech to the Muslim League, Delhi, June 14, 1937, quoted in ibid., p. 141.

47. Hunter, p. 3.

48. Ibid., p. 194.

49. *Moslem Chronicle*, April 25, 1895, p. 177.

50. *Moslem Chronicle*, January 11, 1896, p. 20.

51. *Moslem Chronicle*, January 9, 1897, p. 109.

52. See Ray, p. 129.

53. *Moslem Chronicle*, October 10, 1896, p. 460 and October 24, 1896, p. 472.

54. *Moslem Chronicle*, December 12, 1896, p. 558.

55. *Moslem Chronicle*, May 16, 1890, p. 222.

56. R. Ahmed, p. 83. The *anjumans* also established *madrasahs*, supported local mosques and performed other community services. Ibid., p. 168.

57. Radharomon Mookerjee, *Occupancy Right: Its History and Incident* (Calcutta: Calcutta University Press, 1919), p. 73.

58. Ibid., p. 74.

59. Ibid., p. 78.

60. M. Azizul Huque, *The Man Behind the Plough* (Dacca: Bangladesh Books International, Ltd., 1939), p. 232.

61. Mookerjee, p. 79. 1) *Raiyats* whose rent had not changed for twenty years or since the Permanent Settlement became *"raiyats* at fixed rents" and were entitled to hold forever at those rates; 2) *Raiyats* who had cultivated or who had held land for twelve years were declared to have a right of occupancy in the land, so long as they paid rent. "This rule did not apply to proprietor's private land let out on lease for a term of years or from year to year and the accrual of occupancy rights in any land could also be barred by a written contract." Occupancy *raiyats* rent could be enhanced "if new land was brought under cultivation, or if their rents were lower than the customary rate, or if the value of their produce increased." 3) Other *raiyats*, not having rights of occupancy, were entitled to a lease, or *patta*, only at rates determined in negotiation with their landlords. See Chatterjee, 1984, p. 10.

62. Mookerjee, p. 84.

63. Chatterjee, p. 10.

64. *Report of the Land Revenue Commission*, v. 1, p. 25.

65. *Proceedings of the Indian Legislative Council*, 2 March 1885, cited in Huque, p. 243.

66. Mookerjee, p. 95.

67. *Proceedings of the Indian Legislative Council*, March 13, 1882, cited in Huque, p. 238.

68. Ray, p. 64.

69. K. K. Sen Gupta, "The Agrarian League of Pabna, 1873," *Indian Economic and Social History Review*, vol. vii, no. 2, 1970, pp. 258–260.

70. *Report of the Land Revenue Commission*, v. I, p. 27.

71. Huque, p. 259.

72. Mookerjee, p. 105.

73. Ibid., p. 291.

74. Ibid., pp. 186–187, 298–299.

75. Ray, p. 54.

76. Chatterjee, 1984, p. 148.

77. *Report of the Land Revenue Commission*, v.iii, p. 178–179. See also ibid.

78. Huque, p. 274.

79. Ibid.

80. Ibid., pp. 132–133.

81. Chatterjee, pp. 127–129.

82. R. Ahmed, p. 167.

83. Cited in S. Sarkar, p. 81.

84. Clarke to Le Mesurier, 1 June 1906, para. 14, Home Political Proceedings A, July 1906, cited in S. Sarkar, p. 458.

85. Ibid. Kali *puja* refers to a ceremonial worship of the Hindu goddess, Kali.

86. See in particular Pandey, 1983, pp. 60–129.

87. Pandey, 1990, p. 164; Freitag, 1989, p. 150.

88. See Pandey, ibid., for a discussion of the caste composition of support for cow protection.

89. *Moslem Chronicle,* January 17, 1895, p. 16.

90. R. Ahmed, pp. 171–172.

91. S. Sarkar, p. 411.

92. *Moslem Chronicle,* August 7, 1897, p. 89. Rafiuddin Ahmed has noted that the court which gave the ruling was seen as a "Hindu" court. R. Ahmed, p. 178.

93. Earlier, the *Moslem Chronicle* had complained, "The fact that the police, the village *chowkidars* and the *panchayat* [village council] are almost entirely composed of Hindus not only indicates the probability of the ease with which such scores can be got up, but shows how completely, indeed, is the simple Mussalman cultivator at the mercy and at the terrorisation of the Hindus. What with the Hindu *zamindars,* the Hindu money-lenders, the Hindu *punchayat* [sic], the Hindu village *chowkidars* (watchmen), the Hindu police and the Hindu subordinate magistracy and judiciary, the life of the ordinary Bengal Mussalman peasant is one round of woes and miseries." *Moslem Chronicle,* May 16, 1896, p. 223.

94. See Pandey, 1983, p. 120, for a discussion of this phenomenon with respect to religious "custom."

95. "Regarding the proposal to compel landlords to file copies of the settlement khatians in every rent suit," S.L. no. 417, Dacca Division Commissioner O., Revenue Department File No. 29, Collection No. XVI, 1903–04 (A). National Archives of Bangladesh (NAB).

96. *Abstract of Intelligence,* Bengal Police, week ending 6/May 1905, GOB F. 43(a), 1905 1/6.

97. Literally, "respectable people," the elite of Bengali Hindu society.

98. The motives behind partition have been discussed at length by other scholars, most notably S. Sarkar, 1973, chapter 1. As he argues "Till at least 1903, there can be no doubt that administrative considerations were predominant in all discussions concerning the future map of Bengal. . . . Yet . . . Home Proceedings and private papers alike vividly reveal the importance of political factors in moulding the final contours of the partition plan and in ruling out alternatives which on administrative grounds alone would have been at least equally viable." S. Sarkar, 1973, pp. 12–14. For a discussion of *bhadrolok* politics generally, see Broomfield, 1968.

99. *Report on Bengal and Assam,* p. 8.

100. *Report on Bengal and Assam,* Enclosure 5 in No. 2. From W.C. MacPherson, C.S.I., Offg. Chief Secretary to GOB to Secretary of GOI, Home Department, 6th April, 1904, p. 93.

101. From Babu Sita Nath Roy, Hon. Secretary Bengal National Chamber of Commerce, to Chief Secretary, Government of Bengal, February 3, 1904, in ibid., p. 80–81.

102. *Report on Bengal and Assam,* p. 6.

103. *Public Letters 1905,* vol. 33, p. 7 and p. 2, cited in R. Ahmed, p. 180.

104. *Moslem Chronicle,* October 16 and 21, 1905, cited in Sen, p. 35.

105. *Moslem Chronicle*, October 21, 1905.

106. *Amrita Bazar Patrika*, December 13, 1906, cited in Sen, p. 40.

107. *Mussulman*, January 4, 1907, p. 4.

108. *Mussulman*, February 8, 1907.

109. The most detailed account of the movement is in S. Sarkar, 1973.

110. "Swadeshi Movement Chittagong District," GOB F. 43c, 1905.

111. S. Sarkar, 1973, p. 80. Sarkar also notes that the community of low-caste Namasudras also resisted the *swadeshi* protests because they saw in the government promises of increased positions in public service a chance for their own community to advance. S. Sarkar, 1973, p. 330.

112. *Charu Mihir*, February 2, 1906, cited in *Native Newspaper Reports*, February 10, 1906, p. 106.

113. *Charu Mihir*, January 25, 1906, cited in *Native Newspaper Reports*, February 3, 1906, p. 96.

114. *Mihir O Sudhakar*, January 26, 1906, cited in *Native Newspaper Reports*, February 3, 1906, p. 89.

115. Fortnightly Report from Bengal, No. FAR5, 5 December 1906. Abstracts of Reports from Bengal during the First Half of November, 1906. Home Political Progs A, January 1907, n. 263, February 1907, n. 152–54. Cited in S. Sarkar, 1973, p. 444.

116. Mendicants who have renounced the world; the last and potentially purest stage of life in Hinduism.

117. Bankim Chandra Chatterjee, *Anandamath* (translated from Bengali by Aurobindo and B. Ghosh, Calcutta, 1906), p. 98. Some observers consider the last chapter to be a later addition, written deliberately to appease the British.

118. *Mussulman*, March 29, 1907, p. 8.

119. *Mussulman*, March 29, 1907, p. 3.

120. *Mussulman*, March 15, 1907, pp. 6–7.

121. The case is discussed by Sumit Sarkar as an example of the "flood of argument on the question of responsibility" which broke out after the first incidents of communal and agrarian violence during the *swadeshi* movement. S. Sarkar, 1973, pp. 449–464.

122. This refers to the religious holiday of either 'Id-ul-Fitr, the day that marks the end of Ramadan, the month of fasting, or 'Id-ul-Azha, which commemorates Abraham's offering of his son Ishmael for sacrifice. The dates on which they fall in any given year is determined by a lunar calendar.

123. *Mihir O Sudhakar*, February 16, 1906, in *Native Newspaper Reports*, February 24, 1906, p. 149.

124. Ibid.

125. "The Situation in East Bengal," *Bengalee*, May 5, 1907, p. 3.

126. S. Sarkar, 1973, p. 453; Ray, p. 190.

127. F. A. Sachse, *Final Report on the Survey and Settlement Operations in the District of Mymensingh, 1908–1919* (Calcutta: Bengal Secretariat Book Depot, 1920), p. 29.

128. S. Sarkar, 1973, p. 80.

129. Fraser to Minto, 28 March 1907—Minto Papers, M980, cited in S. Sarkar, 1973, p. 441.

130. Rafiuddin Ahmed has used this literature extensively to understand identity changes in Bengal in the thirty years before partition. See Ahmed, op. cit.

131. Abed Ali Mia, *"Polli-Dosa"* (Panatipara, Rangpur: Abed Ali Mia, 1925) at National Library of India, Calcutta.

132. S. Sarkar, 1973, p. 464.

133. As David Gilmartin has demonstrated, such intermediaries, particularly the rural *pirs*, played a critical role as links between elite politics and rural mobilization in rural Punjab. Gilmartin, 1988.

134. *Mussulman*, April 16, 1909, p. 8, cited in R. Ahmed, p. 169.

135. The decision was based in part on a desire to defuse the nationalist movement. The new arrangement left Bihar and Orissa as one separate province and Assam as another.

136. King George V had suggested the reunification to mark his visit as Emperor, and the move had the backing of a number of officers in the Bengal administration who had opposed partition from the beginning.

137. Syed Abdul Fatah to Secretary, All India Muslim League (AIML), Lucknow, 20 April 1913. Papers of the Bengal Provincial Muslim League (BPML), vol. xxxvi, p. 55. Archives of the Freedom Movement (AFM), University of Karachi, Karachi, Pakistan.

138. Ibid.

139. Ray, pp. 185–186.

140. Sandria Freitag has used this term to describe the British policy of identifying "those exercising power through personal, patron-client relationships, whether operating through residential, occupational, caste, ritual, or extended kinship networks" as their intermediaries. Freitag, 1989, p. 57.

3

The Function of Violence: Renegotiating the Status Order 1918–1926

The agitations that accompanied the first partition of Bengal had made explicit the potential for using religious symbols to mobilize Muslim peasants against predominantly Hindu landlords. In the years that followed, a new class of rural leaders were in a position to use those symbols to frame political debate in terms of both religious identity and tenant interests. This period also saw an increase in official, and non-official, efforts to investigate and report on communal violence. Both efforts sought to identify the causes of the riots and identify the responsible community. What the investigations and reports succeeded in doing was help freeze popular perceptions of Hindu and Muslim identities by portraying animosities between the two communities as a historical inevitability, and casting the rioters as "irrational" mobs.

In colonialist discourse, conclusions about the historical inevitability of communal violence were used to support the government's claims about the benevolence of British rule and the necessity of British presence for keeping the peace between historically "hostile" religious communities. For their part, Hindu and Muslim politicians seeking to blame each other for the violence and claim victim status for their own community forged new political symbols out of the riots in order to unite their community and set it apart from other groups. The analysis of the riots below focuses on Muslim leaders in their roles as agents of this process, but it goes without saying that the leaders of both communities were engaged in a process of constructing each other. By casting themselves as the victimized community, and identifying the "other" as the perpetrators as they testified before government commissions of inquiry, representatives of the many Muslim parties in Bengal, *anjuman* leaders, and other community spokesmen used the violence to redefine relations between Hindus and Muslims and to construct a politically self-conscious Bengali Muslim community. Although politicians on all sides acknowledged that the acts of violence that precipitated the riots of this period were premeditated, and even the official reports by British police officers conceded that the violence was coordinated, leaders on all sides continued to blame the "fanatical mob" rather than the calculating politician for the violence. The riots were understood as unfortunate but inevitable, a by-product of political mobilization of two historically inimical communities rather than as a political tool in its own right.

In fact, the incidents that ignited the major disturbances of this period, and much of the violence of the Calcutta riots of April, May, and July 1926 and the Pabna riots of July 1926, were in large part choreographed events, calculated to bolster efforts to unseat established leaders before the November elections. And each incident imposed new constraints on future political choices. Political leaders manipulated volatile symbols, particularly those like music before mosques that could be evoked in public demonstrations, as part of a strategy calculated to elicit popular support for whichever political party claimed to represent the interests of the newly vulnerable group. Many of the incidents were reconstructed in press accounts and official inquiries, and ultimately re-enacted in the next riot, as previous targets became symbols of martyrdom and resistance. The riots themselves became symbols of the failure of the established Muslim leadership to protect its own community in the public arena, and of the British government's partisan behavior toward one community or the other.

This is not to say that riots are the product of "elite manipulation" as the colonialist writers generally concluded. The subalternists rightly argue against this picture of the "irrational masses" being manipulated by fanatical appeals. However, it would be equally misleading to see these riots as spontaneous protests against the established order. Who constitutes an elite is also open to question. The subalternists define it as "dominant groups, foreign as well as indigenous" as distinct from the "'people' or 'subaltern classes.'" Such a severe dichotomy between elites and subalterns fails to account for the emergence of "subalterns" who had links to the organized arena of politics dominated by "elites." As C. A. Bayly argues, "[d]own almost to the very bottom of society every subaltern was an elite to someone lower than him."[1] Popular religious leaders, peasant activists, and other "subaltern" leaders engaged in mobilizing support around symbols that evoked a more exclusionary Muslim identity and linked that identity to land reform issues which had appeal for the vast majority of Bengal's Muslim cultivators and tenants. A decade later, agitations around these same issues provided a base for the Muslim League's rise to power in the province.

Renegotiating the Status Order

The years following the annulment of the 1905 partition were marked by increasing divisions within the Muslim political leadership in Bengal. Those who had previously supported government policy struggled to reclaim a base in united Bengal, as tensions between Britain and Turkey and other events in the greater Muslim world came to preoccupy religious leaders and attract the attention of others who had abandoned the loyalist position to exploit the government's betrayal of partition. While such issues were unlikely to trouble the majority of Bengal's Muslim population, they did shape the way British authorities perceived Muslim interests and the way they attempted to identify a leadership on which they could rely.

Among Bengali Muslims, the leadership struggle was prompted by the appearance of a newly conscious class of economically mobile Muslims who had sufficient social clout and wealth to challenge the established leadership, represented in Eastern Bengal by the Nawab. The economic and social changes of the previous two decades had supported the rise of this group, whose members used their economic position to carve out a role in local politics through organizing rural *anjumans* and peasant associations. Having embraced the teachings of reformists who preached the message of a purified Islam, they had also become local patrons of mosques and schools. These Bengali Muslims saw a *madrasah* education and adherence to a more orthodox lifestyle as a way to enhance their own social position. Their status derived not only from their economic power as substantial cultivators but from their new respectability as claimants of a new, very visible, Muslim identity.

Both electoral competition and street violence provide occasions for leaders to highlight differences between groups. In elections, that opportunity is governed by institutional mechanisms that determine when and how an election can take place. Other political developments also create opportunities for emerging groups and leaders to claim to represent the "genuine" interests of their group or community. In Bengal, two events in 1922–1923 signaled the end of a brief period of cooperation between Congress and Muslim leaders associated with other organizations in Bengal. In 1922 Gandhi abruptly terminated the first major campaign of the nationalist movement, which he had launched jointly with Muslim leaders who were protesting British policy toward Turkey at the end of World War II.[2] In 1923, a Hindu-Muslim Pact negotiated by the breakaway Swarajist party was defeated by Bengal's Hindu elite.[3] Both events provided the context for increased communal conflict as middle-level leaders exploited opportunities for communal tension to bolster their own standing.

The years between 1918 and 1926 encompass major political changes, including the devolution of powers to provincial assemblies under the Government of India Act of 1919. This act of state created conditions for competition among the Congress, Swarajists, and Muslim parties for control of key provinces. Bengal was one of these key provinces, and the shifting alliances of this period brought about by the changed political circumstances created opportunities for political actors on all sides to reformulate what it meant to be a Muslim in Bengal and to sharpen distinctions among Muslims, as well as between Muslims and Hindus. Such reformulations became particularly important because the 1919 Act significantly raised the stakes for electoral competition while simultaneously freezing representation on the basis of communal affiliation.

In the critical period after the first Non-cooperation campaign (1919–1922) and the Khilafat movement (1919–1924), a number of key leaders within the independence movement began to shape separate political platforms on the basis of religious identity. The Congress in Bengal had long been dominated by a Hindu elite which was uncomfortable with the populist elements of Gandhi's Non-cooperation movement. In the aftermath of the campaign, the party faced new challenges from the Swarajist party,[4] which advocated contesting council elections, and from extremist groups which advocated more violent means. At the same time, Hindu revivalist organizations, particularly the Hindu Mahasabha, gained influence. The Muslim League, discredited because of its loyalist stance during the Non-cooperation movement, found much of its organization in Bengal taken over by a variety of parties, as momentum on pan-Islamic issues culminated in the Khilafat movement and catapulted a new kind of leadership into prominence. While generating effective tactics for political mobilization, both the Khilafat and Non-cooperation campaigns also fostered reasons for mistrust between Hindu and Muslim communities.

The Plasticity of Identity Symbols

It was not self-evident, however, that Hindu-Muslim would again become *the* political cleavage dividing Hindus and Muslims, as it did after 1905. Some of the early peasant organizations formed after 1914 included low-caste Hindus as well as Muslims. And as noted in chapter one, some of the same Muslims who changed their names to "Sheikh" and "Sayeed" and sent their sons to *madrassahs* during this period also continued to participate in Hindu festivals and other local traditions. The fact that these "reformed" Muslims recognized different codes of behavior for public and private lives supports the argument that "communalism" is not a "given" political identity but a deliberate strategy political actors use to secure certain advantages. In 1905–1911, those who sought to mobilize Muslim resistance to the *swadeshi* campaign saw a clear advantage to recruiting preachers who wanted to rid Bengali Islam of Hindu influences. During the Non-cooperation and Khilafat movements, on the other hand, there had been a concerted effort on the part of most leaders to downplay differences in order to insure full participation in the campaign. The Khilafat organizers perceived as useful an alliance with Gandhi's non-cooperators, and for a brief period, the Non-cooperation/Khilafat movements promoted symbols that stressed communal cooperation in the combined effort against colonial rule.

At the same time, both movements introduced techniques of political mobilization that validated the use of religious symbols in the civil disobedience campaign and that gave *anjumans* and peasant associations a role in mobilizing Muslim peasants. In the years before the Khilafat movement, the leadership of Calcutta's Urdu-speaking Muslims had generated local interest around pan-Islamic issues. The Khilafat took this campaign even further by investing in the very kind of popular religious leader the British had dismissed as unrepresentative of the community to mobilize popular anger against British policy. That legacy of the campaigns was not only a new set of tools involving popular protest but also a new set of leaders capable of using these tools for varying purposes. When both Hindu and Muslim politicians finally abandoned civil disobedience for council politics and the elections of 1926, they created an opportunity for new Muslim parties to challenge the Khilafatists as well as the Nawab and vie for government recognition of their status as the proper representatives of Muslim interests.

The renegotiation of social power among Muslims was framed in terms of competition with Hindus in large part because that was how the colonial power had constructed their relationship in formulating its policies. As the census had done previously, official recognition of some groups as speaking for "Muslim" interests and others as speaking for "Hindus" gave them a permanence they would not have had otherwise. The 1919 Government of India Act maintained separate electorates for Muslims while enfranchising thousands of new voters, mostly in rural areas. These provisions gave Muslim parties an incentive to frame their campaigns to appeal to newly enfranchised cultivators who supported land reform measures opposed by Hindu *zamindars* and for whom symbols which evoked Hindu exploitation and dominance would resonate.

The state plays an important role as the force responsible for granting legitimacy to the claims, and by extension the identities, of those affected by the violence. Although the precise motivations behind the Calcutta "riot" of 1918 were unclear, what did matter for Bengali politics was that the incident was characterized as a "communal" riot. Government reports and memoranda on the incident indicate that many officials viewed the disturbance in terms of "communal" identities. By granting legitimacy to the claims and identities of one group over another, favoring those it believed most likely to uphold "law and order," the British gave contested symbols a prominence they would not otherwise have had. The incident also exposed the uneven relationship Bengal's emerging Muslim leadership had with the colonial authorities. In the Calcutta riot of 1918, its efforts to challenge the authorities' view of who constituted a legitimate leader of the Muslims elicited a violent response by the state.

The first council elections since Non-cooperation which were held in November 1926 constituted something of a watershed in communal relations, as Hindu and Muslim parties adopted positions and symbols designed to deepen political cleavages. The election took place in the climate of animosity that the breakdown of the Khilafat and Non-cooperation movements had engendered. The election was also preceded by a bitter debate over reserving government appointments for Muslims, an issue which was exploited by politicians from all parties. It was no accident that the escalation in communal conflict in the mid-1920s accompanied this challenge to the established Bengali Muslim leadership.

The newcomers to the campaign framed their appeals in terms of a version of religious identity that explicitly rejected any accommodation with other groups, and implicitly blamed the established Muslim leadership for its failure to protect Muslim interests. Rival Muslim leaders deliberately emphasized issues that were designed to highlight differences between Hindus and Muslims and calculated to discredit anyone in their own community who sought to minimize those differences. They called in religious symbolism to bolster their positions and win useful allies among religious leaders and others who had influence in the *mofussil*. In their efforts to establish themselves as spokesmen and representatives for the interests and ideals of the community, they rejected the accommodationist positions and conventions of the previous decades, and even those of the previous few months, most notably the Hindu Muslim Pact which had divided the Council up until the death of the Swarajist leader, C. R. Das, in 1925. While the stated target of their attack was the Hindu leadership, the intended goal was to displace the Nawab and others recognized by the colonial authorities as the "natural" leaders of the Muslims. By creating controversy around particular symbols of identity, they challenged alternative understandings of precedent governing processes and other cultural conventions. Religious symbolism had played a part previously in the Non-cooperation and Khilafat movements; in 1926 it dominated all other issues.

The Rise of Pan-Islamic Concerns

With the outbreak of World War I, events in the Ottoman Empire and the rest of the Muslim world began to assume a great significance for Indian Muslims. Britain had relied heavily on Indian soldiers in the war, many of them Muslims who were sent to fight in Turkey—a point which drew protests from many religious leaders.[5] As the Muslim press reported regularly on developments, and Muslim leaders, many of whom were involved in organizing Red Crescent Societies to assist with Turkish relief, grew more strident in denouncing British policy in the Balkans, British officials grew concerned about the emergence of a vocal new Muslim opposition that appeared poised to supplant the leaders they had promoted. Among the most prominent leaders associated with the issue were two Oxford-educated brothers, Mohammad and Shaukat Ali, whose editorials on the issue in Mohammad Ali's Calcutta-based *Comrade* frequently attracted sedition charges. The brothers were both interned during the war. Abul Kalam Azad, a charismatic speaker from a prominent non-Bengali family in Calcutta, and his Urdu newspaper *Al-Hilal*, were similarly viewed with suspicion by the British authorities. Azad was interned in 1916 and his newspaper banned. He was not released until 1920.

Mohammad Ali "and his gang"[6] were also blamed for stirring up popular resentment toward the British during what became known as the Kanpur mosque affair. In 1913, when violence broke out in Kanpur over a British plan to remove a washing place attached to a mosque in order to widen a road, Lieutenant-Governor Meston referred to protests by Ali and others as evidence of "the domination of the false leaders who are gradually paralysing the best instincts of the Indian Mahomedans." He called the leaders "demagogues who now aspire to lead the Mussulman community," as opposed to those who had long advocated the community's "traditional reliance . . . on the British government."[7] To many British officials, his complaint seemed to be the fulfillment of Hunter's concerns of forty years earlier—that a rebellious and "fanatical" element among the Muslims could exert undue influence at the expense of the loyalist class the government had tried to foster.

A 1913 report on the political situation in Bengal raised express concerns within the government:

I have never known a political situation so disquieting. Every day the Muhammadans are coming more and more to the conclusion that they have been betrayed in India and deserted in Europe and that the British Government is asking too much when it expects them to be loyal and contented. Nawab Sir Salimulla Bahadur and some of the older and wiser leaders are working hard to keep the community in the path of loyalty, but the younger members are either toying with Congress or standing aside in sullen disgust.[8]

The Nawab's influence was seen as "still strong enough" to keep Muslims from attending the Bengal Provincial Conference in great numbers,"[9] but his declining health left him less able to "stem the tide of Muhammadan discontent."[10] In the *Bengalee* of 26 April 1913, the rising young politician A. K. Fazlul Huq announced: "Our quarrel is not with the Hindus but with the officials. We are grateful to the Hindus. But it is the officials whose attitude is unforgiveable and we wish to settle our accounts with them." The district officer's reaction was telling: "This is from a man who was a Deputy Magistrate a few months ago and whose father (an old personal friend of mine) was a staunch supporter of government."[11] Other officials expressed the view that "stands like Fazlul Huq's need not disturb us so long as there is no real solidarity with the advanced Hindu agitators."[12] As was the case earlier on with the Wahhabis, the British authorities most feared loyalist Muslims slipping into the hands of "extremists."

The Calcutta 'Riot' of 1918

In September 1918, serious violence broke out in Calcutta following the publication of an article in the *Indian Daily News* condemned as offensive by the Muslim press, Muslim League leaders, and other prominent Muslim organizations in the city. Accounts of the disturbance which have focused on its "communal" elements have characterized the Muslim population of the affected neighborhoods as "easy prey for extremist agitators," a "fanatical rabble,"[13] or an "excited upcountry mob."[14] Other versions, which have been more concerned with its economic determinants, have perceived the participants as embodying the "convergence of community and class identities."[15] In fact, the violent confrontation was neither a communal riot nor an example of nascent class struggle. Instead, the incident represents an example of how a new kind of Muslim leadership was attempting to shape the issues that defined the Muslim community. There was great resistance to this new leadership, particularly on the part of British authorities who remained suspicious of what they believed was treasonous intent among many of those who, like the Ali brothers, were aligned with prominent 'ulama in condemning British policy toward Muslims in India as well as in the Balkans. In Bengal, there was also great resistance on the part of other Muslim leaders, many of whom, though not all, belonged to the loyalist elite of the partition years, and who feared that their influence and patronage would be undermined. In Bengal, as elsewhere in north India, the rival claims led to a battle not only for control of the issues that would define the community's interests, but for the public space in which those issues would be aired and defended.

The article which sparked the confrontation was published on July 17, 1918. Written from the perspective of a visitor to Senegal, Morocco, or Algeria, it described the traveler observing "an Arab with clean cut features and a world of mysticism in his eye gazing down into the gutter as reverently as if it were his prophet's tomb." Participants at the meetings of the non-official commission which investigated the disturbances agreed that the intent of the piece was to portray these "mystical" Muslims as absorbed in other thoughts.[16] Whatever the intent, the article was immediately condemned by two Urdu Calcutta newspapers, *Naqqash* and *Jamhoor*, for disrespectfully comparing the Prophet's tomb to a gutter.[17] On August 4, the Bengal Presidency Muslim League (BPML) also condemned the piece and vowed to bring legal action against the paper.[18] The Anjuman-e-Mainal Islam convened a public meeting on August 10 at which it was resolved to hold an "All-India" meeting on September 8 and 9 to consider further steps. On August 11, the BPML wrote to the *Indian Daily News*, asking that the paper publish an apology for the "resentment that the remark has unfortunately created." The letter was not acknowledged.[19] Instead, on August 21, the newspaper criticized the Muslim press for launching a "campaign of calumny and misrepresentation" and "stirring up racial and religious animosity," and suggested that "there was a good deal more behind the agitation than appeared on the surface."[20] Three days later, the government ordered *Naqqash* to submit articles to the press censor, a move that was interpreted as anti-Muslim given that officials had not made any such moves against the *Daily News*.

Plans went ahead for the meeting to begin on September 8. The organizing committee, under the chairmanship of retired district magistrate Maulvi Najmuddin Ahmed, collected donations, issued invitations, printed and circulated handbills, and erected a platform at the Halliday street pumping ground. Among those invited were the governor and his staff. Within the committee, however, quarrels broke out over assignments, which ended in a split over whether the meeting should go ahead. Maulvi Najmuddin complained that it was rumored that four committee members who were piqued at the allocation of offices were trying to persuade the government to stop the meeting.[21]

On August 31, the police commissioner ordered that the meeting could not be held until he received more information about the invitees. The committee sent a list and program for discussion which included other issues in addition to the original article. In fact, the range of issues covered by the list suggests that the committee was hoping to position itself to represent Muslims on a number of issues of political importance including the internment of the Ali brothers, specifically:[22]

A. Proposed reform scheme from Muhammadan point of view[23]
B. Education of the Muslim[24] public on the present conditions
C. Suggestions for safeguarding Muslim interests and avoiding friction with non-Muslim communities
D. Internment of Muhammadan leaders
E. Protest against attacks by non-Muslims on "Muhammadan susceptibilities"
F. Formation of a deputation to wait upon the Imperial and Provincial government "with the object of laying Muhammadan grievances before the authorities."

On September 3, a delegation comprising Maulvi Najmuddin and some eleven others met with the governor. In testimony before the nonofficial enquiry commission, Najmuddin stated that the governor asked that a deputation meet with him again on September 9 as a substitute for the public meeting out of concern for the impact a public meeting could have on the religious holidays of Bakr-Id, Muharram, and Durga Puja,[25] which were all approaching. Najmuddin promised that no trouble would result from the public meeting, that only a limited number of "renowned ulemas [sic]" would speak, and that the object "was not to create ill-feelings between Hindus and Muslims whose differences were trifling."[26]

The inquiry commission went on to note, however, that most other leaders present at the meeting, among them established Muslim leaders associated with loyalist positions like Nawab Ali Chaudhury, Abdur Rahim, Golam Hossain Kasem Ariff, and Hussein Suhrawardy, a young lawyer from a prominent family who had a short time earlier entered politics, opposed the meeting on the grounds that it would be dangerous and that "all pains which the government had taken to suppress Wahhabism would be destroyed" and that "the object of the meeting as explained by Maulvi Najmuddin Ahmed was not its real object, and that its real object was not being disclosed." The reference to "Wahhabism" was particularly damning and was apparently designed to evoke the very images of 'ulama igniting rebellion among the masses that the government feared. The meeting closed with a plan for the governor to meet with the planning committee to suggest postponing the meeting.[27] In the interim, however, the planning committee decided on its own to send a deputation to inform the government that the meeting would go ahead as planned, and that it would be held "in an orderly fashion." The inquiry commission noted that there was a "widespread feeling" among committee members "that a small group of Calcutta Mussulmans had misrepresented the aim of the meeting to the Government."[28]

On September 4, the government prohibited the meeting and requested the names and addresses of all the delegates. At 8:00 p.m. that day, the government ordered nine outside 'ulama who had arrived for the meeting to leave Calcutta within twenty-four hours. According to a statement by Maulana Mahomed Enayatulla, two of the Muslim leaders who had opposed the meeting, Suhrawardy and Ariff, accompanied by Deputy Commissioner of Police Lahiri, visited the 'ulama shortly after the orders were given and told them that the orders had been canceled. The next day, Suhrawardy and Ariff accompanied four of the 'ulama to see the governor who told them that he "regretted" the externment orders and that he was "acting on the unanimous opinion and advice of Mahomedan leaders" in canceling the meeting. Enayatulla responded that Maulana Abdul Bari and other 'ulama at Farangi Mahal[29]—those in the forefront of the protests against the war in Turkey—would not have agreed with the assessment of the "Mahomedan leaders" the government had sought out.[30] But such an argument could only have reinforced the governor's view that Enayatulla, like Azad, the Ali brothers, and religious leaders at Farangi Mahal, did not genuinely represent the interests of the Muslim community, as the government understood it, and were not to be trusted. Instead, the governor had relied on leaders he wanted to believe were more "representative" in the hope of nurturing their loyalty and undermining the others it considered illegitimate spokesmen.

Sandria Freitag has discussed the changing "crisis of authority" among U.P. Muslims during communal riots over a sixty–year period—from the 1870s through the 1930s, with particular attention to the Kanpur Mosque incident. The ramifications of the violence that surrounded that confrontation are significant for what happened in Calcutta in 1918. In early 1913, with what it considered great consideration for the feelings of the affected communities, the Kanpur administration drew up plans for road improvements in the city that skirted all temples and mosques, and required only the relocation of a bathing place (*dalan*) attached to the mosque. When the chairman of the municipal board toured the site, "he was accompanied by several Muslims, all of whom walked—without incident—through the *dalan* with their shoes on, an event which soon assumed great significance."[31] The administration proceeded with its plans confident that it had garnered the best of Muslim opinion from recognized leaders that the *dalan* should not prove an obstacle to the new road. When another kind of leader within the Kanpur Muslim community began to organize protests, the administration was caught by surprise. The wearing of shoes in the *dalan* abruptly became an issue in the conflict between these different kinds of leaders.

It seems clear, for instance, that while local practice had tolerated the wearing of shoes in the *dalan*, once this became common knowledge it proved an
embarrassment to the Muslim community in general—and for this reason
the new *mutavalli* [managers of mosques] made it their first act to try to find
the culprits. Similarly, an agreement to relocate part of the mosque might be
possible to arrange quietly, locally; but once the cause received some publicity, in an atmosphere already heavily laden with despair over the position of
Islam, this became impossible.[32]

When the *dalan* was removed on July 1, thousands gathered at the
mosque, and at a meeting that evening it was resolved to send telegrams
protesting the removal to the government, the press, and other Muslim
leaders. Muslims across Kanpur then elected an additional nine *mutavalli*
to serve as managers of the mosque along with the original two. Plans
were made for a huge meeting of all Muslims from the city on August 3.
Thousands arrived at the mosque, and when the police tried to stop them
from stacking bricks as if to rebuild the *dalan*, the crowd began to throw
debris at the police. The disturbance ended when police opened fire,
killing at least one and injuring several others.

The incident served to boost the standing of those leaders who had insisted on confrontation with the British authorities, that is, precisely
those the British had considered illegitimate as representatives of the
community. The message they communicated was clear: mass mobilization as a tool of political action worked. And it worked not because the
"masses" could be manipulated by fanatical appeals, as the British and
many other Muslim leaders believed. It worked because these leaders
had taken an issue which would otherwise have been handled quietly
and made it public property;[33] they had taken a local symbol and in-
vested it with political importance for all the Muslims of Kanpur, and
even beyond. The *Mussulman* wrote: "Muhammadans of India will have
no peace until that demolished building is restored. If it is not, let the agitation be carried on from generation to generation, and if we are only
true to ourselves and to our religion, the ultimate victory is ours. It is for
the Government to reassure the public mind . . . "[34]

In Calcutta, there was a similar split between established Muslim leaders who still courted government support and the others, some of them
Urdu-speaking non-Bengalis sympathetic to the protests against British
policy toward Turkey. While the latter saw an opportunity to gain the upper hand by accusing their rivals as government pawns,[35] the so-called
moderates (who had traditionally supported government policy) were
equally interested in discrediting those spearheading the protests. The
way they chose to discredit them was by accusing them of what they, and
the British, feared most: stirring up the "fanaticism" of the masses with

religious appeals. Each group accused the other of misrepresenting Muslim interests.

It was not until September 5 that the *Indian Daily News,* under pressure from the government, published an apology for the July 17 article, explaining that there had been "no intention to hurt anyone's feelings" and that the article had slipped through one night when the paper was short-staffed and the editors had filled up space with clippings from other newspapers.[36] The apology had little impact. On September 7, A. K. Fazlul Huq, a young lawyer who was to become one of the most important political leaders in Bengal, and later, in Bangladesh, and who had attained some prominence for his controversial role in negotiating the Lucknow Pact,[37] met with the planning committee and urged them to cancel the meeting. However, the principal organizers—all non-Bengali editors or sub-editors of the Urdu press—refused.[38]

On September 8, as a crowd assembled around the Nakhoda mosque in Calcutta, the government agreed to another meeting with all the leaders. The next morning, as the delegation met with the governor, the crowd reassembled at the mosque and then moved toward Government House where the private meeting was taking place. Huq attempted to speak to the crowd but was refused permission by the police, who ordered the crowd to return to the mosque. Marwari businessmen,[39] who, fearing trouble, had hired non-Bengalis to guard their shops and houses, ordered the guards to clear the streets near their property. Fights broke out between the guards and protesters when they attempted to do so. When a shot was fired from inside one of the Marwari houses, killing a protester, the crowd attacked Marwari shops. The police responded by opening fire and attacking the crowd with *lathis;* three days later, when the violence was over, forty-three were dead, thirty-six of them Muslim and seven Hindu. Twenty-four of those who were killed died in a single incident when police and army forces fired on a crowd of Muslim mill-hands who were marching into Calcutta on the morning of September 10. According to witnesses who testified before the inquiry commission, the unarmed crowd included boys as young as eight and ten years old.[40] Marwari shops were the principal target of looting, and a number of Marwaris were assaulted.

Arguments have been advanced that the violence was essentially class-based but later became "communal" as part of an expression of popular resentment against price-gouging by Marwari merchants. However, Marwaris were not singled out in the protests that built up in the months before the violence. In fact, there is little evidence to indicate that this was a "communal" riot at all, or that the incident introduced "communalism" as a weapon into Bengali politics.[41] While the principal targets of the Muslim protesters were Marwaris, Marwari property was attacked only after the hired guards tried to prevent the demonstrators from moving outside the grounds of the mosque and after shots were fired from a Marwari house. While it is true that the looting of Marwari shops, which began after the shooting, could have been aggravated by feelings of resentment over the community's control of shops and other businesses in the area, it would be a mistake to view the crowd's response as an example of class solidarity.[42] It is far more likely that the looters took advantage of the outbreak to engage in looting, rather than that they started a "riot" in order to loot.[43]

Although the Urdu journalists who seized on the issue originally framed their protests in the name of defending Islam, as in the Kanpur incident, the target of those protests was not the Hindu community but the British government and Muslim "collaborators" who had failed to protect Muslim interests. In fact, the tactics employed—strikes, mass rallies and heated denunciations of government policy in the press—were aimed primarily against government targets and had all been used before, particularly in the swadeshi campaign. The violence that resulted was thus more a response to government actions than it was a creation of "communal" passions.

The report of the inquiry commission makes clear that the various parties involved were aware of the potential for violence, and that those opposed to the public meeting used the threat of violence to discredit their opponents. There is little question that those organizing the meeting anticipated, even welcomed, a confrontation with the authorities. The Marwari shopkeepers were apparently concerned enough by the rumors of violence that they imported guards from outside Bengal, either because they felt Bengali guards could not to be trusted not to be drawn into conflict or because "up-country" Hindus had a menacing reputation. But of all the incidents of violence recorded by the inquiry committee, most deaths occurred at the hands of city police and army troops, including the killing of the twenty-four millworkers. In fact, the provincial government's heavy-handed approach was criticized not only by the inquiry committee but by the government of India, prompting a reorganization of the Calcutta police.[44] Governor Ronaldshay was so convinced that the incident marked a watershed in communal relations that he was taken aback when Marwaris and Muslims in Calcutta joined together in protests against Gandhi's arrest in 1919. Ronaldshay apparently expected the violence of the previous year to have precluded any such event.[45]

Although the principal participants were all non-Bengali, both Hindu and Muslim, the incident nevertheless had serious implications for Muslim politics in Bengal. The Bengali Muslim leaders involved in the negotiations, Huq, Suhrawardy, and Rahim, were forced to come to terms with a new kind of politics and a new way of framing their community's interests. In the year that followed, as the Khilafat movement was launched, the Bengali Muslim leaders who had backed government policy in 1918 found themselves in an uncomfortable alliance with the very leaders who had opposed it, and were now determined to frame the issues that would be of concern to Muslims not in private meetings at Government House, but publicly—in mosques, meeting halls, and *id-gahs*[46] across Bengal.

The Legacy of Non-cooperation and Khilafat and the Hindu-Muslim Pact

The years between 1919 and 1924 mark the official boundaries of Mohandas Gandhi's first Non-cooperation movement and the Khilafat movement, a campaign launched jointly by Gandhi and Indian Muslim leaders to force the British and Allied powers to maintain the boundaries of the Ottoman empire, and, in so doing, to preserve the Caliph of Islam. Among the principal organizers behind the Khilafat movement were the two brothers, Mohammad and Shaukat Ali. With the support of prominent 'ulama, particularly the Jami'at-i 'ulama-i Hind, the Khilafat movement soon eclipsed the Muslim League in popular appeal. The December 1920 meeting of the Congress at Nagpur overwhelmingly endorsed Gandhi's Non-cooperation campaign and the Khilafat movement, launching nationwide boycotts and other acts of civil disobedience. The movement also thrust the 'ulama into a new position of power, as influential figures like Maulana Akram Khan assumed a leading role in dispatching preachers into the *mofussil* to rally support for the movement.[47] Despite mass arrests, the movement swiftly gained momentum until the murder of twenty-two policemen in the town of Chauri Chaura led Gandhi to abruptly call off the campaign in 1922.[48] The Khilafatists continued on their own well into the 1930s, but the movement essentially ended in 1924, when Kemal Ataturk's new government abolished the Turkish sultanate and, with it, the caliphate.

The tactics employed by the two movements were the same as those used during the anti-partition agitation: boycotts, the promotion of *deshi* (home-made) goods, and resignations from government institutions. British schools, courts, and cloth were rejected and alternatives established and promoted, including arbitration boards, "national" schools, and home-spun cloth. In Bengal, however, these symbols of Non-cooperation were implicated in a recent and violent past. The memory of communal violence and government repression that had followed the *swadeshi* movement made many Hindu leaders reluctant to join with Gandhi and the Khilafatists. The *bhadrolok* had an even greater fear of the of social implication of involving the lower caste "masses" in such a campaign.[49]

More significant, the use of these tactics for political mobilization fostered new reasons for mistrust and bred renewed suspicions that the two communities were not shouldering the hardships of the boycotts equally. While some one thousand students left the Calcutta Madrasah, for example, few Hindu schools in the area participated to the same extent.[50] "The predominantly Muhammadan character of the agitation even at the end of the year was seen in the fact that in the school and college strike of November it was chiefly Muhammadan students who were affected."[51]

Whether or not Bengali Hindus participated less in the boycotts overall is not known, but fears about Hindu motivations were swiftly exploited after the movements fell apart in 1922. In 1924, the Bengali Muslim newspaper *Islam-Darsan* published the poet Saiyed Mohammed Ismail Hosen Siraji's welcoming address to the Bengal Muhammadan Conference at Sirajgunj. Siraji was blunt.

> Nearly all of the government jobs are monopolized by Hindus. My question is, how many of our Hindu brothers have abandoned their jobs while, in the meantime, so many Muslims, abandoning their own jobs, have brought hardship to their communities and their families? . . . While there are hundreds and hundreds of Hindu colleges, especially the famous Benaras Hindu University, left untouched, for what purpose have the cherished Muslim Aligarh College and the Islamia College of Lahore been ruined? . . . Selling *deshi* cloth at an inflated price, Hindu and Marwari shopkeepers have made a great profit. On the other hand, by buying the coarse and expensive *deshi* cloth, Muslims punish themselves.[52]

Six years later, *Shariat-e Islam*, another Bengali newspaper, was still bitter about the boycotts, suggesting once again that the intention had been to prevent "backward" Muslims from competing with Hindus.

> Whatever damage and loss there is, this is the Mussalman's lot. During the boycotts of the schools and colleges, they truly suffered . . . yet the scheming Congressmen with their sinister motives in a flash tore them up by the roots. . . . That swaraj can come by closing the schools, colleges, madrasahs, etc., adding to the unemployment problem and increasing the numbers of thieves and *dacoits* [bandits], this is sheer nonsense. Certainly, by these means, the way is open to crush that backward community by closing off the way to progress.[53]

The movements also stirred deep fears among both the Hindu and Muslim elites about the dangers of mass mobilization, particularly in the *mofussil*. The *bhadrolok* class that formed the backbone of the early nationalist movement in Bengal had too great an investment as land holders to risk taking up any cause that might threaten their stake in it by reforming tenancy laws. The enthusiastic participation of Bengali 'ulama in the Khilafat movement and their success in gaining the support of Muslims in rural Bengal also brought home to Hindu leaders the fact that Muslims would be in a better position to build a bridge with rural voters. Meanwhile, the techniques of the campaign had made rural leaders aware of the possibilities for agitation on agrarian issues. Even the unsuccessful efforts to organize a jute boycott led government observers to comment that the attempt had made "the cultivator think of other methods in which he might improve his position and . . . prepare the way for the no-taxes and no-rent movement which afterwards appeared in Eastern Bengal."[54] By 1923, there were widespread reports of tenants refusing to pay not only the illegal taxes but even the legal rent.[55]

Symbols important to the construction of political identity can be found as much in traditional authority relationships as in institutions like the Khilafat or the mosque. Beginning with the agitations of the *swadeshi* period (1906–1911), the British Government in Bengal began to identify as the agent of this "new consciousness" among Bengali Muslims the "itinerant mullahs," whose activities in stirring up communal passions increased during the Khilafat movement. They continued to be seen as one of the most potent forces capable of mobilizing rural Muslims. The government realized that because of their close relationship to the Muslim cultivators, these *maulvis* occupied a position of considerable influence. The powerful Maulana Akram Khan was known to have his own followers among these mullahs preaching the cause of the Khilafat throughout east Bengal. During the Khilafat and Non-cooperation movements, British authorities tried to counter the strength of the alliance between the Congress and the 'ulama by mounting a counter-propaganda campaign in the *mofussil*. To that end they co-opted local religious leaders and, with the help of some Muslim politicians, including A. K. Fazlul Huq, collected *fatawa* (formal legal opinions) against the Khilafat movement by prominent *maulanas* and distributed them. "It is attacking [the Non-cooperation Movement] with their own weapons," wrote District Magistrate Waddell. "And wherever we fairly join issue with them we are bound to succeed because we have reason and truth on our side."[56] The competition among Muslim leaders and British authorities to win the support of the mullahs says much about the importance of these traditional religious networks in the process of political mobilization.

Even within the Muslim community, however, there were dramatic differences between the politicians and the 'ulama on the nature of such mobilization. The 'ulama supported enthusiastically the religious and emotional appeal of the campaign, but many Western-educated *ashraf* leaders did not. Many of these leaders were also suspicious of the non-Bengali Muslim leaders of the movement.[57] During the *swadeshi* years, the Muslim press had highlighted rural concerns by combining calls for increased Muslim representation on local boards with pleas for relief for the indebted peasantry. It was not until after the formation of a peasant-based political party, however, that the Muslim press took a stand on more controversial measures like support for reforming the Tenancy Act. But because the Muslim League, like the Congress, primarily represented Muslims who had their own interests in the land to preserve, mass mobilization remained perilous.

The Praja Movement

The *praja* (tenant) movement traces its origins to the rise of prosperous peasants. As noted in chapter two, the tenancy acts of 1859 and 1885 had defined the various classes of *raiyats*. "Occupancy *raiyats*" were those who could prove occupancy in their holdings for twelve consecutive years. They could then acquire occupancy rights in any new land taken into cultivation. *Jotedars* were cultivators with substantial holdings of up to 400 acres in which they had occupancy rights. In addition to subletting their land, they often operated as money-lenders. As Chatterjee notes, by the late nineteenth century, provincial politics in Bengal was dominated by this class of middle and small landholders who had purchased shares of larger *zamindaris* and had then sublet parts of them.[58] Much of the Hindu *bhadrolok* elite came from this class.[59]

Favorable trade in jute since 1900 had fostered the rise of a class of prosperous cultivators and *jotedars* also among the Muslims in East Bengal.[60] Profits from this trade tended to be concentrated in certain districts, Mymensingh, Dacca, and Pabna notable among them, at a time which saw a sharp decline in the number of tenant- and owner-cultivators throughout the province, and an increase in sharecroppers and landless laborers.[61] The increase in *bargadars* (sharecroppers) was a direct consequence of the increase in the richer sector of the peasantry who sublet their land. Previously, sharecroppers represented landed cultivators who had spare family labor and were looking for additional income. By the turn of the century, sharecroppers "tended to be drawn from the ranks of cultivating peasants whose holdings were less than required for subsistence or who had been completely dispossessed of their lands."[62]

The increased concentration of the land in the hands of better-off cultivators had the effect of pushing some of their number to turn to education as a way to better their economic position and social status. As the Calcutta University Commission reported in 1918, the more up-looking members of the cultivating classes have ambitions towards a less humble station. . . . Such are some of the new social and economic motives which are stimulating the educational awakening of this part of Bengal. . . . A cultivator with a number of sons sends one of them to the high school with the hope of going on to college and entering a profession. This boy is not wanted on his father's land. The holding is not large enough to support him as well as his brothers.[63]

Cultivators who were able to benefit by expropriating the holdings of less fortunate neighbors[64] began to educate their children in numbers not seen before,[65] and to organize themselves in community groups and *anjumans* and *raiyat* associations which flourished at this time,[66] and which would form the backbone of *praja* organizations and, later, the Krishak *praja* (peasant-tenant) party. These associations sponsored the construction of local *madrasahs* and mosques, and fielded candidates for local union board elections.[67]

The communalization of agrarian issues in Bengal from the 1920s until partition in 1947 appears in some ways to be almost a given. Arguments advanced in explanation of peasant disturbances and communal outbreaks begin with the demographic fact that the majority of large landlords and money-lenders in eastern Bengal were Hindus, and the majority of cultivators and tenants were Muslim. But the dichotomy was not so simple. As noted above, by the early part of the twentieth century, there was a sizeable number of Muslim landholding cultivators who sublet their land to tenants. The leadership of all major parties—the Congress, the Swaraj party and the Muslim League—came primarily from landowning families, so that each of the parties entered into the bitter land reform debates of the quarter century preceding partition with one eye toward retaining its immediate landed constituency and the other toward winning support among the mass of Bengal's rural voters. At the same time, the perception of loyalty, of communal solidarity, became a powerful factor in the politics of land reform, regardless of the reality of land ownership and landlord interests among party leaders. With the rise of the *praja* movement, Muslim leaders became aware of the need to identify themselves with tenant interests, and used the issue against each other while jockeying for position before elections.

After the first Non-Cooperation movement of 1919–1924, politics in Bengal focused increasingly on agrarian concerns. This was largely a result of the growth of the *praja* organizations in the early 1910s, which attempted for the first time to represent the concerns of the substantial cultivators like the *jotedars*, although not necessarily the sharecroppers and other poor tenants. Other reasons included a growing awareness on the part of political leaders of the importance of numbers in the increasingly expanded electorate, particularly after the Montague-Chelmsford reforms of 1919, which, in addition to granting Muslims separate electorates, also enfranchised a larger block of the propertied population, adding some 5.5 million voters for the provincial councils and 1.5 million for the Imperial Legislature, or between 1 and 3 percent of the adult population. That percentage obviously left out the great mass of the Muslim peasantry who would be affected by land legislation in the following years. The reforms of 1935 retained the property requirement but expanded the franchise to thirty million voters, still only one-sixth of the adult population. The efforts of the Non-cooperation and Khilafat movements to involve the peasantry in political campaigns, and, after the late 1920s, the crisis in agriculture during the depression years which had resulted in growing landlessness and rising rural debt in Bengal, also contributed to a growing awareness of the centrality of agararian concerns. Land reform issues—tenancy legislation and amendments, rural debt reconstruction, abolition of *zamindari* and the Permanent Settlement, and rural primary education—dominated Bengali politics and became increasingly the focus of communal divisions during this period.

Praja conferences took place as early as 1914. According to Abul Mansur Ahmed, whose autobiography chronicles the politics of these years, the Kamariarchar Praja Conference in Mymensingh included provincial figures who would go on to play critical roles in shaping Muslim politics in the province. Among them were A. K. Fazlul Huq, Abul Kasem, Mohammad Razibuddin Tarafdar, Maulana Mohammad Akram Khan, and Maulana Maniruzzaman Islamabadi. The conference passed a resolution protesting rent enhancements for Holi,[68] or for changes to the property like cutting trees or installing a tank. Although billed as a gathering for all, the conference featured only Muslim speakers.[69] In 1917, Fazlul Huq, among others, founded the Calcutta Agricultural Association and in 1920, the Bengal Joatdars (*jotedars*) and Raiyats Association.[70]

The *Dinajpur Survey and Settlement Report* of 1934–1940 shows continuing evidence of upward mobility among better-off Bengali Muslim peasants. In the north Bengal district of Dinajpur, Muslims made up a majority and enjoyed a higher standard of living than many Muslims in East Bengal. The census of 1931 reports that 7.4 percent of the Muslims in the district were literate, compared to 5.5 percent of the Hindus. The *Survey and Settlement Report* goes on to note that

> The cultural and economic superiority of the Muslims of the district is revealed by their supremacy in the Union Boards where they consistently have representation in excess of their proportion. In only 5 thanas out of 30 are there fewer Muslim Presidents [of Union Boards] than non-Muslim Pres-

idents. . . . Muslim Presidents and elected members are a decided majority even in such a Hindu *thana* as Kaharul.[71]

As elsewhere, the economic well-being of the Dinajpur Muslims was due to the success of the Muslim *jotedars* in the cultivation of jute. The tendency to identify with a more visible "Islamic" identity is evident among all Muslims of the district, and particularly this class. The report notes that "in common with rustic Muslims throughout the province in the last 30 years, there has been a decided quickening of Islam. This is apparent even in names. The old surname Nasya has now completely disappeared. . . . Now all who cannot attain the social dignity of Choudhury, or Sarkar, or Mandal are 'Sheikhs,' or 'Ahmad.'"[72] The poorer Muslims in the district were still nearly indistinguishable from their poor Hindu counterparts, dressing in *dhoti*, not *lungi*, and unable to bear the expense of a *fez* or *topi*. The well-off, on the other hand, attend Friday *jumna* prayers "decently dressed" and wearing a *topi*, or cap, or possibly a *achkan*, and have a white-washed *pucca* mosque and school built in their neighborhood. In these schools "the village school-master or the *patwari* is likely to reply in Urdu to a question in Bengali."[73]

The report also notes that in the years of expansion in the jute trade, more rich villagers from the district began performing the Hajj.[74] The increased awareness of these markers of a Muslim identity went hand in hand with efforts on the part of the better-off Muslims to be seen as patrons of the community—in building mosques and schools and providing wells—thereby increasing their own prestige and influence in local politics. However, the new consciousness and activities among this class of Muslims did not necessarily interfere with other practices, suggesting that Bengali Muslims may not have perceived the new behavioral rules for being a good Muslim as necessarily excluding other aspects of their culture. For example, *pir*-worship continued to play a dominant role in the religious activities of many Muslims, and *pirattas* (rent-free land dedicated to a *pir*) were frequented by both Hindus and Muslims and were, the report noted, "innumerable." Muslims also continued to participate in Lakshmi Puja and other Hindu festivals, and both communities observed the Nabanna, or harvest ceremony.[75]

This variability in behavior suggests that Bengali Muslims adopted different codes of behavior for the different "communities" to which they belonged—the localized community of a village where it was possible to subscribe to a "private" code of behavior that might include *pir*-worship and *puja*, and the larger "community" bounded by the itineraries of reformist *maulvis* and membership of the *anjuman* where a more "public" set of rules obtained. In the first, the sense of community was mediated in part through collective rituals related to both "religious" identifications.[76] In the second, other behaviors—participating in social and political programs of the *anjuman*, attending *bahas*[77]—reinforced membership in a different community. The seeming contradiction in this dichotomy may be problematic for modern readers; in its historical context the "multi-strandedness" of community identity was not unusual.[78] The emergence of this self-consciously Muslim identity did not necessarily signal the abandonment of all other values and traits. Rather, adopting a more articulated Muslim identity was a strategy for responding to the political and economic changes taking place.

The Swarajists and the Hindu-Muslim Pact

After the suspension of Non-cooperation in 1922, Bengali leaders opposed to Gandhi formed the Swaraj party under the leadership of C. R. Das and contested seats in the provincial council with the aim of pursuing an obstructionist policy that would destroy the British system of dyarchy.[79] They gained the support of many of the Hindu elite who preferred such a strategy to Gandhi's populist methods.[80] At the same time, the Hindu Mahasabha, founded in 1914 by Pandit Madan Mohan Malaviya, and the Hindu revivalist Arya Samaj, stepped up *shuddhi* (reconversion) campaigns to "reclaim" Muslims.[81] These groups also had support among a number of the Hindu elite, as did the extremist *samitis* (groups) which had been revived to carry out the same violent agenda they had preached following the 1905 partition.[82]

The Swaraj party needed Muslim support to carry out its agenda in the council. In 1923, Das and the Swarajist Muslim leaders agreed to the terms of a Hindu-Muslim Pact, which was to go into effect once self-government was attained. The pact included provisions promising Muslims 60 percent of the seats in local bodies to be filled through separate electorates and 55 percent of all government posts. At the time, Muslims made up approximately 52 percent of the total population of Bengal.[83] Music before mosques was to be banned, and no restrictions were to be placed on cow-killing.[84] The pact was short-lived, however. Denounced by the Hindu Mahasabha and opposed by most of the Congress, it lost significant Muslim support as well after one council member demanded that one of the Pact's provisions, that 80 percent of government posts be reserved until Muslims occupied 55 percent of such posts, be implemented immediately. The resolution was moved by a loyalist Muslim member who was hoping to end the Swarajists' control of the council. The Swarajists managed to postpone a vote and hold on to their majority long enough to vote no salary for the government-appointed ministers, Abdul Karim Ghuznavi and A. K. Fazlul Huq, forcing them to resign. When the government appointed two new ministers, the council again voted no pay and dyarchy was suspended until the 1926 elections.[85] With Das' death in 1925, the Swaraj party disintegrated.

The Search for a 'Muslim' Party

At the time of the 1926 election, there was no dominant Muslim political party in Bengal. The Muslim League was moribund, its members having been overtaken by the Khilafat Committee when the League's leadership balked at Gandhi's strategies and at the dangers of injecting religious symbols into the campaign. League leaders had also feared the enthusiasm the 'ulama displayed for reasserting their authority in politics. The success of the Khilafat Committee in supplanting the Muslim League was due as much to the League's internal paralysis as to the Khilafat Committee's ability to win the support of the 'ulama and, through them, a link with the Muslim masses that in 1919 the League did not have.

Fazlul Huq represented part of the young Muslim leadership in Bengali politics that was catapulted into prominence during the Non-cooperation/Khilafat movements.[86] By 1923, however, he had changed sides, and collected fatwas from prominent maulanas urging resistance to the Non-cooperation movement that he passed along to British officers.[87] Huq's standing as a leader among the Muslims remained tenuous. His earlier association with Hindu leaders during the Non-cooperation campaign left the conservative Muslim merchant leadership and the followers of the Nawab of Dacca wary about Huq's political intentions.[88] In his speech to the convention of the All-India Muslim League in Delhi in 1918 he characterized communal violence as an "exception to the happy relations between the two" communities.[89] Huq had better connections in the *mofussil* than did most of the Muslim leaders, having laid the groundwork for what was to become his Krishak Praja Party as early as 1917.[90] In 1923 most of his Muslim colleagues, like their Hindu *bhadrolok* counterparts, largely avoided any contact with the *mofussil*. With the decline of the 'ulama's influence after Chauri Chaura, Westernized leaders lost their only institutional link to influence mass opinion in the villages.

By 1924, it was not at all clear who the League's leaders in Bengal were. Responding to the heightened communal tension in Bengal at this time Wahed Hossain, of the Calcutta High Court, wrote to the Secretary of the Muslim League:

> The present tension of feeling between Hindu and Mahomedan presents a good field for League action. . . . As the League proposes to form a National Pact, I would request you to exert a little to establish a Board of Conciliation in each Province. . . . It is time that the League should move in the matter and try to exercise its influence. As Swami Sradhanand [a Hindu leader] is

laying [the] blame at the door of the Jammat-ul-Ulema-i-Hind [(sic) the organization of Indian 'ulama] and the Central Khilafat Committee, they are
not the proper bodies to exercise influence but the League being neutral I
think it will be able to make its influence felt.[91]

Gandhi also had difficulty with the disputes between the Khilafatists and
League leaders, and complained that "there is a lack of consolidated
Muslim opinion on Islamic questions. Everybody feels keenly and no-
body comes forward with a reasoned and representative statement."[92]

The collapse of the Khilafat Movement in 1924 left behind a profusion
of Muslim organizations in Bengal, but none that had a party organization or much influence outside the immediate district of whatever family
stood behind it. Gandhi was not alone in his efforts to identify a united
Muslim voice. British officials, eager to reclaim a single "representative,"
saw the vacuum as an opportunity to create one that would support the
government. In their efforts, they turned to the established Muslim families who had formed the backbone of loyalist Muslim politics in the past.
In Dacca, the District Officer tried without success to merge the Dacca
Moslem Association with the *anjuman* controlled by the Nawab's family.
As had been the case during the partition years, the government clung to
its promotion of the Nawab as "representative of the Muhammadans of
the city and the district as a whole."[93] In Midnapore, the District Magistrate tried the same tack in his effort to strengthen the association headed
by the Suhrawardis, the prominent Calcutta family, arguing that "the
Muhammadans of Midnapore require strengthening and encouragement
rather than weakening. . . . It would be a good thing to get [the Branch
National Muhammadan Association of Muhammad Khoda Nawaz] to
disband itself and amalgamate it with the District Muslim Association
which is run by the Suhrawardis."[94] It was the policy of the Political Department to maintain a list of "recognized" associations. Only those associations officially recorded on this list could recommend candidates for
public office and help prepare electoral registers,[95] a fact that was not lost
on groups vying for patronage.

The government provided other benefits to loyalist Muslim parties.
When Maulvi Akbar Ali approached the government about holding a
separate conference at the time of the Bengal Muhammadan Conference
at Sirajgunj, Subdivisional Officer Hindley persuaded some Europeans
to donate tarpaulins. Hindley observed that the conference reflected a
"real feeling of disgust" at Muslims voting with Das and the Swarajists,
and "gratitude to Government for what it's done for Muslims locally,
e.g. extra Madrassa buildings, visits by [government officials]" and a desire to attract Government attention to grant a fuller measure of conces-
sion to them

as the majority caste, by definitely ranging themselves against the Swara-jists. . . . The situation is one which the Government should not overlook, and while it can never be the business of this Government to exploit the do-ings of one sect to the disadvantage of another, I do feel that in this case the weight must be given to the representation of a body of men who have dared to declare, at the cost of great personal sacrifice and possibility of their failure, on the side of law and order.[96]

Hindley recommended that other MLAs involved be "consulted by Gov-ernment regarding recognition for their services and possible ways to meet the demands of the Mahommedans assembled here."[97]

Maulvi Akbar Ali sent SDO Hindley a copy of the resolutions passed by the conference, which included forming an association under the name of the All Bengal Moslem Association "with the view to bring about uniformity of action among Moslems of Bengal and to safeguard and advance their interests." The conference also resolved that the Ben-gal Tenancy Act should be amended to safeguard the interests of ten-ants, that legislation offering relief to debtors be enacted, and that gov-ernment recruit more Muslims in government and rail services. The resolution criticized Muslims who "get up bogus meetings of condem-nation", calling such "mischief mongers," "not the opinion or voice of the Moslem electors"—included in this were those Muslim council members who voted against the budget. The Conference condemned them as not acting in accordance with the wishes of the electorate, re-viving the "backwardness" argument to urge "upon them and the Gov-ernment the necessity of saving the grave situation created by the hasty and thoughtless action of the counsellors which is sure to give a death blow to the educational interests of the country and specially to the progress of education of the Muhammadans who are still very back-ward in that respect."[98]

The Communal Violence of 1926:
Symbols, Elections, and Violence

In the months before the general election of 1926, there were major out-breaks of violence in Calcutta, Pabna, and Dacca. Urban violence on such a scale had not been typical, even during the *swadeshi* years. These riots marked a political conjuncture that altered the course of Muslim politics in Bengal, because unlike the "riot" of 1918, these violent outbreaks did represent planned attacks designed to polarize the Hindu and Muslim populations. More important was the fact that these contests over sym-bols and public space took place in the months immediately preceding the general election. The intra-Muslim aspect of this competition was particularly intense, as rival would-be representatives attempted to generate political consensus around these particular symbols of identity.

The issue which precipitated the violence in all three places was the playing of music during Hindu processions past mosques. Conflict over the playing of music before mosques was not much in evidence before the late 1890s. In fact, nearly every editorial that dealt with the problem made note of the conflict as a very recent phenomenon, a betrayal of the sense of community that had seen Hindus and Muslims willing to accommodate one another's beliefs and even participate to some extent in one another's festivals. The *Moslem Chronicle*, for example, published in 1895 a number of letters of protest against those it suspected of using the issue to get back at Muslims for the killing of cows. The newspaper condemned leaders on both sides who seemed bent on undoing the long-standing co-existence of the two groups, and included music before mosques in a list of issues Bengali Muslims ought to "rally around," including *waqf* legislation,[99] rights to cow slaughter, and hostels for Muslim schoolboys.[100]

Early, sporadic incidents of music before mosques could not have prepared either community for the violence the issue touched off in the mid-1920s. According to one report, the casualty figures for the six riots in and around Dacca and Calcutta and the week of rioting in Pabna in July ran into the hundreds.[101] Discrepancies in local custom regarding processions past mosques plagued British administrators, whose approach toward resolving the custom was to establish precedence. Such attempts were futile, for a telling feature of the riots was the deliberate disregard for prevailing customs and the reinvention of traditions that one side or the other claimed were authoritative for relations between the two communities. In fact, the government's attempts to establish prevailing custom as law merely contributed to both groups' willingness to rewrite history to suit their own interests. Gyanendra Pandey rightly observes that this phenomenon marks a "destabilization of custom," a "process encouraged by the very fact of the colonial attempt to record [it]," a factor which played an important role in the growing number of clashes over communal symbols and issues during this period.[102] Official recording of a group's right to public space implied official sanction; thus, groups vied with each other to win an official ruling. If they lost, and the authorities ruled in favor of another version of custom, government obstruction became an additional target of protest.

As Freitag points out in her discussion of riots in U.P. in 1923, 1924, and 1925, British policy toward quelling disturbances changed during this period in large part because local officials were no longer able to count on traditional intermediaries to maintain law and order. They could no longer control local leaders by limiting them to "approved institutional outlets," because these new leaders took their demands and protests into public spaces.[103] British administrators made little effort to disguise their frustrations. The commissioner of Lucknow complained that "[t]he leaders, moreover, are split up by personal and party jealousies, e.g. amongst the Hindus both Swarajists and Liberals are bent on preventing the other from getting the credit of effecting a settlement. . . ." The provincial chief secretary agreed: "Political rivalry, always latent, is now the dominant factor. . . . Causes of dispute are capricious and local. . . . In modern conditions, moreover, the influence of individuals changes with kaleidoscopic rapidity."[104]

The bitterness of one district magistrate who had attempted to record once and for all the custom governing practice and belief in his district is made clear in his letter to the chief secretary, government of Bengal:

> The question only having arisen during the last two years or so, there are no records, and the witnesses available are prejudiced. . . . In some places the Muhammadans have recently erected new mosques by the roads and the Hindus immediately wish to take processions by them with music though probably they never did so in the past. In others, mosques have been stuck down beside a road where processions have passed, and I think it perfectly clear that any Muhammadan objection to music must be ruled out in such cases as the mosque did not previously exist . . . and it cannot be said that there was no practice of stopping music before the mosque, when there was no mosque before which to stop it.[105]

What British administrators failed to grasp was that leaders in both communities were deliberately creating issues where none had previously existed. In large part, processions past mosques—and opposition to them—became critical symbols because they involved a claim on public space. As in 1918, leaders on both sides appealed to the authorities to legitimize their claims and, by extension, their status as leaders of their community. As Hobsbawm has noted, such "invented traditions" play a critical part in the construction of the ideologies of nations and movements. In the process, history is "not what has actually been preserved in popular memory, but what has been selected, written, pictured, popularized and institutionalized by those whose function it is to do so."[106]

The Calcutta Riots of April–July 1926

The first major communal violence that took place in Bengal in the post Non-cooperation-Khilafat period occurred in Calcutta. On April 2, 1926, the Arya Samaj held its annual procession in north Calcutta. When the procession passed in front of the Dinu Chamrawalla mosque at the time of evening prayer, a police escort ordered the group to stop playing music, as had been done when passing mosques earlier along the procession route. The music was not stopped until some Muslims came out of the mosque to complain, and even then, one drummer continued to play, prompting a number of Muslims to pelt clods of dirt and an empty packing crate at the procession. The processionists retaliated until they were driven off when more Muslims joined the group at the mosque, which then began stopping trams and buses and assaulting Hindu passengers. Within minutes, groups armed with *lathis* appeared and both Hindu and Muslim neighborhoods were attacked. Later that day, a Saivite temple was damaged and a number of shops looted. The fighting and looting stopped briefly on April 15, but broke out again on April 24 and was not completely quelled until May 9. The next wave of riots broke out on July 11 and lasted until July 25. While some mosques were attacked, the damage was limited mainly to stone-throwing.[107] In the two riots, more than 138 people were killed and some 1,200 injured.[108]

The official report into the causes of the April riots began by blaming the violence on the "age-long rivalry between the Hindus and the Muhammadans." It went on to catalogue a series of incidents in which trouble had broken out over the passing of processions playing music past mosques. Contributing events which served to increase the "inherent rivalry between the two communities" included the increased activities of the *shuddhi* movement and the formation of a "League for the Protection of Hindu Women from Attacks by Muhammadans" and a Cow Protection Society. Speeches made at a meeting of the All-India Hindu Mahasabha in April 1925 reportedly "provoked considerable resentment among the Muhammadan community,"[109] and were followed by further "provocative" speeches by Arya Samajists at a meeting in Calcutta in November 1925 and by the Jamiat-ul-Ulema-i-Hind, the organization of Indian 'ulama, in March.[110] Political leaders also explained the outbreaks as the inevitable product of the bitter political fights over the Hindu-Muslim Pact and other issues that had dominated council politics during the preceding months. Their analysis began from the same assumption colonial authorities made in writing up their reports: that the Hindu and Muslim masses were naturally prone to irrational motivations. How competition between Muslims and Hindu in the council was translated into Hindu-Muslim street violence was not made clear.

Government officials also saw the July violence as "inevitable" after the April outbreak, and thus did not take seriously evidence of planning on either side: "In the existing state of tension . . . a further clash between the two communities was inevitable and it was impossible to do more than to postpone the evil day. Both communities were prepared to break out into violence on the slightest alarm, and the most that could be expected of any precautionary measures adopted by the police was the postponement of serious conflict as far as possible and a speedy suppression of open rioting, when the clash should come."[111] Pandey has noted that this description forms part of the communal riot "narrative" which has been used to demonstrate the benefits of British rule. "The point of the exercise . . . was to describe the 'native' character, establish the perverse nature of the population and the fundamental antagonism between 'Hindus' and 'Muslims.'"[112] Violence was thus understood as an essential component of the "native" character; in describing it, the official reports on the riots were laying out for their readers the rationale for the British presence in India.[113]

It followed from this logic that nationalist politics would also be held responsible for the riots. The police report on the riots blamed "the general spirit of lawlessness which has grown up during the past few years," first openly appearing "during the Non-cooperation movement, when the disciples of Mr. Gandhi publicly preached defiance of Government and took every opportunity of promoting or fomenting resistance to lawful authority." It singled out the vernacular press for promoting "an atmosphere of general disobedience." Violence between Hindus and Muslims was seen as the predictable result of the political reforms:

> The possibility of an elected Government divorced from a control such as is exercised by the British Government in India, which acts and has always acted as a buffer between all opposing communities in general, and the Hindus and Muhammadans in particular, must inevitably have caused latent apprehensions in the minds of all politically-minded Indians of both the major factions and these apprehensions must have increased in direct ratio to the increasing imminence of the new form of Government.[114]

The British were enthusiastic at the prospect of undermining the nationalists; they could then confidently argue back that special political arrangements were needed because of "communal" hostility. Sir Abdur Rahim, a Bengali judge and a fierce opponent of the Congress and the Swarajists, saw in the suspension of dyarchy an opportunity to gain concessions from the British in the form of increased official appointments for Muslims. In a speech to the All-India Muslim League in December 1925, he called for Muslims to reject Congress and elect persons who had the interests of the Muslim community at heart.[115] British police reporting on the riot described that same speech as "the truest diagnosis of the situation" of Bengali Muslims under the Reforms Scheme, and Rahim as a "far-sighted" and "staunch protagonist of the claims of his community" who "would not have dared to take the responsibility of provoking so grave a crisis between the two communities, if he had realized the true facts of the situation." In fact, most scholars agree that the Muslim leaders Abdur Rahim and H. Suhrawardy, on the one hand, and the Arya Samajists on the other, were principally responsible for provoking the violence. Broomfield acknowledges that there was evidence of organization and premeditation by both Muslim and Hindu leaders, but he comes down harder on the Muslim leaders, contending that Rahim, assisted by British officials, "called the pace," beginning with an act of "outright provocation" in his speech at Aligarh in December 1925 that was echoed in the "fiercely communal tone that characterized all writing in the Muslim press at the time."[116] In fact, most of the Hindu press was equally partisan; the editors and publishers of six Hindu and four Muslim newspapers were prosecuted for publishing inflammatory material. Official reports also describe the Arya Samajist speeches of the same period as "provocative."[117]

Rajat Ray, while accurately perceiving that the "inflammatory electoral campaigns" like that of Rahim and H. Suhrawardy, Rahim's son-in-law and then Deputy Mayor, lay behind the violence, argues that it was not so much the "leaders of the Rahim brand [who] deliberately made inflammatory appeals," but the "intolerant social and religious aspirations" to which they appealed which were responsible for "the murderous riots of 1926."[118] He likewise appears to treat communalism as a given, a force which required only the right kind of leader to bring it to the surface. "Mass communalism," he writes, "arose from the eruption of the masses in politics after the war." It was a phenomenon that, in his view, could also be imported, as when up-country Hindu Mahasabha leaders carried out a propaganda tour during the riots.[119] Because he also regards communalism as a problem that afflicted the masses, Ray excuses senior Muslim leaders from responsibility for planning acts of violence,[120] presumably because most of the actual attacks were delegated to neighborhood leaders, notably those with criminal reputations who were recruited by Suhrawardy and others. For his part, Rahim blamed the Arya Samaj and the Hindu Mahasabha for instigating attacks on Muslims.[121]

Blaming the violence on outsiders was characteristic of government reporting on such incidents,[122] thereby removing primary responsibility from local leaders by making them appear to be pawns in the hands of *agents provocateurs*. The tendency on the part of the colonial authorities to assign full responsibility for the violence to "criminal elements" "den[ies] the involvement of those who employ and support the 'criminal elements,' as well as the fears and feelings of the community at large which sometimes looks upon these elements as protectors and even heroes."[123] In fact, the recruitment of participants by those involved in planning the violence is an essential part of the process of accomplishing a riot.

A clue to how the April 1926 riots in Calcutta got underway can be found in the description of Suhrawardy as a leader connected with two known criminals, Mina Peshawari and Allah Baksh Peshawari. On the night of July 14, Suhrawardy and Allah Baksh Peshawari "visited Mechuabazar, which is the stronghold of the Mahomedans in north Calcutta, and incited the Mahomedans to resist the procession and abused other Mahomedans who sought to dissuade them."[124] "Hooligan" leaders like the Peshawaris feature consistently in post-partition accounts of communal "riots" as well as accounts from the pre-partition period. Such figures are patronized by politicians because of their criminal networks, which provide the necessary organization for coordinating attacks, breaking strikes, and distributing arms or petrol.[125] As an observer of contemporary incidents of such violence has observed, "[t]he role of 'antisocial' elements always surfaces into consciousness during politically turbulent periods. Yet it is often forgotten that state power is frequently secured in normal times on the strength of such 'anti-social elements.' The political patronage that they enjoy gives them immunity against the criminal justice system."[126] There are other identifiable elements in staging a riot, including the selection of targets, the circulation of inflammatory accusations through leaflets and rumor, the allocation of blame, and claims and counter-claims for redress for the victimized community. All of these are designed to create solidarities and cleavages within a political community, and all were features of the Calcutta violence.

British officials held some Hindu leaders responsible for much of the violence in April. In the previous year, the police had ordered the Arya Samaj to change its procession route; in 1926, the organization appeared determined that such interference would not be repeated. The police report concluded that it was "morally certain that Arya Samajists desired that there should be a mosque on the line of route, in order that their experiment of passing it with music might be fulfilled," and that therefore, they "arrange[d] that a mosque should fall on their line of route."[127] The report also speculated that the group's leaders voiced fear about the possibility of trouble as a way of protecting themselves from being held responsible.

Shortly after the violence began in early April, Marwari and Bengali Hindu leaders convened a meeting at which they decided to stop employing Muslim laborers. Although Muslim leaders retaliated by calling for a boycott of Hindu shops, the fact that a high proportion of Muslims were normally employed by Hindus and that Hindu traders far outnumbered Muslim traders left them at a distinct disadvantage. One government report blamed Madan Mohan Barman, a leader of the Hindu Mahasabha, and Swami Biswananda, both "up-country" activists associated with the cow protection and *shuddhi* movement of U.P. and Bihar, for instigating violence and then "keep[ing] in the background when the actual trouble comes."[128] Barman's house was used as a base for some of the Hindus participating in the violence, from which they threw bricks at Muslims.[129] Muslim leaders organized counter-attacks. During the first phase of the riots on April 3, Suhrawardy "was found on the spot when the police arrived and the looting was over, and his attitude was such as to create the suspicion that he had encouraged the looters."[130] After the riots were underway, Suhrawardy told officials that "if things did not improve he would be obliged to exhort his co-religionists to reprisals."[131]

The leaders recognized by the colonial authorities had little influence with the violent crowds. The report of the official inquiry notes with some satisfaction that "Mr. J. M. Sen Gupta, Maulana Abul Kalam Azad, and other *soi-disant* leaders of the contending communities visited the disturbed area and attempted to pacify the rioters, but their efforts produced no effect whatsoever, and, in fact, in many instances they were abused."[132] Sen Gupta was Mayor at the time, but was clearly seen by the British as a leader only of the Hindus. The violence continued through April 14, characterized principally by stabbings and attacks on mosques and temples. In fact, many of the most violent attacks were not the acts of a crowd or mob at all, but of individuals. The police report noted that the attacks on religious buildings had not previously been seen on such a scale in Calcutta.

The incident that set off the July outbreak was a procession held in connection with the Barwari Puja of Raj Rajeshwari, a festival observed by merchants on Cross Street in Calcutta. The procession had originally been scheduled for June 1, but was rescheduled after the organizers rejected a government order to redirect the route. Organizers were originally licensed to hold the procession on the understanding that it would include only seventy-five participants and forty bandsmen. It was postponed when the authorities reported that

> attempts were being made to utilise the procession as a Hindu demonstration, and that large numbers of Hindus had collected with the object of participating in the ceremony. The procession was widely advertised both in the press and by means of leaflets and the Hindu public were requested to join the procession in large numbers. . . . Moreover, the possibility of the procession becoming a Hindu demonstration had thoroughly aroused the Muhammadans residing in the area through which the procession was required to pass, and any attempt to take the procession along this route without adequate escort would unquestionably have resulted in a violent and widespread conflict between the two opposing communities.[133]

The commissioner of police prescribed an alternate route, which was rejected by the organizers. Some Hindu leaders arranged a *hartal* (strike) on

June 3 in protest of the postponement, and a public meeting was held at which the government was accused of bias in favor of the Muslims. The procession was then rescheduled for July 15 on the understanding that the participants would be limited to five hundred and that it should not be used as a "Hindu" demonstration.

When the procession set out at 8:15 a.m. on July 15, it had about three hundred participants. As it approached the first of four mosques along the procession route, a group of Muslims who had gathered near the mosque demanded that the music be stopped. When the police attempted to disperse the group, the crowd threw brickbats and bottles at the processionists as well as at the police. Some of the processionists then threw the brickbats at the mosque. Under police escort, the procession moved on, but the crowd at the mosque continued to throw brickbats at passing trams, and one group "dressed in khaki and wearing Turkish caps," gathered in front of the house of a prominent local Hindu, and pounded on the gate with *lathis* but were unable to get in. The procession again came under attack as it continued along the route, and the police opened fire repeatedly, injuring at least eighteen persons. The Muslim crowds also attacked police stations. The procession eventually grew in number as Hindus from local areas joined in. As it moved into areas that were predominantly Hindu, participants attacked Muslim shops, and a Muslim passer-by was assaulted.

After the procession reached the Mirbahar Ghat, Muslim boatmen gathered to disrupt the crowd. "At this juncture the whistle of the ship S.S. Kohistan was blown loudly and continuously, evidently to rally the Muhammadan sailors and boatmen, and in a few minutes the number of Muhammadans had swelled to four or five hundred."[134] The processionists then attacked the Muslims, until the police intervened to disperse the crowd. The processionists completed the rite by immersing the images in the river, and the procession ended. Between 8 a.m. and 3 p.m., stabbing incidents occurred in neighborhoods along the procession route, leaving two dead.

There was clear evidence of design by Muslim leaders during the July disturbances as well. The use of the steamship whistle to rally Muslim boatmen at the the time of the immersion of the images is one example of planning. As the police report noted,

> it is impossible to avoid the conclusion that the opposition offered by the Muhammadans to the Raj Rajeswari procession was deliberate and pre-arranged. There is reason to believe that the original intention was to offer passive resistance (Satyagraha), but this intention was accompanied by a firm determination that the resistance thus offered must achieve its purpose, and the leaders who counselled this plan of action cannot have overlooked

the dangers of the course which they advocated. There is most reliable information that Mr. H.S. Suhrawardy, whose aggressive attitude in the earlier
period of the riots has been mentioned in previous reports, visited the
neighborhood shortly before this occurrence and that his temper before he
did so was such as to cause more cautious leaders to warn him. His conduct
and that of the other leaders concerned cannot, therefore, be too strongly
condemned. That trouble was likely to occur was apparently foreseen by
other Muhammadan leaders, as is evident from the text of the telegram sent
by Mr. A.K. Ghuznavi from Allahabad to the Moslems of Bengal. There is little doubt that on this occasion Mr. Ghuznavi had begun to realise the disas-
trous effects of his uncalled for enquiries from all districts in Bengal about
the practice relating to music before mosques. . . . It is beyond question that
his message inspired a sense of grievance amongst his followers by adum-
brating the possibility of "grave provocation and persecution."[135]

A more sinister example of premeditation was found on July 20, when
the authorities discovered that a number of Hindu (Bengali and Marwari) houses had been soaked in oil along the route to be taken by the
Muharram procession.

Oil had also been freely poured on the lanes which bound three sides of the
buildings, evidently with the intention that the blazing roads would not
only prevent the escape of the inmates of the burning building, but would
also delay the Fire Brigade in entering the lanes for rescue work and for ex-
tinguishing the fire. . . . The oil was laid with the utmost secrecy and was not
noticed by anyone until the morning of the following day, but fortunately
very heavy rain fell on the night of the 20th July and a terrible tragedy was
providentially averted. A thorough inquiry was instituted immediately after
the discovery of the oil, but no clues of any description were available and it
can only be surmised that the plot was contrived with the object of exacting
revenge for the shots fired at Muhammadan processions in this area.[136]

Official correspondence was blunt in assigning much of the blame to
Suhrawardy as "more than any one else responsible for the resistance of
a lawful procession."[137] In a meeting at Rahim's house on July 13,
Suhrawardy urged taking strong action to obstruct the procession, until
Rahim had to caution him against further violence.

The day after the Raj Rajeshwari procession, July 16, was the fifth day
of Muharram. Several processions were attacked by crowds throwing
brickbats. On July 18, however, the seventh day of Muharram and the
biggest day for processions, passed without incident after troop reinforcements were deployed. The next day began with another Hindu procession. Police traveled the route beforehand to warn residents against
causing any trouble. According to the police report, the processionists en-

gaged in "provocative music when passing" one mosque, but proceeded without incident until it reached Paikpara where some Muslims threw brickbats and the processionists retaliated. When they approached another mosque and the police ordered them to stop the music, the processionists chose instead to wait until 5:00, when prayers were ended. At 5:00, the police ordered the Muslims in the mosque to disperse immediately. The processionists threw brickbats at the empty mosque and at some Muslims who had remained in the area. At that point, several explosions were heard, which the processionists claimed were caused by bombs thrown from the mosque. After dispersing the crowd, the police searched the mosque but found nothing.

On July 20, another Muharram procession was attacked. One Muslim died when shots were fired at the procession from a Marwari house. Local Hindus protested when Muslims were allowed to join police in searching houses in the vicinity, and the government justified the move by arguing that "only two such Muhammadans were admitted and . . . [b]oth were respectable men . . . [T]he reason why Muhammadans were selected as search-witnesses was that it was essential that there should be some one present at the search who would represent the interests of the Muhammadan complainants, particularly as all the police officers, with the exception of the Deputy Commissioner, were Hindus."[138] Once again, the authorities' categorization of local officials on the basis of their religious affiliation eroded any possibility that the state would be seen as a neutral force.

The last day of Muharram, July 21, was the bloodiest. The police report observed that this was only "to be expected" since the day was "the tenth and most important day of the Mohurrum festival." In addition to stabbings and other assaults which left two dead and at least fourteen wounded, the police were "compelled to open fire" in eight incidents, killing five and wounding ten. The total number of those killed in police firings during the two weeks of violence was six; total dead from the riots was twenty-eight. In justifying the resort to police firing, the report observes that since "a large proportion of the disturbances during the present riots were occasioned by, and took place during, the holding of religious processions, it is self-evident that numerous conflicts between large bodies of the opposing communities occurred and that the police were frequently faced with the necessity of immediately dispersing large crowds of persons who were keyed up to the highest pitch of religious and communal frenzy."[139]

It was widely accepted by both the Hindu and Muslim press that the riots were not spontaneous eruptions, but were planned and organized. One newspaper, the *Forward*, insinuated that the rioting was prolonged in order to insure that Rahim's supporters were elected to the Council.[140]

On April 29, the *Statesman* noted that, in addition to the speeches, inflammatory leaflets were "distributed in the thousands . . . suggest[ing] that somewhere in the background is somebody with funds and a rudimentary kind of organization."[141] Some of the leaflets accused Muslims of "brutally assaulting fourteen-year-old Bengali children" and urged Bengali Hindus to take their *lathis* and teach a lesson to the "eight *crores* [eighty million] of Muslims in India."[142] Other pamphlets printed at local Bengali presses exhorted the Hindus not to ride in taxis driven by Muslims. One of the taxis identified in the leaflet was set on fire and its driver driven off by a group of Hindus.[143] Leaflets distributed among Muslims accused Bengali Hindus of betraying the Hindu-Muslim Pact and called on Muslims to retaliate for the killing of any Muslim by taking "the heads of 100 *kafirs*."[144] Leaflets distributed in the second phase of the April riots urged Hindus to "Silently destroy the (Islamite) bugs. . . . Demolish their houses. Set fire to their abodes and destroy them. . . . Where are the *salas* Rahim and Suhrawardy? . . . If Malaviya or Birla were to give us orders, we would light a holy fire and burn you all in it. . . . You *salas*, you are saved only by the strength of the British Government; otherwise we would have smashed your Nakhoda Mosque [in Calcutta] and made the battlefield crimson with your blood."[145] Another claimed that while Muslims supported Hindu shopkeepers, Hindus never bought from Muslim shops, and then went on to repeat the usual complaints about Hindus benefiting more from government jobs.[146] The persistent distribution of inflammatory pamphlets by parties on both sides and the use of hired *goondas* (criminals) "impl[ied] funds spent to keep the riot going."[147]

Rumor played an important role in sustaining the violence, acting as a form of communication quite beyond the reach of the police and other state authorities who were trying to quell the violence. Subalternist scholars have analyzed the function of rumor as a signal of solidarity for those participating in acts of resistance. Gayatri Spivak, in her introduction to *Selected Subaltern Studies*, notes that the power of rumor derives from its function as "not belonging to any one voice-consciousness. . . . Rumour evokes comradeship because it belongs to every 'reader' or 'transmitter.' No one is its origin or source. [It is] . . . always in circulation with no assignable source."[148] While it is clear that rumors have no identifiable author, their dissemination follows a pattern that indicates a significant degree of preparation. The state also plays a role in giving legitimacy to rumors. Deliberately planted rumors also help create an "aura of spontaneity" around "carefully orchestrated initiatives."[149] As Basu points out, creating an atmosphere of spontaneity is one of the goals of a successful riot.[150] The very anonymity of rumors is itself a matter of design. If the press and local administration give credence to rumors, it is even more likely that ordinary residents would believe them.[151] Most of the rumors during the April 1926 riots in Calcutta had to do with attacks on mosques, temples, and *gurudwaras* [Sikh temples]. On April 3, a number of Sikhs, hearing a rumor that the Mechuabazar *gurudwara* had been damaged, attacked the Jumma Pir Dargah. Muslims of the area retaliated by setting fire to a temple and threatening another.[152] On April 8, Calcutta Muslims gathered at the Nikasipara mosque because they had heard that some Hindus were about to attack it; at about the same time, a Hindu crowd had assembled because of a rumor that Muslims were about to loot their shops. Both groups were dispersed without incident.[153]

A consistent feature of these riots was the accusation, by one side or the other, that state actors—police or other officials—played a part as perpetrators of the violence, or took sides in favor of one community or the other. Shortly after the violence in Calcutta first broke out in April, Rahim complained that Hindu police were siding with Hindus,[154] a charge that echoed the one leveled against Muslim police during the *swadeshi* years.[155] There is some indication that Rahim may have had reason to be concerned. When the police commissioner recommended that any volunteer force set up to protect mosques and temples be recruited from both communities, Mayor J. M. Sen Gupta "expressed considerable doubt regarding his ability to provide the necessary Muhammadan contingent."[156] On April 5, a group of Muslims who had assembled at the junction of Maniktolla and Narkeldanga Main roads accused the police of guarding Hindu temples and generally assisting Hindus, and called on Muslims to attack them. Government intervention also played a part in giving the July procession a prominence it might not have had had it been held as originally scheduled. The government's efforts to redirect the route of the procession provided the organizers with an opportunity to take a very public stand against such an encroachment on their traditional right. Ironically, the date chosen for the rescheduled celebration coincided with Muharram, with the result that back to back religious processions laid claim to the same Calcutta streets.

After the April riots in Calcutta, Muslim League members accused the Bengal government of having "failed in safe-guarding the lives, properties and interests of the poor Muslim inhabitants. . . . Poor, innocent Muslims are being butchered every day, by the police and the Hindus." [157] In May 1926, Abdur Rahim formed the Bengal Muslim Party whose aim was to prevent domination "by a class of monopolists and intelligentsia" and "unembarrassed by the limitations of caste and . . . untouchability" to "contribute our best to the realisation of the true ideal of government of the people, by the people, for the people."[158] As Shila Sen has observed, Rahim wanted to deny "the All-India Muslim League the representative character it claimed" and ensure that Bengal Muslims' interests were not

ignored in any future constitutional set-up. He was not prepared to compromise on Bengal Muslims' majority position for the sake of Hindu-
Muslim unity or for the sake of Muslim interests outside Bengal.[159]

While many Congress leaders and Swarajists accused Rahim and
Suhrawardy's "communal" strategies of being antagonistic toward nationalism, Rahim and other Muslim leaders charged that the nationalists'
tactics were also "communal" and biased against Muslims. After the riots
were over, the government commented that

> both sides are still equally insistent on what they hold to be their ancient
> and inalienable religious rights and it is unfortunately a fact that they are be-
> ing encouraged to persist in this attitude by leaders who might have been
> expected, from their education and standing, to do their best to heal the
> present deplorable rift between the two communities. There is, moreover, an
> equally unfortunate tendency among the several political parties at present
> existing on either side to face the coming elections in a frankly and uncom-
> promisingly communal spirit.[160]

Muslim leaders associated with Rahim's group attempted to elicit popular support for themselves as the only Muslim leaders capable of defending the interests—and lives—of a community newly perceived as
very vulnerable. In Calcutta in 1926, Hindu and Muslim leaders established relief committees which, while providing genuine humanitarian
assistance, were also instrumental in promoting a version of events in
which their community was endangered by the other. After the riots
were over, both committees established defense funds to assist defendants who faced prosecution for participating in the riots.[161] The violence
inspired the Khilafat Committee to change its constitution. In addition to
working to rid the Holy Places of non-Muslim control and promote the
welfare of the Muslims of India in religious, educational, social, political
and economic matters, it passed a resolution to safeguard Muslim property and lives.[162]

The Pabna Riots of July 1926

Serious violence in Pabna broke out just before the last phase of the Calcutta riots, and overlapped with it. In fact, the incidents were closely
linked by rumor and participants. An increase in communal activities in
the area preceding the July 1926 riots had followed the establishment of
the Anjuman Islamia, an organization that reportedly had links with
Rahim, and its visibility increased as competition for public service jobs
and local bodies sharpened. In addition, following the Calcutta riots, an
Arya Samajist was said to have delivered inflammatory speeches in

Pabna, and Muslim speakers had distributed pamphlets inciting Muslims to violence.

The incident that sparked the week's rioting in Pabna in July 1926 took place on the grounds of the Sitlai *zamindari* six miles from the town of Pabna, where images had been removed from a temple and vandalized. On July 1, the *zamindar*, Babu Jogendra Nath Maitra, and Indujyoti Majumdar, the chairman of the Pabna municipality, complained to the district magistrate that the images had been removed and left "in a mutilated condition" on the road near the *zamindar*'s house. Maitra told the magistrate that "they would most probably immerse the images," as would be necessary to keep them ritually pure, but the officials asked that he "consider the matter as the images might be required for identification in case the culprits were detected." Majumdar told the subdivisional officer they would inform the authorities of their decision, but in the end, he did not.[163]

Late on the evening of July 1, Maitra, Majumdar, and others took the images in a procession with music into the town of Pabna just as evening prayers at the mosque began. According to the police report, officials who reached the scene saw part of the procession attacking the Khalifapatti mosque. A report by the superintendent of police recorded the statements of a witness who testified that Muslims who were in the mosque at the time came out and pleaded with the processionists, who numbered about one hundred, to stop the music, but were told that the music "must go on." The processionists then threw brickbats and, after collecting bamboo sticks from a shop, began to assault the Muslims, who fled back inside the mosque. The witness claimed that the processionists sang "Bande Mataram"—the song linked with the Hindu revivalist elements of the *swadeshi* campaign.[164] After the incident, a large number of armed Muslims from nearby towns and villages were reported to be moving toward Pabna, but were dispersed by the police.[165]

On July 2, the government prohibited all processions, meetings or assemblies of more than five persons in public places under section 177 of the penal code. *Lathis* and other weapons were also banned. Despite the order, looting was reported to be widespread by July 5, and another Hindu image was desecrated.[166] Police who tried to stop the looters were also attacked. Rumors of looting outpaced the actual crime, with government officials trying to dispel exaggerated reports of "500,000" looters in Pabna.[167] According to one government official, "what gave the original impulse to the looting was probably the false rumours of looting that came from Hindu sources on the 2nd and 3rd. This put the idea of looting into heads already excited, and as Pabna was a center of *hat*-looting in 1917–18, the seed fell on good ground and looting began and spread rapidly."[168] The looting and other subsequent violence occurred almost entirely in villages and *hats* outside the town of Pabna.[169] On July 7, the district magistrate arrested "some fanatical *maulvis* of the local madrasahs who were concerned in the attempt at forcible conversion."[170]

The police report clearly reveals that the confrontation at the mosque was planned by prominent Hindu figures in the town. Following Maitra and Majumdar's meeting with the deputy magistrate, the men convened a secret meeting at the *zamindari* where they decided to bring the procession into town at the time of evening prayer and to collect *lathis* and conceal them in Hindu shops, "evidently with the intention of attacking the mosque."[171] Two of the organizers of the procession were arrested on charges of abetting the attack on the mosque.[172]

In the weeks before the incident, government files recorded the activities of itinerant *maulvis* in the area preaching against un-Islamic practices and, in some areas, advising local Muslims to desecrate Hindu temples.[173] They also spread reports about Hindu attacks on Muslims in Calcutta, and called for retaliation.[174] The reports continued to refer to them as Fara'idi or Feraizi, linking them with the nineteenth-century reformist movement, and with official fears of treasonous "Wahhabis." Indeed, this association was exploited by the *maulvis* themselves, a move that helped to legitimize them in the eyes of Muslim tenants and cultivators. The Hindu press further elaborated on the role of the *maulvis*, linking some to outside 'ulama in a manner reminiscent of the 1918 Calcutta incident.[175] The newspaper *Amrita Bazar Patrika* blamed Maulvi Abdul Hamid for generating communal tension to further his efforts to get on the district board.[176] The later attacks also showed explicit signs of organization; government reports speculated that outside Muslims were involved in much of the looting and that they also spread rumors of desecrations of mosques in order to gain the support and participation of the local population.[177]

In tracing the roots of the Pabna violence, Partha Chatterjee suggests that they need to be understood in terms of the very different worlds of "organized" and "unorganized" politics, the former being the world of "Councils, municipalities, district boards, . . . parties, associations, Anjumans, . . . representations . . . conferences, editorials and press releases," and the latter being the "autonomous subjectivity of the mass of the people," their collective actions and the "consciousness which informs them."[178] In his framework, the actions of Maitra and Majumdar fall into the category of organized politics, as do the Hindu and Muslim press. The actions of the "itinerant *maulvis*," according to this theory, belong to the world of "unorganized politics" because these figures acted "on behalf of a collectivity . . . a community threatened."[179] While the distinction between these two spheres of politics may be helpful in throwing some badly needed light on aspects of subaltern history too long overlooked, the line between the two is drawn somewhat arbitrarily.

To argue that one of these *maulvis* was not "a mobiliser organising support among the masses in order to promote sectional interests in the world of organised politics"[180] is not right. The *maulvis* who urged the Muslims of Pabna to desecrate temple images or refuse to pay taxes to support Hindu festivals were engaged in mobilizing support to promote interests which included creating in Bengali Muslims a greater sense of their Islamic identity. To the extent that this identity was enhanced through attacks on Hindu images and Hindu patrons of festivals, the *maulvis* were successful. As was the case in the *swadeshi* years, the fact that they could forge links between the impoverished state of most Bengali Muslims and the Hindu sources of their oppression only strengthened their position.

But it would also be a mistake to see the actions of these *maulvis* as isolated from the actions of all of the other institutions that make up the world of organized politics. These religious leaders were patronized by local *anjumans*, which in turn provided a base for many emerging leaders to enter district board or Council politics. A number of the *maulvis* had important connections to the prominent Muslim religious centers of Lucknow, Deoband, and Delhi, many of whose 'ulama had entered politics in a dramatic way during the Khilafat movement. By investing the "masses" with a collective consciousness that is "fundamentally religious" and giving them credit for all collective, "spontaneous" political acts, Chatterjee's thesis is not very far from the colonial/nationalist argument that the masses are inherently irrational and given to mob violence.

This is not to say that economic motives were not a factor in the Pabna violence. But it is unlikely that any looting or other attacks on Hindu merchants would have occurred in the absence of the initial confrontation over the images and procession.[181] The widespread nature of the looting was evidence not necessarily of a "jacquerie—an entire rural community combined for violent action"[182] but of a planned act of retaliation, which the presence of outside participants who moved from village to village, strategically circulating rumors, tends to confirm. The fact that in such instances of collective violence, local leaders never completely control the behavior or direction of the crowd does not mean that such leadership was lacking or that the crowd's actions were, from the outset, spontaneous. As studies of collective violence have demonstrated, not everyone in the crowd is engaged in the same activity. Crowds may include people with personal or economic motives for participating, as well as those carrying banners, shouting slogans, or directing others to the target of attack.[183] Ghanshyam Shah points out that an individual who has internalized the "communal consciousness" of the crowd "may or may not participate directly in riots" but may still act as a force to legitimize the violence.[184] To speak of the "language of the crowd" or the "politics of the crowd" may misrepresent the actions and motives of many of those present.[185]

Government efforts to regulate processions and music before mosques prompted leaders on both sides to seize upon the issue to challenge the authorities and assert themselves as protectors of their communities. A Hindu conference held shortly before the violence broke out had raised protests against police efforts to restrict processions past mosques.[186] The Hindu Mahasabha had been active in the area since 1921. In May, a prominent Muslim paper had urged the government to prohibit music before mosques at all times.[187] These were not the groups to which the government appealed to restore order. Instead, "one leader each of the Hindu and Muhammadan communities [were] sent to areas to dispel panic and prevent trouble."[188] Such leaders were unlikely to be the ones who had publicized the issue in the first place; thus, their ability to have much influence in the affected areas is dubious. Those who hoped to reap gains from the conflict were engaged in tours to dispense relief and petition the government on behalf of the "victims" of the violence.

As Chatterjee observes, the Pabna incident provides an example of the extraordinary lengths to which the government would go in categorizing communities as a means of managing conflict. After the Pabna violence had been brought under control, and a number of persons arrested, the government insisted on retaining a Muslim pleader to prosecute the Hindus, and a Hindu to prosecute the Muslim accused.[189] Following the proceedings, the government imposed a punitive tax on both communities within the municipality of Pabna, and on Muslims in the surrounding countryside. Both communities protested, with the Secretary of the Anjuman-i-Islamia objecting that "since the Mussalmans of the town did not do anything to break the public peace in spite of the gravest provocation by the Hindus and as the Muhammadans of the town suffered most at the hands of the Hindus, their mosque desecrated and damaged. . . . " they should be exempt from the tax. The better-off Hindus of the town complained that the tax burden fell unfairly on them, leading the chief secretary to observe that "the doctrine of collective responsibility has produced results that were probably not contemplated and will be hard to justify before the public." However, the officials decided that the Hindus could not be exempted, but had to pay only the cost of deploying additional police in the area.[190]

Conclusion

Increasing divisions in the Muslim political leadership in Bengal, between those who had previously supported the government and new leaders struggling to claim a political base, shaped the way British authorities perceived Muslim interests and the way these Muslim leaders attempted to identify themselves and their would-be constituents. These new leaders emerged in the aftermath of the Khilafat and Non-cooperation movements, which had granted legitimacy to popular religious leaders who had been able to mobilize local support for national or even international issues which were not of immediate concern for Bengali Muslim peasants. These strategies for political mobilization served to boost the standing of the very leaders the British authorities had considered illegitimate as representatives of the community.

The "riots" that erupted in Calcutta in 1918 and 1926, and in Pabna in 1926, were largely the product of this leadership struggle, but there are important differences among the three. Generally portrayed as Calcutta's first communal "riot" or even as an uprising against Hindu exploitation, there is another story behind the violent outbreak of 1918. The motivations of the various actors come into sharper focus when the riot is seen as being about political power and its repressive exercise. The protests organized around the derogatory article in the *Indian Daily News* were aimed at the British authorities and, by extension, those who collaborated with them. In a manner which foreshadowed the agitations of the next few years, the organizers successfully turned a relatively obscure matter—the derogatory article—into one which attracted widespread public concern. To understand the motivations of the crowd, the fact that the assembly eventually engaged in looting is less significant than the reason they gathered at the mosque in the first place. The assembly at the mosque, whose leaders the authorities refused to recognize as legitimate, acted out of a sense of grievance. If the crowd was not persuaded by what these leaders had told it about the wrongs inflicted on Muslims by the British in Turkey and Kanpur, the behavior of officials in Calcutta was probably enough to convince them of British bad faith. The ensuing violence was not so much motivated by class or "communal" interests as it was by political interests: The riot constituted an act of resistance to state power, a response to the authorities' refusal to permit the public meeting, and, in particular, the efforts by police and guards to prevent the crowd from moving outside the confines of the mosque and proceeding through the streets to Government House.

What is striking about Calcutta's series of violent outbreaks in 1926 was that the leaders who had opposed public protests in 1918 were at the forefront of efforts in 1926 to take public action to the streets. The evidence indicates that the 1926 incident was an organized event, calculated in large part to bolster various groups contesting the November elections. By this time, Muslim politicians hoping to advance their cause traded freely in charges of "communalism" with both Hindu and other Muslim leaders. In 1918, the crowd was assembled to challenge restrictions put in place by the colonial authorities; in 1926, Hindu and Muslim organizers contested constraints imposed in response to demands for either no music before mosques or no restrictions on processions. Their opposing claims to public space were designed to demonstrate that they could make that space unsafe for the other community.[191] Those most actively involved in planning the violence attempted to reap gains from it by representing the interests of the "victims" of the violence.

The violence in Pabna was also well planned by both parties but represented a different kind of power struggle, particularly on the Muslim side. The *maulvis* responsible for instigating the desecration of the images were also engaged in an effort to establish their own authority over the Bengali Muslim population by trying to construct new rules for Muslim behavior—rules that prohibited paying taxes that could support Hindu images, rules that authorized attacks to avenge the killing of Muslims in Calcutta. How much their interest in creating such a culture was shared by their congregation is not entirely clear; but with the growing political role of the *anjumans*, and the growing political influence of status-seeking Muslim cultivators, there is no doubt that they had an audience. As in Calcutta, government efforts to impose new regulations only encouraged efforts by all parties to profess to speak for and represent the interests of a Bengali Muslim "community."

The use of religious symbols and loyalties by political leaders was a precarious undertaking in the highly charged atmosphere of Bengal in the 1920s. The political leadership of Muslim Bengal was far from united either in its goals and strategies for protecting its own interests or on what those interests should be. In the years before the Khilafat movement, the leadership of Calcutta's Urdu-speaking Muslims had generated local interest around pan-Islamic issues. The Khilafat movement went further in mobilizing popular support around religious symbols, and, in doing so, legitimized a new kind of leadership capable of challenging British policy and the old Muslim leadership which supported it. As the first partition of Bengal had made clear, religious symbols could be used in conjunction with economic grievances to mobilize Muslim peasants against the Hindu landholding elite. Middle-level leaders who had come into their own positions of power in the countryside responded to and furthered this effort by promoting visible markers of Muslim identity. In the power struggle that followed the end of the Khilafat/Non-cooperation movements, these leaders seized on issues of symbolic significance—like music before mosques—to challenge the rules, both customary and official, that governed public life.

The "communal" riots that erupted in Bengal in 1926 were not the result of a "natural" enmity between Hindus and Muslims or the unfortunate but unavoidable consequence of either the constitutional transformations taking place or of the increase in tensions over land issues. While all of these informed the context in which the riots occurred, the violence that came to define Hindu-Muslim relations during this period was part of a deliberate strategy pursued by both Hindu and Muslim leaders in order to distinguish themselves from other contenders for power before the upcoming elections by constructing the other community as a threat to their own and their rivals as being unable to counter that threat.

The construction of this community was distinct from the patterns of the past. Events which had the blessings of custom were challenged as insults to Islam; a single attack on a Muslim was exploited as evidence of a threat to all Muslims. Muslim leaders evoked fears of a "Hindu *raj*" with images of Bengali Muslims as an aggrieved and endangered community. Not all of the grievances were manufactured, but by combining long-standing complaints regarding land reform and Muslim representation with dark hints about the vulnerability of Muslims under leaders who were incapable of protecting them, these leaders distanced themselves from both the Khilafatists, who had cooperated with Congress' Hindu leaders, and the established, accommodationist position of the Nawab. These leaders and the organizations they established filled a vacuum left by a state which they perceived or portrayed as unable to protect their communities. Their ability to generate popular discontent around symbolic issues and mobilize people on the basis of fear enabled them not only to challenge the competence of the British authorities to regulate disputes but also to discredit their rivals and establish support for themselves as the only leaders capable of defending the interests of Bengali Muslims.

Notes

1. He points out that resistance by no means characterized most of the peasantry during this period, and that sectionalism among different classes and communities for the most part worked against their joining forces against the dominant classes. See C. A. Bayly, "Rallying Around the Subaltern," *Journal of Peasant Studies*, 16, no. 1 (October 1988), pp. 119–120.

2. Mohandas Gandhi's first civil disobedience campaign was launched jointly with a campaign by Indian Muslim leaders to force the British and Allied powers to maintain the boundaries of the Ottoman empire, and in so doing, preserve the Caliph of Islam. Khilafat is the Persian rendering of caliphate. Indian Muslim leaders had been organizing protests around the issue years before Gandhi joined them. Gandhi's goal was to win self-rule for India.

3. Unlike the Congress, which refused to cooperate with any scheme short of complete self-rule, the Swarajist ("self-rule") party planned to wreck the system of dyarchy from within. The Hindu-Muslim pact was to go into effect once self-government was attained. For a fuller description of the pact, see also Broomfield and Gordon.

4. The Swarajists rejected Gandhi's Non-cooperation campaign and took the position that it was better to stand for election and fight the government from within the councils than to refuse to participate at all. Motilal Nehru and C. R. Das led the breakaway movement from Congress to launch the party in 1923.

5. Hodgson, pp. 339, 342.

6. This is how they were described by the viceroy, Lord Hardinge. See Hardy, p. 183.

7. Letter from Meston to Hardinge, dated August 25, 1913, enclosed with letter no. 43 of *Letters to Secretary of State*, January–December 1913, no. 119 of *Hardinge Papers*, p. 117, cited in Peter Hardy, *The Muslims of British India* (Cambridge: Cambridge University Press, 1972), p. 184. Sandria Freitag has analyzed the question of leadership arising out of the Kanpur incident at length. See Freitag, 1989a, pp. 71–73 and pp. 210–219.

8. Ibid.

9. "Report on the political situation in Bengal," DO Beaton-Bell to Stevenson Moore, April 6, 1913, GOB F. 67\1913, s.n.1.

10. DO Beaton-Bell to Cummings, May 7, 1913, GOB F. 67/1913.

11. Ibid.

12. Duke's comments on Beaton-Bell's report on the situation in East Bengal, May 5, 1913, GOB 67/1913.

13. Broomfield, p. 122.

14. Ray, p. 224.

15. Broomfield, p. 119.

16. *Report of the Non-Official Commission on the Calcutta Disturbances, 1918* (Calcutta: Bangiya Jana Sabha, 1919), p. 4. Hereafter, RNOCCD. The description is a classic example of Orientalist romanticism.

17. Ibid., p. 4. Both editors were non-Bengali.

18. Ibid.

19. Ibid., p. 5.

20. Ibid., pp. 5–6.

21. Ibid., p. 8.

22. Ibid.

23. This referred to the Montague-Chelmsford reforms, which in Bengal awarded Muslims only 40 percent of legislative seats even though they comprised over 50 percent of the population. The arrangement was based in part on the Lucknow Pact, which had been negotiated by Fazlul Huq and other leaders in 1916. The Muslim negotiators lost a great deal of credibility afterwards.

24. The list used both "Muhammadan" and "Muslim" to describe the Muslim population.

25. Bakr-Id, more commonly known as 'Id-ul-Azha, commemorates Abraham's offering of his son Isaac for sacrifice; Muharram is a Shia day of mourning for the death of Husein, the son of Muhammad's cousin and son-in-law, Ali, who was murdered. In Shi'a tradition, only members of Muhammad's family could assume leadership of the Muslim community. Durga Puja is the biggest Hindu festival in Bengal, celebrating the homecoming of the goddess, Durga.

26. RNOCCD, p. 9.

27. Ibid., p. 10.

28. Ibid., p. 11.

29. Farangi Mahal was one of the most prominent centers for Islamic scholarship in British India. Some of its most prominent 'ulama were active leaders in the Khilafat movement.

30. RNOCCD, p. 12.

31. Freitag, 1989a, p. 212.

32. Ibid., p. 215.

33. Freitag, who has done some of the most valuable work in this area, defines this "public arena" as a realm of "coherent, consistent . . . symbolic behavior . . . providing legitimacy and recognition to a range of actors and values denied place in the imperial order." Freitag, 1989a, p. 6.

34. Extract from "The Cawnpore Scandal," *Mussulman*, 22 August 1913, in "Report regarding the present state of Muhammadan feeling in Bengal," F. 66/1913, s.6–8. WBSA.

35. Broomfield, pp. 119–121.

36. RNOCCD, p. 6.

37. The Lucknow Pact was negotiated by leaders from Congress and Muslim Leaguers as an effort to pressure the British for constitutional concessions. Adopted in Lucknow in December 1916, it provided for the over-representation of Muslims in provinces where they constituted a minority, like the Central Provinces, United Provinces, and Bihar, and under-representation in Bengal and Punjab where they constituted a majority. In Bengal, the pact awarded Muslims forty percent of the legislative seats; Muslims made up fifty-two percent of the population. See *Simon Commission*, vol. IV, p. 139, cited in Broomfield, p. 114.

38. Habib Shah, a Punjabi, editor of *Naqqash*, Fazlur Rahman, a Bihari, sub-editor of *Jamhur*, and Jafar Husain Kalami, a Madrasi, sub-editor of *Millat*. Ray, p. 224; Broomfield, pp. 120–122.

39. The Marwaris were Hindus originally from Gujarat and Bombay who, as a community, were prominent in the commercial sector of Calcutta.

40. RNOCCD, p. 35, cited in S. Das, p. 236, n. 75. It would not be at all unusual for mills to hire children of that age, even today.

41. See Broomfield, p. 123.

42. As S. Sarkar notes, "Narrowly economic interpretations are of no help at all in understanding the multiplicity of types of subaltern activity and their interpenetration." Sumit Sarkar, "The Conditions and Nature of Subaltern Militancy: Bengal from Swadeshi to Non-Cooperation, c. 1905–22," in Ranajit Guha, ed., *Subaltern Studies III* (Delhi: Oxford University Press, 1984), p. 286. See also Bayly, pp. 119–120.

43. Basu convincingly argues that the mere fact that looting took place during riots in Bijnor, U.P., in 1990, does not mean that economic motivations were at the root of the violence. Indeed, the fact that Hindu shopkeepers had apparently planned for such a contingency by removing goods from their shops is further evidence that the riot was planned. Amrita Basu, "When Local Riots are not Merely Local: Bringing the State Back In, Bijnor 1988–92," *Economic and Political Weekly*, vol. 29, no. 40, October 1, 1994, p. 2,614.

44. RNOCCD, p. 29; Government of Bengal, Police, 2C(4–6), B15–19, Dec. 1918; *Essayez, the Memoirs of Lawrence, Second Marquess of Zetland* (London, 1956), p. 116, cited in Broomfield, p. 124.

45. *Bengal Diary*, March 21 and April 4, 1919. *Zetland Collection*, cited in Sarkar, p. 289.

46. A place, usually a park or other open area, where the prayers for the two important Muslim holy days of *'Id-ul-Azha*, which commemorates Abraham's willingness to sacrifice his son, and *'Id-ul-Fitr*, which celebrates the end of the month of fasting (Ramadan), are held.

47. "Mohammadan agitation in connection with Allies' settlement with Turkey" (Report on *hartal* of 19 March 1920), GOB Home Poll. (Conf.) 106/1920 (Appendix A).

48. Gandhi, genuinely shocked by the violence, believed that more work needed to be done to prepare the masses for civil disobedience. He did not return to political work until 1929. For more on Gandhi's thinking on this, see Amin.

49. Broomfield, p. 159. See also Barbara Southard, "The Political Strategy of Aurobindo Ghosh: the Utilization of Hindu Religious Symbolism and the Problem of Political Mobilization in Bengal," *Modern Asian Studies*, v. 14, no. 3, 1980, pp. 353–376.

50. From the Quinquennial Report on the Progress of Education in India 1917–1922, Bureau of Education, cited in P. C. Bamford, *Histories of the Non-Cooperation and Khilafat Movements* (Delhi: Government of India Press, 1925), p. 106.

51. "History of the Non-cooperation Movement and Khilafat movement in Bengal," 3.c. 395/24, pp. 3–5 (7–9).

52. *Islam-Darsan*, August-September, 1924, published in Mustapha Nurul Islam, *Samayikapatre Jibana o Janamata, 1901–1930* (Life and Public Opinion in Periodical Literature, 1901–1930) (Dacca: Bangla Akademi, 1977), pp. 220–221. [Trans. P. Gossman]

53. *Shariate Islam*, July-August 1930, in ibid., pp. 223–224. [Trans. P. Gossman]

54. GOB Home Poll. "History of the Non-Cooperation Movement and Khilafat Movement in Bengal," 3.c.395/24 p. 5 (9).

55. *Report on the Administration of Bengal, 1921–22* (Calcutta: Bengal Secretariat Press, 1923), p. 153.

56. GOB Home Poll. 209/1921 WBSA.

57. GOB Poll. "History of the Non-Cooperation Movement and the Khilafat Movement," File 395/1924, p. 1.

58. As Chatterjee observes, this subinfeudation was so pervasive that by the mid-1930s there were 17.82 intermediate tenures for each estate. Chatterjee, 1984, p. 16.

59. Ibid., p. 13.

60. See Huque, Chatterjee, 1984, and R. Ahmed.

61. Huque, pp. 55–56, and 132–133.

62. Paul R. Greenough, *Prosperity and Misery in Modern Bengal: The Famine of 1943–44* (New York: Oxford University Press, 1982), p. 66.

63. *Calcutta University Commission 1917–1918 Report*, Vol. 1 (GOI, 1920), pp. 202–203.

64. Ibid., pp. 132–133.

65. *Calcutta University Commission Report*, GOB, p. 11.

66. Le Mesurier to Lyon, 2RJ, 6 June 1906, para. 10, Home Political Progs A, July 1906, n. 124, NAI, cited in S. Sarkar, 1973, pp. 454–455.

67. Ray, p. 72.

68. A Hindu festival which takes place generally in March or April during which family members and friends reenact a courtship ritual of the god Krishna and his lover, Radha, by throwing colored powder or water on each other.

69. Sumit Sarkar, 1984, p. 284.

70. Broomfield, p. 157. At this time, Congress also realized the importance of establishing a link to peasant groups, and began organizing *krishak samities* (peasant organizations) in the 1920s. At the same time, caste associations among low-caste cultivating Hindus—Namasudras for the most part—began to demand reserved seats in the Council for themselves.

71. F. O. Bell, *Final Report on the Survey and Settlement Operations in the District of Dinajpur, 1934–1940* (Alipore: Bengal Government Press, 1941), p. 9. Hereafter, Dinajpur SSR. A *thana* is a police precinct.

72. Ibid., p. 10.

73. Ibid. A *dhoti* is a wrapped lower garment worn primarily by Bengali Hindus; a *lungi* is a single piece of cloth wrapped like a skirt and worn principally by Muslims; *fez, topi,* and *achkan* are hats worn by Muslims; a *pucca* mosque would be built of brick or stone; *para* is neighborhood.

74. The annual pilgrimage to Mecca. Ibid.

75. Ibid.

76. Freitag, 1989a, pp. 188–189.

77. Rafiuddin Ahmed has analyzed the role these religious debates played in creating public consciousness about what it meant to be Muslim and in linking Muslims from different localities. See R. Ahmed, pp. 74–82, 103.

78. Susanne Hoeber Rudolph, "Now You See Them, Now You Don't; Historicizing the Salience of Religious Categories," paper presented at conference on "Religious Forces in the New World Disorder" at University of California at Santa Barbara, February 23, 1995, p. 5.

79. The system of dyarchy began with the Government of India Act of 1919 which granted certain powers to the provincial assemblies while retaining all important powers in the central imperial government. For a fuller discussion of the Swarajists' efforts to destroy dyarchy, see Broomfield and Gordon.

80. Broomfield notes that throughout 1922, Hindu Bengali *bhadrolok* leaders repeatedly warned of the dangers of Gandhi's methods which, by "reawakening" the masses, threatened to destroy the middle classes. Broomfield, pp. 159–162.

81. The Muslim counterpart was the *tabligh* campaigns which sought conversions to Islam, particularly among low-caste Hindus.

82. Broomfield, p. 238.

83. Simon Commission, vol. IV, p. 139, cited in Broomfield, p. 114.

84. For more on Das and the pact see Broomfield, 1968; Gordon, 1974; and Ray, 1984.

85. For a detailed discussion of the political maneuvering of this period, see Broomfield, pp. 244–281. On the second vote, Huq voted with the Swarajists. Broomfield, p. 263.

86. "Mohammadan Agitation in connection with Allies' settlement with Turkey" (Report on *hartal* of 19 March 1920), GOB Home Poll. (Conf.) 106/1920 (Appendix A).

87. District Officer Waddell to Emerson, July 18, 1921, GOB 209/1921 sn. 17–37.

88. Kenneth McPherson, *The Muslim Microcosm: Calcutta 1918 to 1935* (Wiesbaden: Franz Steiner, 1974), pp. 31–32.

89. A. K. Fazlul Huq, Presidential Address to All-India Muslim League, Delhi, December 20, 1918, in "Sectarian Nationalism and Khilafat," in A. M. Zaidi, ed., *Evolution of Muslim Political Thought in India*, v. 2 (New Delhi, 1975), p. 144.

90. Broomfield, p. 157.

91. "Correspondence of Qaid-e-Azam Mr. M. A. Jinnah and other papers," Bengal Vol. 1:2. Shamsul Hasan Collection, Qaid-e-Azam Academy, Karachi, Pakistan. Hereafter QAA.

92. Mohandas Gandhi, *Collected Works of Mahatma Gandhi*, v. 15 (Delhi: Publications Division, Ministry of Information and Broadcasting, Government of India, 1958–), p. 272.

93. H. C. V. Philpot, District Magistrate, Dacca to Commissioner, Dacca Div., 9 May 1927. GB Poll. File 8A–5, Progs. B451–61, September 1927. WBSA.

94. G. H. W. Davies, District Magistrate, Midnapore to A. W. Cook, Commissioner, Burdwan Div. GB Poll. File 8A–1, Progs. B393–406. August 1925. WBSA.

95. Broomfield, p. 272.

96. "Report on Sirajgunj Conference," Hindley, Subdivisional Officer (SDO) Sirajgunj to Mitter, District Magistrate (DM) Pabna, June 8, 1924, GOB 219/1924, sl.9.

97. Ibid.

98. Maulvi Syed Akbar Ali to Hindley, SDO Sirajgunj, 10 June 1924, in ibid.

99. A *waqf* is a trust in which property is donated for religious purposes.

100. *Moslem Chronicle*, January 1895, passim.

101. *Report of the Working of the Reformed Constitution*, GOB, 1927, pp. 104–6.

102. Gyanendra Pandey, "Rallying 'Round the Cow—Sectarian Strife in the Bhojpuri Region, c. 1888–1917," in Ranajit Guha, ed., *Subaltern Studies II* (Delhi: Oxford University Press, 1983), p. 120.

103. Freitag, 1989a, p. 76.

104. Bombay Confl. Progs., vol. 71, progs. no. 1, serial no. 6, p. 3, par: 3, as cited in Freitag, 1989a, p. 76.

105. GOB Home Poll. 117/1927 sl. nos. 1–3, WBSA.

106. Eric Hobsbawm, "Inventing Traditions," in Eric Hobsbawm and Terence Ranger, eds., *The Invention of Tradition* (Cambridge: Cambridge University Press, 1983), p. 13.

107. J. E. Armstrong, Commissioner of Police, "Report on the Calcutta Riots of July 1926, 11th to 25th July"(Calcutta: Bengal Government Press, 1926), p. 22, in "Hindu and Moslem Rioting at Dacca, 8th–12th September, 1926," P&J 2764/1926. Hereafter, RCR–July 1926.

108. S. Das, p. 81.

109. J. E. Armstrong, "Report on the Calcutta Riots of April 1926, First Phase, 2nd to 15th April" (Calcutta: Bengal Government Press, 1926), p. 1–2. Hereafter, RCRFP.

110. Ibid.

111. RCR–July 1926, p. 1.

112. Pandey, 1990, p. 39.

113. See ibid., p. 45.

114. RCRFP, pp. 1–2.

115. *Hanafi,* February 5, 1926, cited in Broomfield, p. 276.

116. Broomfield, pp. 264–267.

117. J. E. Armstrong, Commissioner of Police, Calcutta, "Report on the Calcutta Riots of April 1926." GB Poll File 174/26, WBSA, cited in Chatterjee, 1984, p. 68.

118. Ray, p. 356.

119. Ibid.

120. Broomfield, pp. 277–278, and Ray, pp. 356–357.

121. Broomfield, p. 279.

122. Pandey, 1994, pp. 199–200, 212–213.

123. Ibid., p. 200.

124. Government of India, Home Political File 209/1926, cited in Ray, p. 358.

125. In the Sikh massacre in Delhi in 1984, for example, Congress-I leaders and police tapped well-known criminal figures to coordinate the killings mainly in the *bustees* and neighborhoods where poor Sikhs lived. These men were protected from prosecution. In this light, Das' comment that these "[p]roducts of social alienation . . . probably participated in the violence for expressing their sense of frustration resulting from uncertainty of existence and an identity crisis," must be viewed with skepticism. In fact, these "products of social alienation" were probably well paid. See Das, pp. 93–94.

126. Upendra Baxi, "Reflections on the Reservations Crisis in Gujarat," in Veena Das, ed., *Mirrors of Violence: Communities, Riots and Survivors in South Asia* (Delhi: Oxford University Press, 1992), p. 237.

127. RCRFP, p. 4.

128. GOB Chief Secretary to GOI Home, 5 August 1926. GOI Home Poll. File 209/26, NAI, as cited in Chatterjee, 1984, p. 69.

129. RCRFP, p. 5.

130. Government of India, Home Political File 209/1926, cited in Ray, p. 358.

131. J. E. Armstrong to L. Birley, Chief Secretary, April 4, 1926, GOB Poll File 174/26, WBSA, cited in Chatterjee, 1984, p. 68. See also chapter two.

132. RCRFP, p. 6.

133. RCR–July 1926, p. 3.

134. Ibid., p. 1.

135. RCR–July 1926, p. 7.

136. Ibid., p. 23.

137. Ibid.

138. Ibid., p. 10.

139. Ibid., p. 17.

140. *Forward,* April 29, 1926, cited in Broomfield, p. 278, and Ray, p. 357.

141. *Statesman,* April 29, 1926, cited in S. Das, p. 87.

142. RCRFP, p. 24.

143. RCRFP, p. 11.

144. A *kafir* is an unbeliever, a non-Muslim. RCRFP, p. 24.

145. *Sala* is a derogatory term in Hindi. RCRSP, pp. 24–25.

146. Ibid., pp. 25–26.

147. *Indian Quarterly Register,* vol. II, July-December 1926, p. 77.

148. Gayatri Chakravorty Spivak, "Subaltern Studies: Deconstructing Historiography," in Ranajit Guha and Gayatri Chakravorty Spivak, eds., *Selected Subaltern Studies* (Oxford: Oxford University Press, 1988), p. 23.

149. Basu, pp. 2,613–2,614.

150. Basu, p. 2,613.

151. Ibid.

152. RCRFP, p. 6.

153. Ibid., p. 11.

154. J. E. Armstrong to L. Birley, Chief Secretary, April 4, 1926, GOB Poll File 174/26, WBSA, cited in Chatterjee, 1984, p. 68.

155. See chapter two.

156. RCRFP, p. 25.

157. Letter from Gulam Imam, member, All-India Moslem Council, to Secretary, All-India Moslem League, April 28, 1926. Archives of the Freedom Movement, vol. 37, no. 67.

158. *Modern Review*, May 1926, vol. XXXIX no. 5, p. 601, cited in Shila Sen, pp. 59–60.

159. Sen, p. 65.

160. J. E. Armstrong, Commissioner of Police, "Report on the Calcutta Riots of July 1926, 11th to 25th July" (Calcutta: Bengal Government Press, 1926), p. 25, in "Hindu and Moslem Rioting at Dacca, 8th–12th September, 1926," P&J 2764/1926.

161. RCRFP, p. 28.

162. *Indian Quarterly Register*, vol. II, July-December 1926, pp. 77–78.

163. "Report regarding Pabna Disturbances," GOB Home Poll. 317/1926, p. 1. WBSA.

164. "Special Report Case No. 15/26," GOB Home Poll. 317/1926, sl. 1–31. WBSA.

165. Ibid.

166. "Report regarding Pabna Disturbances," GOB Home Poll. 317/1926, p. 1. WBSA.

167. Report of District Magistrate, Pabna, July 6, 1926, and communique from GOB, Political Dept., July 6, 1926, GOB Home Poll. 317/26. WBSA.

168. *Hats* are rural markets. W. A. Marr, Commissioner, Rajshahi Division, to A. N. Moberly, Chief Secretary, GOB, July 25, 1926, WBSA, cited in Chatterjee, 1984, p. 236.

169. Telegram from the Commissioner of Jalpaiguri and Rajshahi to GOB, Political Dept., Calcutta, July 7, 1926, GOB Home Poll. 317/26. WBSA.

170. "Report on Pabna Disturbances," GOB Home Poll. 317/26, p. 6. WBSA.

171. "Special Report Case No. 15/26," GOB Home Poll. 317/1926, sl. 1–31. WBSA.

172. Telegram from the Commissioner of Jalpaiguri and Rajshahi to GOB, Political Dept., Calcutta, July 7, 1926, GOB Home Poll. 317/26. WBSA.

173. GOB Home Poll. 317/26 WBSA, cited in Chatterjee, 1984, p. 69.

174. Report by District Magistrate, Pabna, July 24, 1926, L/P&J/2116/26, IOR, cited in S. Das, p. 76.

175. *Statesman*, September 8, 1926, cited in S. Das, p. 77.

176. *Amrita Bazar Patrika*, August 15, 1926, cited in ibid.

177. W. A. Marr, Commissioner, Rajshahi Division, to A. N. Moberly, Chief Secretary, GOB, July 25, 1926, WBSA, cited in Chatterjee, 1984, p. 236.

178. Chatterjee, 1984, pp. 105–107.

179. Ibid.

180. Ibid., p. 109.

181. Chatterjee acknowledges that these incidents would probably not have occurred without "mobilisation efforts" from the world of "organised" politics. Ibid., p. 115.

182. Ibid., p. 109.

183. See John Stevenson, *Popular Disturbances in England, 1700–1832* (London: Longman, 1979), p. 11.

184. Ghyanshyam Shah, "Identity, Communal Consciousness and Politics," *Economic and Political Weekly*, vol. XXIX, no. 19, May 7, 1994, p. 1,133.

185. Stevenson, p. 11. See also Rudé.

186. *Indian Quarterly Register*, July-December, 1926, cited in Ray, p. 358.

187. GOB Home Poll. 317/26, cited in Chatterjee, 1984, p. 236.

188. Report of District Magistrate, Pabna, July 4, 1926, GOB Home Poll. 317/26. WBSA.

189. Marr to Moberly, 10 July 1926, GB Poll. File 317/ 26. WBSA; see Chatterjee, 1984, p. 72.

190. GOB Home Poll. 317/26, cited in Chatterjee, 1984, pp. 72–73, 237. As Chatterjee points out, the colonial doctrine of collective punishment led to absurd calculations: Christians and Buddhists were exempted from the tax, as were Brahmos, members of a religious reform movement that incorporated elements of Christian monotheism and social service with Hinduism. Ibid., p. 237.

191. For more on this analysis of the use of public space, see Basu, p. 2,612.

4

The Politics of Violence:
Patterns of Organization
1926–1941

Constructing a political community self-conscious of its identity and capable of making successful political demands depends on a leader's skill
at making objective differences between that group and other groups
matter. By giving these differences symbolic meaning, leaders reinforce
political cleavages and group solidarity.[1] Given that the process of identity formation is variable, as those who might be presumed to belong to
any one "identity" also respond to many different claims on their loyalty,
violence is an effective tool for political mobilization because it cuts
across other divisions. Bengali Muslims who were divided among themselves over the specifics of land reform and the benefits of loyalty or resistance to British rule could be united against perceived aggression
against themselves as Muslims.

This is not to say that communal outbreaks merely represent the outcome of elite efforts to manufacture mass support. Looking for the causes
of any communal riot in the broader political or socio-economic forces at
work needs to be coupled with an analysis that stresses human agency—
the violence itself, viewed "from below"[2]—to understand changing popular perceptions of identity and why "certain targets and symbols of
unity were chosen and why various groups of conflicting interests so
readily rallied around them."[3] The continuity of certain symbols, like music in front of mosques, is a reminder that politicians operate within constraints in choosing symbols of identity. Not all symbols will work all the
time; changing alliances may render some symbols irrelevant or may
reignite interest over issues that had all but vanished. Without understanding the political context, the actors jockeying for position before the
elections and what they stood to gain or lose from the riot, as well as the
discursive process in which these actors articulated this identity in con-

test with each other, it is impossible to understand why particular outbreaks occurred when and where they did.

The escalation in communal conflict in the mid-1920s in Bengal grew out of a struggle among rival leaders, both Hindu and Muslim, to establish themselves as spokesmen and representatives for their community. To do this, they had to first create their version of what that community should be. The violent confrontations that accompanied this rivalry had two distinct but related aims. The Muslim leaders who challenged existing custom by organizing processions or protests over religious and political symbols sought to usurp the authority of the reigning Muslim leadership and rival parties. To this end, they attempted to prove themselves as more representative of Muslim interests by the distance they could put between themselves and the largely Hindu leadership of the nationalist movement. Courting government recognition, they competed for control over public space with Hindu leaders. They constructed Hindu leaders, and Hindus in general, as biased and as threatening to the physical security of Muslims. Hindu leaders did the same, playing on Hindu fears of being reduced to a minority in the political arena. Each new confrontation provided opportunities to create martyrs and other symbols of community identity. For Muslim leaders, the symbols increasingly evoked the sufferings of the Muslims, their victimization at the hands of Hindu militants, and the failure of both the government and unscrupulous Muslim leaders to protect them.

The Representation of Violence and Victimization

The means by which violence becomes ritualized is also constitutive of the process of identity formation. In the communal outbreaks that followed the mid-1920s, the representation of violence took on a critical political role. Through rumor, inquiry reports, and political propaganda, leaders on both sides sought to portray the other community as the aggressor and their own as the victim. Through repetition, these representations became "facts" for the next confrontation, freezing popular perceptions of identity. What people believed about how a riot started then fed into the design of the next confrontation: rumors about the desecration of temples and mosques or atrocities against one group or the other were revived to justify reprisals in the next round. In many cases, in areas where images had been desecrated, the incidents received far greater attention in the local press than they had in the place where the incident actually took place.[4] And each incident imposed new constraints on future political choices. Having popularized a certain construction of Hindu or Muslim identity, political leaders on both sides found themselves limited in their ability to draw on symbols other than those that evoked polarization and exclusion.

As noted in chapter three, the "communal riot narrative" represented a form of colonialist knowledge used to explain violent outbreaks in terms of "historic" antagonisms that the British believed existed between different religious "communities" in India. Such antagonisms were used to justify the British presence as the only force capable of maintaining the peace. What the investigations and reports succeeded in doing was to help freeze popular perceptions of Hindu and Muslim identities by portraying animosities between the two communities as an historical inevitability, and casting the rioters as "irrational" mobs. But the colonial authorities were not the only ones to construct such narratives to explain riots in terms favorable to their own political objectives. Political parties on both sides also constructed "facts" out of every incident—about who was the aggressor, the number of casualties, how the police or other state agencies behaved in a partisan manner, or how the "victimized" community resisted provocation. For violence to be effective, these "facts" had to be made believable. This was accomplished through several different mechanisms: through repetition in party propaganda, rumor, and sympathetic press reports, and through the sanction of the state as when official reports blamed one side or the other.

The Choreography of
Violence in Public Spaces

The way in which Bengal's Muslim leaders manipulated communal outbreaks reveals that the violence was more calculated than impulsive, as emerging leaders appropriated public space to assert the rights of communities they claimed to represent. Processions and other public demonstrations were important because they were a way of acting out the political power struggle by laying claim to public places. When leaders on all sides made a deliberate effort to take processions and other demonstrations beyond these general areas into Muslim or Hindu neighborhoods, it was a way of letting the residents know that they were not safe even in their homes. Temples and mosques attacked during one riot became symbols of power or victimization in the next round as organizers replicated the choreography. In isolation, any one incident of violence had little meaning for community identity; linked, every new outrage implicated the past of both groups, adding new martyrs and making fast the boundaries that described each community's vulnerability and fear of the other.

In the later years examined in this chapter, the processions in question are funeral processions. Funeral processions combine the symbolic functions of the procession in bringing the community together publicly in an activity exclusive of other groups, and of the martyr in the body of the person being mourned as a symbol both of vulnerability and resistance. Such patterns were not unique to Bengal, nor even to India, and, in fact, have become a hallmark of popular protest movements.[5] In Liverpool in the early 1800s parades by the Orange Order and the Catholics institutionalized a tradition of sectarian violence that has remained in place for nearly 200 years. In both settings, processions became a show of force by the dominant community, evoking both the terror of the mob and the sanctity of religious authority.[6]

The violence that erupted in Bengal in 1926 certainly represented an attack on the status order, but it was a planned attack, carried out by leaders who perceived an advantage in using occasions of public ceremony, usually involving processions, to assert the rights of communities they claimed to represent. In doing so, they sought not only to pick a fight over Muslim and Hindu "rights" to that public space, but to differentiate themselves from leaders who had "compromised" on those rights. Issues which previously had been resolved through the quiet diplomacy of the Nawab were made public property.

The September 1926 riot in Dacca—the worst outbreak of communal violence in its history—represented an example of this kind of political maneuvering by the emerging Muslim leadership in Bengal. Like its predecessors in Pabna and Calcutta, the Dacca outbreak was sparked by a procession, but unlike those incidents, the Janmastami celebration in Dacca was an event that had a long tradition as a symbol of Hindu and Muslim cooperation. As such it was a symbol of accommodative practices of the "old order" and was therefore targeted by new leaders who wanted to give it a new interpretation, and thus take that function away from the Nawab and other representatives. Challenging the symbols of customary authority and customary agreements regarding processions and other uses of public space was part of challenging the old leadership. The protests against the Janmastami procession in September 1926 were aimed at discrediting the Nawab, who had conceded the right of the Hindu organizers to proceed with the celebration.

The violence of 1927 and 1930 was largely aimed at discrediting "nationalist" Muslims—those who had joined the Congress party. In 1927, Muslim leaders blamed the government for permitting a Shivaji procession, celebrating the militant Hindu hero, to take place in Dacca. These leaders used the fact that symbols of Hindu militancy were evoked during the celebration to challenge the Congress Muslims who participated. The funeral procession that sparked the May 1930 riots in Dacca further bolstered the standing of the "fanatical" element within the Muslim parties that the British authorities most feared. These leaders had accused local officials of failing to act forcefully against Hindu stone-throwers in the days before the outbreak, and they used the funeral to communicate the message that Muslims were not safe under the present government. The patterns of violence were replicated in yet another outbreak of violence in Dacca in 1941, by which time it was clear that this ritualized ceremony of violence and the politics of fear would ultimately determine the national identities of the Hindus and Muslims of Bengal.

In 1926, Muslim leaders competing in the year-end elections challenged established authority by organizing public protests against accommodationist conventions, like permitting Hindu processionists to play music while passing mosques. At issue was not only the authority to determine what issues would define the community's interests, but where and how those interests would be made public. Rival Muslim parties deliberately emphasized issues that were designed to highlight differences between Hindus and Muslims and calculated to discredit anyone in their own community who sought to minimize those differences. They called in religious symbolism to bolster their positions and win useful allies among religious leaders and others who had influence in the *mofussil*.

The leaders also had an interest in ensuring that the community's collective memory of the incident did not fade. Major incidents were relived first in press accounts and then in official inquiries established to determine culpability and award compensation. Frequently the next violent outbreak saw previously identified targets taking on new symbolic significance. This re-enactment was a matter of political design, not historical accident, setting a pattern for violence that was ritualized and reiterated in disturbances over the next twenty years.

The Dacca 'Riot' of September 1926

In 1925 and early 1926 there were a number of incidents involving the playing of music in front of mosques in Dacca. In 1925, a confrontation was narrowly averted following the playing of music past a mosque in Amligola. According to the *Report of the Dacca Disturbances Enquiry Committee*, after that incident "three prominent leaders of the Hindus were induced to apologize at a public meeting," and this was generally resented by the Hindu community. "It is said that these gentlemen entirely lost their influence as a result."[7] In the aftermath of the violence in Calcutta and Pabna, leaders on all sides were in no position to compromise.

When Hindu leaders began to make arrangements for the September Janmastami celebration,[8] the atmosphere was tense. After some negotiation, the authorities decided to allow the procession to take place. A group of Muslims who opposed it persuaded Muslim workers to boycott the procession, particularly the cart and carriage drivers traditionally employed during the festival. The procession went ahead as planned, with Hindu organizers employing workers from their own ranks to fill in for the striking Muslims. Processionists shouted *"Bande Mataram"* and other provocative slogans while passing one of the main mosques. The procession itself passed in relative calm, but, according to government records, immediately after the festival Hindu leaders organized a counter-strike against Muslim drivers for participating in the boycott.[9] The spark that set off the riot was the refusal of the Muslim drivers and laborers to work for the procession, and the Hindu counter-boycott. Some Hindus claimed that there was in fact no counter-boycott, but that Hindus feared attack by Muslim drivers and so refused to use the carriages.[10] As Clayton, Commissioner of Dacca, observed, "the hackney-carriage drivers, either under compulsion of their communal organization, or because they had been made to believe it was a religious duty, had sacrificed the two best days' of earnings of the year. . . . It seems reasonable to believe that it was the picketing against hackney-carriage drivers that started the disorder on this morning."[11]

Clayton's language is revealing. He suggests that the drivers' "communal organization" directed their action, an organization that could muster the authority to challenge the customary and lucrative participation of the carriage drivers in the festival. The organization behind the boycott, and the subsequent attacks on Hindu establishments, was located in the *mohalla sardars*, the neighborhood leaders.

"[E]laborate arrangements were made with the aid of the Mohalla Sardar system to organise a Muhammadan Hartal [strike] for the two days of the procession . . . to prevent Muhammadans from rendering any sort of service in connection with the procession and to turn away any Muhammadans who came in to see the show."[12] Not all Muslim leaders supported the boycott, however. There was also evidence that Hindu leaders had also planned for some kind of violence. On August 8, the police and district magistrate raided a house in which *lathis* were being made; the next day more arms were found in a boat belonging to a local Hindu.[13]

For three days following the counter-boycott, there were outbreaks of violence throughout Dacca, with Hindu neighborhoods the main targets. The violence began on the morning of September 10, when a group of Muslims attacked Hindu houses near Yusuf market. This was followed by several other attacks on Hindus. A group armed with *lathis* and daggers broke into a printing press; a crowd of Muslims attacked two officers of a match factory, killing their Gurkha attendant;[14] and there was an attack on a medical students' mess hall in which one student was killed.[15]

In Dacca, as in other outbreaks, it was not possible to resolve the conflict by determining what custom had been permitted regarding processions in the past. In part, this was because the conflict centered not so much on the violation of established tradition, as on who was entrusted to interpret that tradition. Attempts by the British to take on this role only cast the two communities more firmly into antagonistic positions. Within the Muslim leadership itself there was conflict over precisely this question of authority. The debate is reflected in the contemporary Bengali press. *Dhaka Prokash*, an influential Hindu weekly, carried an editorial that stated that

> The Janmastami procession is an historical event. For nearly three hundred years, the procession has been performed in a grand way—from the time of Islam Khan, the Nawab of the age, and by the enterprise of the Hindu community of Tanti Bazar and Nawabpur, and with the cooperation of the local Muslims. From the beginning, the procession has been conducted with music on the main road without any opposition, but the terrible disturbance it has created in Dacca this year on the taking out of the procession has its roots in the sudden religious conscientiousness which has agitated the Muslims lately to stop music before mosques. These Muslims are succumbing to sinister influences. Even though this procession has gone on for hundreds of years with music before mosques, this year certain obstinate members of the Muslim community were determined to cause trouble. For a long time, the Nawab's family in Dacca has patronized this procession—and even this year the present Nawab Bahadur tried to pacify the Muslims by acknowledging the right of the Hindus, but his efforts failed.[16]

In his *Notes on the Races, Castes and Tribes of Eastern Bengal*, James Wise confirms that the Janmastami procession was a showpiece of the Nawab's rule in Bengal, and notes that "the processions are preceded by a string of elephants, and a 'Panja' or model of a hand, presented by a former Nawab, is borne aloft as at the Muharram pageant."[17]

The procession had other symbolic interpretation. Partha Chatterjee has noted that the festival held particular fascination for the artist Paritosh Sen, who describes it his autobiography, *Zindabahar*.

> Nowhere else in the subcontinent could one have seen such a gorgeous, immense and spectacular event. One could see in this procession the extraordinary artistry of those magic hands that had created the world-renowned muslin. For two days this intricate multi-colored pageant, constantly shifting and changing, would pass before my eyes like a huge tapestry. It was like looking through a kaleidoscope. The active organisers were Hindu, but quite literally, the procession was for all to join.[18]

As these sources indicate, the procession was part of a tradition in which both Hindus and Muslims used to participate.

Sandria Freitag describes a similar coalition "protecting and extending the shared local culture" in connection with the observance of Bharat Milap in Banaras.[19] She notes that "such ceremonials constituted statements of shared civic identity . . . as much as they did a specific religious identity."[20] In Dacca, those trying to keep Dacca Muslims from participating in the Janmastami procession were operating from an outsider's perspective and were trying to link these Bengali Muslims with an identity that was larger than Dacca and larger than Bengal. To do so, they needed to break the symbolic ties they held to a Dacca ethic. Boycotting the procession was one way to do that. Raising the issue of custom also gave rival leaders the opportunity to contravene long-standing agreements between the two communities, by changing procession routes and erecting new mosques. In the 1926 Janmastami riot in Dacca, the evidence points to an abrupt break in a tradition that had been built on the cooperation of both communities.

It is critical to remember, however, that the Dacca riots of 1926 constituted an attack on recognized authority figures and institutions, and as such did not always follow clear-cut religious lines. The riots following the Janmastami procession in Dacca reveal an underlying conflict over the issue of authority within the Bengali Muslim community, and a rivalry for the right to claim to represent that community. The *Dhaka Prokash* editorial complains about a new Muslim "conscientiousness" about religion that represented another voice, another claim on Bengali Muslim identity. The culture that had embraced the Janmastami procession was an inclusive one; those speaking for this new Muslim solidarity threatened to undo it.

The Muslim press blamed the government for violating not only customary practices but its own policies. On September 24, the *Mussulman* published an article entitled "The Dacca Riots: A Muslim Version." In it the paper claimed that the district magistrate had decided that music would be permitted "against the established custom and in spite of the standing order of the then lieutenant governor passed sometime in the year 1905," after a disturbance involving music before mosques.[21] The Hindu press blamed Muslim leaders for refusing to accept the government's decision on the matter. An editorial published in *Dhaka Prokash* on September 26 commented that, "[c]ompetition with the administrative power of the King was the clear message from those opposing the Janmastami procession in Dhaka . . . Whenever the King's rule is defied publicly like this, there is bound to be trouble everywhere."[22]

Claiming precedence—and gaining official recognition of that precedent—was crucial to securing political advantage. The historical evidence for what had customarily been permitted during the Janmastami had little to do with what leaders from both communities were arguing.

The government hoped that by determining precedent, and by locating leaders to speak for that precedent, they could convince all interested parties (of which there were more than simply Hindu and Muslim) to reach agreement on the basis of that precedent. All groups had previously gone along with the Nawab's interpretation of how the Janmastami was celebrated but, in 1926, groups challenging his authority would no longer recognize as valid that version of history. The fact that the Nawab's stand in favor of allowing the procession put him in alliance with Hindu leaders was also used against him. Subgroups within each community were determined to see the boycott and counter-boycott carried out in such a way as to ensure retaliation. What had changed was not custom but the tools used to refashion the boundaries of community, and the fact that these were now in the hands of leaders whose power depended on their ability to define Bengali Muslims as a threatened community.

In writing to his superiors in Delhi, the chief secretary of the government of Bengal fell back on the "ancient hatreds" formula to explain the violence when he observed that the question of music before mosques had "aroused the latent antipathy" between Hindus and Muslims.[23] Clayton, the commissioner of Dacca, blamed "the criminal element among the Muhammadans" for "being ready to take advantage of such a situation." The government's account of the riot reveals the same prejudice in favor of "natural" leaders like the Nawab who "acted wisely" in advising those Muslims who would be offended by the procession to stay home.[24] Official inquiries into the cause of the riots in Dacca back up *Dhaka Prokash*'s claim that the Nawab had confirmed that the procession was a long-standing tradition.

Chief Secretary Moberly observed that opposition to the procession amounted to an attempt to challenge the Nawab because of his association with the procession. "Someone seems to have been undermining the Nawab's influence," Moberly wrote. "Hakim Habibur Rahman [Secretary of the District Moslem Association, a rival body to the Nawab's Anjuman Islamia] is very probably at the bottom of this trouble in the hope of discrediting the Anjuman."[25] The District Moslem Association for its part claimed that there had never been any music before mosques in Dacca, and that the Hindus had only claimed this right since the advent of the Hindu Mahasabha on the political scene.[26] The Nawab pleaded for stopping the music at prayer time as a conciliatory gesture, but extreme Hindu opinion refused to yield on the issue.[27]

The debate over custom centered on who should have the authority to interpret tradition and speak for the community on such questions. As Moberly's letter indicates, the machinations behind the District Moslem Association's claim that music before mosques had never been permitted in Dacca reveal an effort to circumvent the Nawab and establish itself as the authoritative voice for Bengali Muslims by questioning the authority of the Nawab to permit the procession, that is, to interpret for Bengali Muslims what their relationship to their celebration should be. By questioning "customary" practice, the DMA was challenging the Nawab's traditional function in that role. The DMA presented the Government with a petition stating:

> It is not sufficient to consider only custom in arriving at a decision on a point which is so seriously agitating the minds of the leaders of the Hindus and the Musulmans all over India, totally ignoring the religious point of view about which the Musulmans present (the Nawab and others who met with Government to discuss the procession) were not competent to give any opinion, nor has this Association any such right, except the learned Ulemas [sic].[28]

While the Association denied itself the same authority, it made clear that it knew who had it, and in saying so, linked itself with the only "organization" capable of deciding what had now become a religious matter— the 'ulama. The association attempted to cast itself as an organization closer to the interests of Muslims as Muslims, challenging the traditional authority of the Nawab with another kind of authority.[29] For his part, the Nawab had also contacted 'ulama in Delhi and Lucknow and "obtained instructions to the effect that though the playing of music before mosques must be offensive to Muhammadans it would not be proper to offer resistance to a procession supported by the Government."[30]

The 1926 riot was largely contained within the city of Dacca itself, but when outside volunteers from both communities came into the city, ostensibly for relief work, the Hindu volunteers were all from Calcutta, and the Muslims mainly from the villages. In fact, Hindu leaders frequently voiced their concern about the threat of Muslim reinforcements coming in from the *mofussil*, and even the Secretary of the District Moslem Association conceded that it was only the efforts of the Nawab that prevented what otherwise would have been a massacre of the Hindu population.[31]

The District Moslem Association had made earlier attempts to unseat another Muslim organization, the Provincial Muhammadan Association—an organization which was listed in the government's official list of Muslim organizations in Bengal. As noted in chapter three, the Political Department exercised considerable influence over political organizations through its list of "recognized" associations. The benefit of being "listed" was increased influence with government officials, including being able to recommend candidates for public office.[32] In 1920 the DMA petitioned the Government for recognition:

When the Khelafut [sic] movement was in its full swing in Dacca the Provincial Muhammadan Association which is a body recognized by the Government was sleeping a sound sleep and its office bearers had joined the movement and took a leading part in that, an Association of loyal Musulmans was thought of [as] a necessity to cooperate with the commissioner of the Division and with kind approval of the officials, the Dacca District Moslem Association was started by the rallying round all loyal Musulmans. . . . If a survey is done of the work it did shaping the minds of the people to remain loyal by the issue of literature and otherwise, it would be found that the Association did inestimable service in this connection. . . . The recognized Association had no sitting during the last three years, and though it stands in name, it has no influence over the Muslim public and it has therefore lost its representative character. But a perusal of the list of the office bearers and members of the Executive Committee of the Dacca District Moslem Association would convince anyone that this Association is not one of Mushroom growths destined to die on the coming morrow but to stand for years and years to do useful service owing to its representative character.[33]

The DMA bolstered its case for recognition by promising to work to keep the public on the side of law and peace. On October 13, 1920, Lindsay, the District Magistrate for Dacca, reported that the Provincial Moslem Association was moribund since its leaders had joined the Khilafat movement. He noted that "the new Association gave most valuable aid to the Government in keeping local Muhammadans from losing their heads and should certainly be recognized by Government."[34] The same Hakim Habibur Rahman who would agitate against the Janmastami procession in 1926 pleaded for the DMA as an organization "representing all the subdivisions of the district and men who have real control over the Muslim public have been elected as members."[35] The majority of these members were landlords, *jotedars*, pleaders, and merchants. Rahman's final criticism of the Provincial Muhammadan Association was that it had abandoned its principles of loyalty and the bounds of Islamic law and had "accepted extremism to the detriment of the welfare of the Muslim community."[36] In the end the government decided to recognize the DMA, and struck the PMA from its list.[37]

In the 1926 elections, "music-before-mosques" continued to be a volatile campaign issue. Hindu voters in Midnapore were warned in anonymous leaflets that they should "be careful," and that "for the safety of Hindu religion, caste and society" they should not vote for B. N. Sasmal, a Swarajist who had been active in the peasant movement, because he had supported prohibitions on music before mosques, had shown respect to Mohammedans who had desecrated temples and had supported reserving eighty percent of government posts for Muslims.[38]

Rahim was ultimately unable to launch the new Bengal Muslim party as he had planned. Huq refused to join, choosing instead to keep with his East Bengal group.[39] Suhrawardy organized the Independent Muslim Party with a number of political activists who had been prominent in the *praja* conferences. The membership of the Independent Muslim Party, founded in September 1926, included Abdur Rauf, Mujibur Rahman of the newspaper *Mussulman*, Mohammed Maniruzzaman Islamabadi of the *Soltan*, A. and H. S. Suhrawardy, Nazir Ahmad Choudhury of the newspaper *Muhammadi*, and Y. C. Ariff. The party described its aims as safeguarding the rights of the community and securing political advancement for Muslims.[40] A. K. Ghaznavi also split with Rahim and, together with Nawab of Dacca and other leaders, formed yet a third party, the Central Muslim Party.[41] However, Rahim's party still did better than any of the others, although it was unable to form a ministry because no other parties would work with it.[42] But the message had gotten through: of the thirty-nine Muslim seats in the council, thirty-eight pledged that they were there to work not for the united Hindu-Muslim interests espoused by the Swarajists but for the interests of the Muslim community.[43]

One indication of the general fear of further violence was the stockpiling of stones and bricks on the roofs of both Hindu and Muslim houses in Dacca.[44] In the countryside, the government continued to point to the activities of preachers in provoking confrontations.[45] In April 1927, Chief Secretary Prentice noted that the governor had received complaints about the efforts of itinerant preachers in encouraging "claims which threaten to endanger the public peace,"[46] and that

> [T]here are signs too that claims are becoming more extreme, e.g. the claims to stop music not only before mosques, but also in the neighborhood of secular buildings . . . and that intolerance is deliberately practiced, e.g. the reported killing of a cow at Feni in reply to Saraswati Puja. . . . events at Patuakhali have shown how a purely local agitation [which] would probably die down if the local people were left to themselves is being fomented by outsiders who arrange for the supply of men and money.[47]

Prentice suggested that the legal authorities be consulted as to whether "under the existing law we can deal with itinerant mollas [mullahs] and outside agitators, and if not whether there is any amendment of law he would suggest for the purpose" to deal with "outsiders who fish in the troubled matters of religious intolerance and stir up trouble."[48] An official from the government's legal office noted that it was probably not possible to make use of anything "more drastic" than preventive detention, and Prentice acknowledged that if the government were to take stronger action, it would be "difficult to avoid the charge of interfering with religion, and so perhaps the remedy will be worse than the disease."[49] Prentice then suggested ways in which "these troublesome people" (the mullahs) might be detained under a preventive detention law: If they were sending or receiving inflammatory letters; or were associating with "local firebrands;" or if they made speeches or distributed writings that could be directly attributed to them (pamphlets being difficult to trace to a single person); or if they could be called "hazardous to the community" (difficult to prove); or if they were involved in a provocation at a mosque which was "likely to cause a riot" (difficult to prove if there were no riot).[50] A month later Liddell responded that "it might be possible to justify . . . to punish the agitator as a result of whose activities an unlawful assembly or riot takes place," and advised looking at sections 154/155 of the penal code under which a "religious riot may be as serious as an 'agrarian' riot."[51]

Mohammad Afsaruddin Ahmed, a preacher and the brother of a prominent Congress-Khilafat leader, Shamsuddin Ahmed, gave a speech at Nadia in 1927 in which he warned Muslims that Hindus were out to destroy them by boycotting them and prosecuting them for slaughtering cows, while they were permitted to play music before mosques. "The Hindus have said we shall not buy from Muslims; that is a declaration of war."[52] Afsaruddin had been an extremist in the Non-cooperation movement, according to the authorities, and was convicted of violations of the penal code in 1922. "Though he still calls himself a swarajist, he is believed to be behind all local communal agitation."[53]

After September 1926, the Janmastami celebration became a symbol of the changed political order and set a pattern for violence that was replicated in later disturbances. During the Janmastami celebration of 1931, for example, the procession had to be dispersed. According to the government report, "the procession, timed to start at 4:30 p.m., was not ready till after 6." The superintendent of police (a European) had ordered it delayed so as not to interfere with prayer time, and the processionists gave it up. But the fact that the city superintendent of police was a Muslim was given great prominence by Hindu organizers who accused the government of being partisan in interfering with the celebration.[54]

The Shivaji Disturbance

The riot that followed a procession in Dacca in 1927 was noteworthy in that it represented an innovation that could make no claim to tradition. On May 5, 1927, a Shivaji procession was held "for the first time" in Dacca, according to the *Report of the Dacca Disturbances Enquiry Committee*, and Muslims opposed it as a "militant procession."[55] The government licensed it on the understanding that there was to be no music before mosques, but the symbol of Shivaji was clearly chosen to provoke a confrontation. Shivaji celebrations in Maharashtra that glorified Hindu militancy and demonized India's Muslim rulers had alienated many Muslims.[56] The Hindu Mahasabha resented the fact that the government had placed restrictions on the procession, and at least some of the leaders claimed that the procession had been canceled as a result. However, it was brought out anyway. Muslims attacked the procession when it stopped to play music in front of a mosque.[57]

The very fact that the Hindu leadership won government approval in securing a license for the Shivaji procession points to another important factor in the stakes for which the various leaders were gambling: government recognition of their rights. The music before mosques controversy became a symbol for both communities' subjective efforts to close ranks and consolidate the support of their own. The counterpart to that process was the effort at objectification. Recognition by the governing power has always been critical; indeed, the politics of identity, or nation-formation, requires that kind of recognition as a reason for mobilization. Government's recognition of a group's rights and identity fuels new demands and competition among other groups for such recognition, and new groups quickly acquired the tools to win such recognition—petitions, protests, the press, and public opinion.

> Central to the process of objectification have been the hundreds of situations that Indians over the past two hundred years have experienced in which precedents for action, in which rights to property, their social relations, their rituals, were called into question or had to be explained. It was the act of questioning the need for explanation to themselves or to the British which lies at the heart of the process.[58]

Even more important than the act of questioning was the competition among groups who used the process to challenge the status order. The efforts by British administrators to obtain explanations of the rules governing processions past mosques or the criteria for leadership in the Muslim community made apparent the discrepancies prevailing in local custom in the former case, and the basis for authority within the community in the latter, and called into question the validity of the old order and opened the door for new groups to claim an authoritative position within the community.

The Independence Day 'Riot' of 1930

The outbreak of violence which followed the Congress-organized celebration of Independence Day on January 26, 1930, marked a significant change in the symbolism of communal confrontations. The disturbances were for the most part limited to Dacca, providing further evidence that local political concerns, not historic enmity, lay behind the conflict. Calcutta celebrations of Independence Day were free of violence and flags were raised to cries of both *"Allah-o-Akbar"* and *"Bande Mataram."*[59] The processions were organized around explicitly political events, not only religious celebrations.[60]

The official report on the "riot" is revealing in the way the perpetrators were identified. After noting that all unlicensed processions had been prohibited, it notes that the "supposed Hindu leaders"—here equated with the Congress leadership—had also issued notices ordering that no processions take place, and that the All Bengal Students' Association followed suit. However, as a confidential letter from the chief secretary clarifies, the Bengal Provincial Students' Association, a rival body to the All Bengal Students' Association which had been formed in December, challenged both the Congress leadership and the government ban by insisting on holding a procession.[61] The government decided that it would be better to arrest the leaders afterwards than to "risk disturbances in the streets" by stopping it. While they hoped to block the display of any "seditious" matter, officials did not anticipate any effort to "foment communal trouble."[62]

The students' procession began with a number of small groups carrying national flags and shouting *"Bande Mataram"* and other slogans, which one official report referred to as "the Hindu war cries." The groups eventually coalesced and massed in front of the Narinda mosque in Dacca at about 5:00 p.m. where they continued to shout. Muslims who had gathered for prayer began to throw stones at the processionists, and in retaliation, some of the students ran into the mosque and tore apart a copy of the Quran. The commissioner of Dacca believed that because the processionists were "armed with revolutionary banners" they may have taken that particular route not necessarily to disturb the Muslims but to avoid being seen by the police.[63] Once again, a group out to project itself as a more representative body, a truer exponent of Bengali Hindu students in this case, sought to do so by challenging a government order that their rival organization and ostensible leaders had respected. The Muslims at the Narinda mosque were not the original target of the BPSA; the government and the Congress leaders who had backed down and agreed to the ban on processions were. But it was well known by 1927 that bans on processions had come about principally because of the conflict over music before mosques. By creating a noisy disturbance at Narinda, the students were able to flaunt their defiance of the government in front of the very group that, they would argue, the government had appeased in imposing the ban.

The day after the procession, the government called Hindu and Muslim leaders to establish a peace committee. While the Nawab was, as usual, given credit for controlling the Muslims, Congress leaders were criticized for having "entirely failed to control the rowdy elements of their community."[64] The report paints the Nawab as the hero in the incident, concluding that "all classes of Muslims felt that their religion had been deliberately insulted. . . . The Magistrate reported that only the strenuous efforts of the Nawab saved the situation."[65] But the peace committee, which included the Nawab along with six other Muslim leaders and six Congress leaders, was unable to prevent further violence.

The Dacca Riot of May 22–30, 1930

Further outbreaks in Dacca in May 1930 demonstrate how divisions among Muslim and Hindu leaders made the acquisition of certain symbols of authority crucial for success. Tensions between Congress and Muslim leaders were aggravated by the lack of interest among Bengali Muslims to participate in the salt agitation[66] of March and April 1930. Government officials reported that "the areas chosen for the agitation have been selected because of the small Muhammadan population in them."[67] When Congress leaders claimed Muslims among their speakers and picketers, non-Congress Muslims objected that "those Muhammadan speakers were men of no education and no status and that their speeches were directed as much against the real leaders of the Muhammadans as against the Government,"[68] the implication being that by 1930 no real leader of the Muslims in Bengal would have anything to do with the Congress.

The official report also suggests that the Muslims "as a whole were annoyed and frightened at the partial success of the Congress in gaining the cooperation of a section of their community. They decided that they must close up their ranks at all costs."[69] As was the case in the Independence Day demonstration, the official version of events was concerned with imposing some kind of solidarity on the Muslim community with its references to "all classes of Muslims" and "Muslims as a whole." But such solidarity did not exist. When violence broke out in early May after a Muslim driver injured a Hindu child, a peace committee set up to settle differences between the two communities found its way obstructed by the fact that there were two rival factions among the Muslims.[70]

These last incidents demonstrate how the procession as a symbol came to acquire new meaning as both communities attempted to appear unified in the face of a perceived threat. During the Janmastami procession of 1926, government files record that students and others in the procession supplemented the music with shouts of *"Bande Mataram,"* the notorious slogan associated with *Sakta* militancy during the *swadeshi* years, *"Hindu dharma ki jai"* and *"Muslim dharma ki khai"* ("Long live Hindu dharma"; "Ruin to the dharma of the Muslim").[71] The 1927 Shivaji procession, new to East Bengal, had obvious reference to Hindu militancy. In the charged atmosphere following Congress' rejection of the Muslim League's Fourteen Points,[72] the Congress' 1930 Independence Day celebration harkened back to the same militancy, perceived by Muslims in Bengal as a challenge and a threat. Conflating Hindu militancy and Congress nationalism, the report on the Independence Day disturbance accused the Congress students of crying "the Hindu war cries." According to the official report, resentment over the public apology made by the three Hindu leaders after a procession was taken past a mosque in Amligola in 1925 sparked a frenzy of activity among Hindus organizing themselves and setting up training camps to teach Hindu youth martial arts. The Dacca People's Association claimed that these were to be used only for self-defense, but Muslim leaders saw it as evidence of less honorable intentions.[73] According to the report on the 1930 disturbances, the teaching of *lathi-khel* (fighting with bamboo batons) and dagger drill, in particular, "made a great impression upon the Muhammadans," for while sword play had been a tradition for Muslims practicing for Muharram, "[w]ith the Hindus the habit is new and the dagger can hardly be looked on as a weapon of defence."[74]

The disturbance of May 1930 introduced yet a new element in the by now ritualized confrontation over processions. During the celebration, a fight between Muslim and Hindu boys grew into a more serious confrontation when crowds on both sides intervened. It ended with a Muslim crowd attacking the houses of four prominent Hindus, including that of a police officer, burning two of them as well as a printing press. The Nawab set up a peace committee, consisting of five Hindu and five Muslim men, but before they could submit their report, violence broke out again. Local Muslims anticipated further trouble. One coachman took the precaution of removing his carriage and horse from the vicinity.

On the night of May 24, a Muslim man was stabbed to death.[75] One group, described in the official report as "the fanatical Muslims," decided to declare the man a martyr, and began to organize a funeral procession for him. The Nawab prohibited it, as did the police, who only reluctantly permitted the relatives to claim the body from the hospital and take it to their home village for burial. The body had been taken out of the city on the morning of May 25, but was brought back that afternoon and carried in a procession through the main streets of the town. Walking in front of the procession was a professional crier who called on all "devout" Muslims to attend the funeral. Some Hindu witnesses claimed that the crier also called for revenge on Hindus; witnesses from the police claimed not to have heard the crier at all. Although the procession it-self reportedly moved through the town quickly, "hangers-on and the people who joined in on the way" began looting. Brickbats were thrown from the house of a prominent Hindu, Ballav Babu, until those carrying the body eventually abandoned it in the street. By the time armed police arrived on the scene, several houses had been burned. Stabbings and in-cidents of arson continued over the next several days. One temple and several mosques were damaged and the stables and carriages of Muslim drivers attacked. In many of the incidents, no police force arrived in time to intervene.

Witnesses told the inquiry committee that resentment over the govern-ment's handling of the 1926 incidents in Dacca and Pabna lay behind the 1930 violence. A general amnesty granted to Hindus and Muslims charged in both previous incidents did not extend to Muslims who had attacked Hindu medical students at the Minerva mess hall, and a number of Muslim leaders had demanded that the government grant a pardon.[76] At the same time, the Hindu press was keen to paint the government as responsible for failing to protect Hindu lives. By mid-June, when distur-bances had largely died down, the *East Bengal Times* continued to publish articles about the state of fear in which Hindus were forced to live. *Ananda Bazar Patrika* published exaggerated "eye-witness" accounts by the head of the Hindu Mahasabha about Hindus facing starvation be-cause of looting. The newspaper also published letters from other "re-spectable citizens" alleging that the police had allowed Muslims to attack Hindu homes and shops and that Hindus were arrested without warrant. One writer, in a letter headlined "Hindus Must Help Hindus," urged "all Hindus to come [to Dacca] at once as volunteers for the rescue of their mothers." According to official sources, the inflammatory press reports and the continuing attacks on Muslims seemed designed with the "delib-erate intention on the part of the Hindus to try and provoke the Muham-madans to break out with the idea of proving that the authorities have not done their duty and brought the city under control."[77] Hindu leaders also advised boycotting the committee of inquiry in protest; Congress leaders appealed to residents to testify before the Congress commission of inquiry instead.[78]

In a letter to the government, a Congress party member of the legisla-tive assembly (MLA) accused "local officials" as being "largely responsi-ble for the gruesome incidents." Claiming to have interviewed "leading citizens of Dacca," including the president and secretary of the bar asso-ciation, he argued that Muslims had not opposed the civil disobedience campaign until local officials stepped in to create divisions. In his ver-sion, a May 3 incident involving Hindu Sankharis [shell-workers] and Muslims had set the stage for the riots that followed a few weeks later. In that incident, a Muslim hackney-carriage driver struck and injured a child in the Sankhari quarter of the city. A number of Sankharis chased down the driver and then attacked a mosque. The MLA argued that tensions during the incident had been aggravated by the partisan behavior of the police. As an example, he cited the police response to the Sankharis when they appealed for protection from attacks by Muslims. Superintendent Hudson, the MLA charged, "said that he did not understand the mentality of the Hindus; having declared Civil Disobedience they should not come to the police for protection."[79]

Shortly after the incident, Congress called a nation-wide *hartal* to protest Gandhi's arrest on May 4, and Syed Abdul Hafiz, a cousin of the Nawab, tried to prevent Muslim shops from participating. At about the same time, the Anjuman organized a strike to protest the failure of the authorities to take action against Hindu shell-workers who had thrown stones at a mosque on May 3. "Maulvi Syed Abdul Hafez who desires to be regarded as the leader of all the Muhammadans of the town [and] issued a notice calling on Muhammadans to observe a Hartal on the 6th May on the grounds of outrage on the mosque."[80] The district magistrate decided that Maulvi Hafez "was not generally acceptable to the Muhammadans as their representative" and called in the Nawab to settle the conflict with the Sankharis. The meeting was held on May 18 "at the Ashan Manzil [Nawab's palace] at which it was resolved that he should be accepted as the leader of the community. There ha[d] for some time been three separate associations of Muhammadans in Dacca known as the Anjuman, the Moslem Association and the Bais Panchayat which were proposed to be amalgamated."[81] The district magistrate himself attended the meeting.[82] The Panchayat and the Anjuman agreed to merge and Nawab was again made president—a resolution for which the authorities did not hide their enthusiasm. The inquiry report stated that "the proposal for uniting all the Muhammadans under their hereditary leader, the Nawab, which had been advocated ever since the termination of the Khilafat agitation by those leaders who were prepared to subordinate their personal aggrandisement to the common interest of the community, was at last brought to a successful issue."[83] With the Nawab reinstated, the authorities had new confidence that they could keep in check both the disorder of the Congress campaign and the fanaticism of those Muslims who, unlike the Nawab, were not seen as "natural leaders" of the community.

In the end, however, it was not the Nawab but the "fanatical" leaders of the Anjuman and their tactics that succeeded. By organizing the protest against the shell-workers who stoned the mosque, the Anjuman succeeded in discrediting the Bais Panchayat, tainted by its association with Congress, and forced it to capitulate to the pressure to merge. The same "fanatical" elements organized the funeral procession for the murdered man. Ironically, it was by using the very tactics that the authorities found abhorrent in the civil disobedience campaign that the parties united under a "natural leader" whom the British respected as genuinely representing the interests of his "community."

In his letter, the Congress MLA's letter noted that the Bais Panchayat led by Abdul Munuff had been "sympathetic toward the [civil disobedience] Movement and made an earnest effort to bring about a compromise" in the Sankhari bazaar incident.[84] At the meeting held at the Nawab's palace to unite the Muslim groups "speeches were delivered emphasizing that all the Mahomedans should make common cause. . . . and that [t]he present movement was pernicious and detrimental to the interest of the Mahomedans. . . . It is further reported that the Magistrate himself cheered some of the speakers. . . . The combination of Hafiz, Mannuf and the Magistrate under the leadership of the Nawab was ominous."[85] The MLA went on to accuse the police of siding with the Muslims in the riot, and the government of allowing the funeral procession to take place. While clearly biased, the MLA's report does provide further evidence that Muslims were divided over the civil disobedience campaign, and that the British were determined to back whichever Muslim group resisted the nationalist movement.

For its part, the government did not disguise its intention to hold Congress' civil disobedience campaign responsible for the violence, even though there was little evidence to support such a link. Officers investigating the incident asked the Hindus who had been attacked whether their own encouragement of the civil disobedience campaign was in any way responsible for their fortunes. The meeting ended with cries of "British Raj ki jai" ["Long live British rule"] and "Nawab ki jai"["Long live the Nawab"].[86] The report bluntly dismisses charges that the government sided with the Nawab: "We cannot see that there is any serious objection to Government officers engaging in propaganda against the Congress in certain circumstances, and in a village populated by "Pals" [low-caste Hindus] only propaganda of a simple and possibly crude character could have any effect."[87] Criticized by witnesses about the government's slow reaction to the violence, officials again blamed that failure on the Congress campaign:

Many witnesses have told us that they could never have believed that the prestige of the British government could fall so low as to permit of such serious calamities befalling the peace-loving inhabitants. They admit that for weeks a large section of their community had been doing their utmost to undermine that prestige by teaching contempt of the rights of private property, the flouting of authority, and disobedience to law. . . . The better class Hindus have no illusions as to the object of the civil disobedience campaign, and yet they profess to be surprised that the police found it more difficult to do their duty than in January last.[88]

The report concluded that if all *zamindars* had "done their duty" in "putting down breaches of the peace . . . these communal riots could never have occurred."[89]

In its description of events leading up to the May violence, the report went to great lengths to argue that the Muslims of Dacca were irritated by the boycott of shops and other aspects of the campaign, but the examples provided in the report concern only Europeans and, in one case, a police officer.[90] Although the inquiry committee conceded that there was no evidence that Congress workers participated to any great extent in the violence, it argued that "[t]he organisers of the civil disobedience campaign were satisfied with what they had done to let loose the forces of disorder and retired from the struggle."[91] The report goes on to cite one Muslim witness who argued that

the whole course of events since 1926 and more especially the partial success of the Hindus in securing the participation of Muhammadans in the civil disobedience campaign strengthened that party among the Muhammadans who ever since the revocation of the Partition in 1912 had believed that their very existence as a political party was being threatened and that there was a real danger of the country being handed over to a Hindu Raj. The failure of the Government to take strong measures against the authors of the civil disobedience campaign further alarmed the holders of these views.[92]

The "holders of these views" were not troubled so much by the civil disobedience campaign itself, but by the threat that they had lost ground to Muslim parties who had participated in it. The increased visibility of the Hindu Mahasabha and other symbols of Hindu militancy, like the singing of "*Bande Mataram*" at Congress activities, gave them the opportunity to discredit Congress Muslims and attract defectors. Although the District Moslem Association and the Anjuman had merged after 1926, a third party, the Bais Panchayat, "composed of young pleaders who lean to Congress' views,"[93] had re-emerged after the January riot.[94] The Bais Panchayat, which participated in the civil disobedience campaign, was, in the words of the government, "revived by those people who were jealous of the Nawab and who had no inclination to see his efforts in the cause of peace result in the consolidation of his position as the undisputed leader of the community whose word was law."[95] In the meantime, with the merger of the District Association and the Anjuman, the Nawab had lost influence with the new combined organization. In the government's view, the new party "fell under the control of the more fanatical Muhammadans who disliked the Nawab's policy of conciliation of the Hindus and co-operation with the Government."[96]

The May riots had the effect of alienating more Muslims from Congress. In June, the Provincial Moslem Conference in Faridpur declared itself against the civil disobedience campaign. A prominent religious leader, Sir Badsha Mian, whom Congress had been courting, spoke out against it.[97] Local board elections in Bakarganj in July 1931 were "run on communal lines" and Hindus lost ground as a result.[98] For their part, Congress activists continued to use religious ceremonies to launch political demonstrations, a practice which contributed to Muslim disaffection. "A noticeable feature of the [Saraswati (a Hindu goddess)] Puja in Calcutta was the way in which this religious ceremony was utilised for political purposes, the opportunity being taken for the national flag to be carried in some of the processions and for objectionable speeches to be made."[99]

The government, meanwhile, continued to see in violent outbreaks the opportunity to drive a wedge between Muslims and nationalist leaders. The assassination in August 1931 of a Muslim police officer named Ahsanullah by a Hindu youth in Chittagong evoked just such a reaction from local authorities. "Signs of communal tension at once manifested themselves after Sunday's murder, and looting broke out . . . If the effect is to rally Mahomedan feeling to the side of authority and to instill fear into the minds of the Hindus who are known to be aiding the revolutionaries actively or passively, the situation may change for the better."[100] Although the official report suggested Ahsanullah was murdered not because he was a Muslim but because he was a police officer,[101] the official response to the killing cast the incident in communal terms. British officials seized on it as an opportunity to court Muslim support and condemn Hindu nationalists. Some of the most serious damage was the work of European "special constables" who destroyed a nationalist printing press and beat its Hindu staff. The official report also acknowledged that the police beat students who were classmates of the suspect. The reason given was that "the boys took part in politics and . . . the schools are a recruiting ground for the terrorist party."[102] A number of Hindu youths taken into custody were also beaten.[103] According to the Congress commission of inquiry, several other residents of Chittagong were assaulted by policemen shortly after Ahsanullah was shot.[104] That night, police came after "those who had incurred the displeasures of the local authorities, including political 'suspects,' pleaders who are engaged in the defence of persons accused in the Chittagong Armory Raid Case, and the men employed in at least one well-known printing press."[105]

However, some Muslims clearly saw an opportunity to rally community feeling around the murder. During the display of the body, there were cries for revenge.[106] A *hartal* was proclaimed, and a large number of shops owned by Hindus were looted. In many cases the goods were not taken away but simply left in the road or burned.[107] Nelson, the Commissioner of Chittagong, concluded that,

> the particular form which the outbreak took, namely, looting of Hindu shops, was the result of an organised plan. . . . There is no doubt that some sort of order emanated from the Muhammadan community proclaiming a hartal on Monday. The fact that the main looting occurred from 12 to 1 when about the whole police force officers and men [sic] were preoccupied with the funeral arrangements and with the large crowd there present suggests premeditation.[108]

There seems to be little question that in many cases the police did not intervene to stop the looting. Even in the official report, witnesses who do not otherwise accuse the government of bias complain of "purposeful inactivity" of the police during the disturbance. The district magistrate was accused of telling one lawyer who had been assaulted, "Why have you come to me? I can't do anything. Go to your Hindu brethren and Bar Library. Organise yourselves and arrange for your own protection."[109]

Because of the partisan behavior of many police and officials, Congress leaders conducted their own inquiry into the incident. The unofficial report accused the police and local magistrate of purposefully creating the trouble and calling it a "communal" riot as a pretext to attack nationalist groups. The report claimed that the authorities expected "the victims of assault and looting . . . to retaliate against their assailants, so that the rather too frequent story of 'Communal riots' may be told again with impunity" to explain subsequent events.[110] The report singled out for blame the European community and "loyalist" Indians who had advocated repressive methods to deal with extremist nationalist groups: "[F]or at least one month previous to the terrible happenings at Chittagong, a certain number of people, with easy access to firearms, and with a sense of security that is not warranted, at any rate, by the letter of the law, have been openly advocating the formation of murder-gangs."[111] By playing a blatantly partisan role, the government succeeded, at least temporarily, in accomplishing what the local officers had wanted: securing Muslim loyalty and instilling fear among Hindu nationalists. "An undercurrent of serious alarm is manifest in the indignation which is daily voiced by the Hindu newspapers at the doings of the Mahomedans and the "apathy" of the officials."[112]

The 1941 Dacca 'Riot'

The disturbances in Dacca in 1941 need to be understood in the context of constitutional developments which had dramatically altered the balance of power between Hindu and Muslim parties in the mid-1930s, and had left Hindu leaders abruptly aware of their constituency's minority status. The Communal Award of 1932 granted Bengali Muslims 119 seats in the Bengal Legislative assembly; Hindus and "depressed classes"[113] were allotted eighty seats. The Bengali Hindu leadership protested against the award, arguing that it had "made it impossible for the Hindus who are the most influential community in the Province to have the representation in the Legislature to which they are entitled . . . leaving them in a perpetual minority unable to influence the course of legislation."[114] At the local level, the increase in Muslim leadership on the union boards was believed to be a direct result of the award. At the same time, Congress agitations against the boards did nothing to hurt Muslim candidates.[115] The Government of India Act of 1935 went even further, granting Hindus only seventy-eight seats out of 250 in a reconstituted assembly, and requiring that thirty of those be reserved for scheduled castes. Hindu leaders again protested on the grounds that Hindus deserved representation commensurate with their status in the cultural and economic life of Bengal. Their protests went unheeded, and in Dacca, the struggle for dominance was played out once again in the streets.

While the riots that broke out in Dacca in 1941 did not center on a "music-before-mosques" incident, violence surrounding processions and violence against temples and mosques became part of the choreography. The Dacca "riot" was not so much a single incident as it was a series of violent outbreaks that lasted over a period of seven to eight months. The first incident occurred during Holi festivities when a Muslim woman in a *burqa* (cloak covering the entire body worn by conservative Muslims) was splashed with colored water. Street fighting broke out, and once again Muslim drivers began removing their horses and carriages from the streets in anticipation of further trouble.[116] Complaints by both groups focused attention on temples and mosques, and unsubstantiated rumors of such attacks were rife. "Hindu witnesses speak of an attack on a temple or Akhara at Malitola on the 17th. The Police received no specific report of any such attack . . . from the persons concerned. . . . The Muslims also allege that the Haji Moinuddin Mosque was attacked on this occasion."[117] On March 17–18, a Muslim named Faiz Khan was stabbed to death by a Hindu mob. What followed is not entirely clear. According to the Enquiry Committee Report, "The Hindus allege that the body of Faiz Khan was taken in a procession from the Mitford Hospital through some

of the main streets of town, and past the Chowk Mosque to the Mohammadan burial ground in Azimpura."[118]

Earlier, the family of the murdered man had requested permission to
hold a procession and had been refused because it was thought that such
a public display would only contribute to ill-feeling. Additional Superintendent of Police Purdy, Superintendent Jenkins, and the Circle Inspector
all refused to grant permission for the procession. Instead, a Sub-inspector of Police and two constables were deputized to accompany the body
to the cemetery. They were ordered to ensure that only pall-bearers were
present. According to the Sub-inspector, the "procession included only
15–20 people, who claimed to be relatives and who accompanied the
body from Mitford Hospital from 4 pm to 7 pm. No shouting of slogans
occurred; the pall-bearers only muttered some religious texts."[119] According to Hindu complainants, the funeral procession for Faiz Khan began
in the early hours of March 18th, and was accompanied by "great noise"
and shouts of "Allah-o-Akbar" and "*Hindu sala log ko maro*" (Die, Hindu
bastards)." The RDREC concluded that

> The Adami Report refers to a procession in 1930 by which the relatives of a
> murdered Muslim roused their community and which was a contributing
> factor in starting the disorders. Many of the details were similar to those
> now alleged and it is not improbable that Hindu witnesses recalled the inci-
> dents of 1930 and grafted them on to the funeral of the Kaviraj Lane victim
> as one explanation of the subsequent disorders.[120]

The conflation of the two incidents is suggestive. The committee could
not be certain how much of the similarity was intentional on the part of
the Muslim mourners, and how much became so in the retelling by
Hindu witnesses testifying after the fact. In either case, it was clearly to
the advantage of leaders in both communities to link the incident with
the previous one, to create the kind of symbols needed for the group's
sense of its own history, real and mythical.

The clashes that followed Faiz Khan's funeral occurred on the dividing
line between Hindu and Muslim *paras* (neighborhoods), often on the road
dividing their two bazaars. The report described damage to temples and
mosques in detail, noting that, as with the funeral procession, buildings
that were the target of earlier attacks again came under fire. The reports
themselves, and the behavior of the police during the riots, contributed to
the perception of certain places as symbols to be defended or destroyed.
The defense scheme Dacca officials devised after the 1926 riots called for
police guards to be posted at several mosques and temples thought to be
particularly vulnerable. Measures taken by the authorities in this way
identified for the fighting parties the symbols of solidarity for a particular

Bengali Muslim or Bengali Hindu community, not necessarily the larger community as identified by its religious affiliation, but a subset of that—group united by the memory of more recent events in its own immediate past. By the time the March 1941 riots were brought under control, three mosques had been damaged, although one was reported to be in such bad repair when attacked that a proper assessment of the damage could not be made. A Hindu temple was partially burned, and two of the mosques were later desecrated with the head and body of a pig.[121] Disturbances continued for another two months, and the report blamed the renewal of hostilities on the desecration of the two mosques with the body and head of a pig and the "intense feeling" this generated among Muslims. The report stated that "this incident was far more provocative than the placing of a cow's skull in a Shiva Temple" some weeks later, because there was evidence that in the latter case, a Muslim may not have been responsible.[122]

The calculated circulation of provocative rumors reached levels not seen in previous riots. From the first outbreak of violence, the Muslim League newspaper *Azad* began publishing unsubstantiated reports about atrocities against Muslim women and students.[123] Such reports and rumors were believed to have been behind the rapid spread of violence to the rural areas. At one *madrasah*, "certain unknown Maulvis incited the congregation to drive away the Hindus in retaliation for the oppression committed on Muslims in the Dacca city."[124] Residents of Dacca were seen in the villages spreading rumors about attacks on Muslims. The official report concluded that the authorities were "satisfied that the organisation, whatever its composition, did in fact not only incite the local Muslims by false reports of oppression, but also by assurances that retaliation on the Hindus had been sanctioned by their leaders."[125]

The violence was seen as having a particularly dramatic effect on the Hindu middle class, who "showed a definite tendency to close their ranks and unite under the shelter of the Hindu Mahasabha to combat any attack, political or otherwise, from Muslim quarters." There was evidence too that extremist Hindu groups also supported the Mahasabha.[126] The Mahasabha had only recently made significant inroads in Dacca, filling a vacuum left by the Congress party following the defection of Subash Chandra Bose in 1938.[127] Bose resigned the presidency of the Congress in May 1939 after first winning it over Gandhi's chosen candidate, an election that divided Congress and left Bose without sufficient support in the party to push through any program. Subash and Sarat Chandra Bose then founded the Forward Bloc party in Bengal, which was banned as a terrorist organization the following year. The Bengal Provincial Congress Committee, always reluctant participants in Gandhi's civil disobedience campaign, used the violence in Dacca as a pretext to suspend the civil disobedience campaign in the province.[128]

In its efforts to assign blame for the violence, the report went no further than to identify "the Hindus" as the aggressors. Nothing more specific seemed to be intended, nor was there any indication that this was considered wanting in the report.

> The Superintendent of Police, Mr. Jenkins, and Mr. Purdy, the Additional Superintendent of Police . . . are both satisfied that the Hindus were the aggressors in the earlier stages. . . . We have no doubt that the Hindus were the aggressors in the initial stages and there is considerable evidence to support the theory that the aggression started with the incidents during the Holi. . . . Mr. Purdy who saw both the major incidents on the evening of the 18th March, viz., the brickbat fight at Malitola and the riot at Manohar Khan Bazar, is quite convinced that the more aggressive mob was the Hindu . . . and there is evidence which in our opinion, shows clearly that the Hindu mob was the attacking party. That evidence was not shaken in cross-examination and there is no doubt that a person of Mr. Purdy's knowledge and experience could form an accurate idea from the demeanor of the crowd as to which of the two was attacking and which was on the defensive.[129]

The arrogance on the part of the authorities about their ability to determine responsibility for the riots contributed to perceptions that the government was biased. In addition, the fact that each population perceived of itself as a vulnerable minority meant that any security force taking action would be seen as protecting one community at the expense of another. Early on in the progress of the riot, the superintendent of police and the additional district magistrate met with Hindu leaders to discuss the earlier incidents of trouble between the two communities. The meeting did not go well, and the report does not elaborate on the reasons beyond stating that it was "clear from the outset that the Superintendent of Police and the Hindu community were unlikely to collaborate for the public welfare."[130] To curb the violence, the civil administration in Dacca instituted "wholesale arrests . . . of male members of the community believed to be responsible for the disturbance."[131] While admitting that such a procedure "inconvenienced many innocent and law-abiding persons," the arrests were seen as "an effective method of curbing the activities of the community at fault . . . i.e., the opposite community to the victim." Because the riots occurred in congested urban areas, and often in Hindu neighborhoods, many more Hindus than Muslims were arrested.[132] Witnesses had made similar charges during the 1930 Dacca riot, while Muslim organizations complained that one of the principal causes of the riot was the fact that the only group which had not been pardoned after the Pabna disturbances was Muslim.

Conclusion

The years between 1926 and 1941 opened up new opportunities for Muslim leaders in Bengal to position themselves as leaders of a community which was self-consciously Muslim. In order to do this they needed first to challenge the "moral authority" of the existing political order, represented principally by the Nawab. This generation of Muslim leaders represented a constituency with its roots in rural east Bengal which was newly conscious of its "Muslim" identity and which had seen the benefits of that identity in status and power. Using public space to organize protests over religious symbols was an important way to prove themselves as more representative of Muslim interests and cast Hindus as a threat. Hindu leaders increasingly did the same, as constitutional changes made them aware of their status as a political minority.

The incidents examined here concern three riots that took place in Dacca in 1926, 1930, and 1941. Like the Calcutta and Pabna riots which preceded it, the 1926 Dacca riot was organized to garner support for a new set of Muslim leaders who challenged long-standing traditions in order to discredit established leaders and who used public demonstrations to evoke symbols calculated to elicit popular support for themselves as protectors of Muslims and representatives of their interests. Funeral processions, in particular, became demonstrations of power, evoking both moral authority and the threat of further violence.

Throughout this period, the Muslim leadership in Bengal remained fragmented among a number of parties, each of whom approached the problem of popularizing political issues in its own way and with its own set of symbols. The problem of constructing one political community, a problem crucial for crystallizing objective differences as the basis of a separate political culture, involved a complicated series of alliances among various political actors, each attempting to draw together the symbols necessary to change popular perceptions about what a Muslim Bengali identity should be. These symbols then became reified along communal lines. The communal "riot" itself, and the narration of it, became ritualized so that processional paths, targeted sites, and rumored atrocities exhibited a choreography that helped freeze popular perceptions of identity. What people believed about how a riot started imposed new constraints on political leaders on both sides. The "communal riot narrative" was a construction of "facts" used to "explain" relations between the two communities. Just as the British used such a narrative to vindicate their rule, both Muslim and Hindu leaders created their own version of events to blame the other as the aggressor.

The conflicts that grew out of this struggle represented an effort on the part of an emerging Muslim leadership to challenge the established leadership by questioning precedents and organizing protests around religious and political symbols. As they competed for recognition and for control over public space, these political leaders created martyrs and other symbols calculated to evoke the sufferings of the Muslims, the aggression of Hindu militants, and the failure of the British and the old Muslim leadership to protect the Muslim community.

The protests against the Janmastami procession were aimed at discrediting the Nawab because of the royal family's long patronage of the festival and his perceived appeasement of Hindu organizers to proceed with the celebration. The Janmastami celebration was one which showcased the Nawab's authority and patronage, and brought together all the residents of Dacca in a celebration which was as much civic as it was religious. In 1926, Muslim leaders who attempted to block Muslim participation in the procession were attempting to wrest from the Nawab not only his political status as the leader recognized by the British as representing Bengali Muslims, but the moral authority he possessed to interpret symbolic questions, such as music before mosques.

In 1927, the government was the target of protests because it had permitted the Shivaji celebration, and had failed to act forcefully against Hindu stone-throwers in May 1930. Because the government and the Congress had banned the Independence Day procession, one faction of the student activists saw an opportunity to enhance their position by defying the order. The evocation of symbols of Hindu militancy during the celebration, as much as the protests by some Muslim groups, was aimed at discrediting the Congress Muslims who participated. The funeral procession that sparked the May 1930 riots in Dacca further bolstered the standing of the "fanatical" element within the Muslim parties that the British authorities most feared. As the patterns of violence were repeated in 1941, it was clear that the traditions invented and routinized by such leaders had given them legitimacy that could not easily be dismissed. Leaders on both sides made use of symbols which evoked fears of their community's minority status to either portray Hindus in Bengal as unsafe under a Muslim League ministry, or Muslims in the whole of India as disadvantaged and vulnerable to attack from the Hindu majority.

Internal divisions within Muslim society in Bengal determined to a great extent the steps that would be taken to forge a Bengali Muslim political identity. These same divisions limited the options available for achieving that end. As competition between rival groups claiming to "represent" Bengali Muslim interests increased, agitations over the Bengal Tenancy Act and other agrarian reform efforts exposed divisions within Muslim parties in Bengal. The politics that characterized the next twenty years saw the Muslims rebuilding a political base that reflected their numerical strength in the *mofussil*. With the birth of A. K. Fazlul

Huq's Krishak Praja Party, Bengali Muslim politics found new and compelling symbols—the symbols of radical agrarian reform. The *praja* movement and the failures of the Congress and Swaraj parties to accommodate Muslim concerns cast *mofussil* concerns and those symbols into the very center of provincial politics in Bengal.

Notes

1. Brass, 1991, p. 22.

2. Basu, p. 2,605.

3. Pandey, 1983, p. 63.

4. *Indian Quarterly Review*, vol. vii, July-December 1926, p. 85.

5. Any number of examples may be cited. In Indian-controlled Kashmir, funeral processions for men killed in the custody of the security forces have been ritualized as protests against Indian policy toward the territory. In August 1987 in Bangladesh, a funeral procession mourning an opposition activist killed in a confrontation with police so unnerved officials that they halted the procession and confiscated the body, only to find that they had succeeded in strengthening the opposition by doing so.

6. Frank Neal, *Sectarian Violence: The Liverpool Experience, 1819–1914, An Aspect of Anglo-Irish History* (Manchester: Manchester University Press, 1988), pp. 58–62.

7. *Report of the Dacca Disturbances Enquiry Committee* (Calcutta: Government of Bengal Press, 1930), p. 10. Hereafter noted as RDDEC.

8. Janmastami is celebrated by Hindus on the eighth lunar day of the dark fortnight of the Hindu month of Bhadra, when the god Krishna was born. *Samsad Bengali-English Dictionary* (Calcutta: Shahitya Samsad, 1972), p. 466.

9. RDDEC, p. 10.

10. *Dhaka Prokash*, September 1926, passim. [Trans. P. Gossman] This strategy is a good example of efforts by both sides to claim "victimization."

11. GOB Home Poll. 501/26, WBSA.

12. Report from Clayton, Commissioner of Dacca Division, to Chief Secretary, Government of Bengal, Political Department, on the disturbances, October 4, 1926, in P&J 2764/1926. IOL.

13. District Magistrate Philpot to Chief Secretary, Government of Bengal, Political Department, on the disturbances, October 2, 1926, in P&J 2764/1926. IOL.

14. The Gurkhas, an ethnic group from northern Bengal and Nepal, were valued by the British for their reputed militaristic skills.

15. RDDEC, p. 11.

16. *Dhaka Prokash*, September 12, 1926, p. 4. [Trans. P. Gossman]

17. James Wise, *Notes on the Races, Castes and Tribes of Eastern Bengal* (London: 1883), p. 381.

18. Paritosh Sen, *Zindabahar* (Calcutta: Papyrus, 1979), pp. 66–68, translated by Partha Chatterjee in Chatterjee, 1984, p. 238.

19. The celebration commemorates the god Ram's reunion with his brother Bharat. Bharat is the Sanskrit name for India. Sandria Freitag, "State and Community: Symbolic Popular Protest in Banaras's Public Arena," in Sandria Freitag,

ed., *Culture and Power in Banaras: Community, Performance and Environment, 1800–1980* (Berkeley: University of California Press, 1989), pp. 206–209. Hereafter, Freitag, 1989b.

20. Ibid., p. 206.

21. *Mussulman,* September 24, 1926, p. 14.

22. "Why Did it Happen?" (editorial) *Dhaka Prokash,* September 26, 1926.

23. Copy of letter No. 4539 Pl., dated October 19, 1926, from the Chief Secretary, Government of Bengal, to the Secretary, Home Department, Government of India. Also, report from Clayton, Commissioner of Dacca Division, to Chief Secretary, Government of Bengal, Political Department, on the disturbances, October 4, 1926, in P&J 2764/1926. IOL.

24. Copy of letter No. 4539 Pl., dated October 19, 1926, from the Chief Secretary, Government of Bengal, to the Secretary, Home Department, Government of India. P&J 2764/1926. IOL.

25. GOB Home Poll 501/26. WBSA.

26. Ibid.

27. Ibid. See also Chatterjee, 1984, p. 74.

28. GOB Home Poll. 501/26. WBSA.

29. Some fifteen years later the same kind of thinking would lead the council meeting of the All-India Muslim League to pass a resolution recommending that Muslim League members make use of such traditional institutions of authority—mosques, *madrasahs,* and festivals—to preach the cause of Pakistan. Muslim League Council Meetings, Vol. 253, Part 2, p. 60. Archives of the Freedom Movement (AFM), University of Karachi, Karachi, Pakistan.

30. Report from Clayton, Commissioner of Dacca Division, to Chief Secretary, Government of Bengal, Political Department, on the disturbances, October 4, 1926, in P&J 2764/1926.

31. GOB Home Poll. 501/26 sl. no. 28.

32. Broomfield, p. 272.

33. GOB Judicial File no. 6, 1920, NAB.

34. Ibid.

35. Ibid.

36. Ibid.

37. Ibid.

38. Letter from Sasmal to the *Bengalee,* December 14, 1926, cited in Ray, p. 364.

39. Ray, p. 362.

40. *Mussulman,* September 3, 1926, p. 5.

41. Ray, p. 362.

42. Ibid.

43. Broomfield, p. 280.

44. "[I]t has become the custom in Dacca to keep a store of bricks and stones on the roof of about every house for use as missiles in a disturbance." Minute of July 3, 1930 from the commissioner of the Dacca division, in L/P&J/6/1996. IOL.

45. GOB Home Poll. 117/1927 sl. 1–3. WBSA.

46. W.D.R. Prentice, Chief Secretary, GOB, to all commissioners of divisions, February 18, 1927. File 117/1927, sl. nos. 1–2. WBSA.

47. Ibid.

48. Prentice, February 14, 1927, in ibid.

49. Prentice, April 4, 1927, in ibid.

50. Prentice to commissioners, April 14, 1927, in ibid.

51. H. C. Liddell to Prentice, March 19, 1927, in ibid.

52. Speech by Mohammad Afsaruddin Ahmed at Kushtia, Nadia, February 28, 1927, cited in Partha Chatterjee, "Agrarian Relations and Communalism in Bengal," in Ranajit Guha, ed., *Subaltern Studies I: Writings on South Asian History and Society* (Delhi: Oxford University Press, 1982), p. 21.

53. A.F.M. Rahman, Subdivisional Officer, Kushtia, to L. G. Durno, District Magistrate, Nadia, March 13, 1927, Government of Bengal Political File 140/27, WBSA, cited in ibid., p. 22, n. 21.

54. Local Government Reports for the first half of September 1931 (Confidential), L/P&J/12/25.

55. RDDEC, p. 11.

56. The celebration was inaugurated in 1895 by Congress leader Balwantrao Gangadhar Tilak to honor the birth of the Maharashtrian leader Shivaji (1627–1680), who had fought against the Mughals.

57. RDDEC, p. 11.

58. Bernard S. Cohn, "The Census, Social Structure and Objectification in South Asia," in Bernard S. Cohn, *An Anthropologist among the Historians and Other Essays* (Delhi: Oxford University Press, 1987), p. 230.

59. *Mussulman*, January 31, 1930, p. 9.

60. The government banned processions on January 26, 1931, but the radical Congress leader Subash Chandra Bose led one in Calcutta in deliberate defiance of the order and was promptly arrested and convicted of "rioting." Local government reports for the second half of January 1931 (Conf.), L/P&J/12/25. IOR.

61. Copy of confidential letter No. 710, P.S., dated February 4, 1930, from the Chief Secretary to the Government of Bengal, to the Secretary, Government of India, Home Department in L/P&J/6/1966. IOL.

62. Ibid.

63. Ibid.

64. "Copy of confidential letter No. 710, P.S., dated February 4, 1930, from the Chief Secretary to the Government of Bengal, to the Secretary, Government of India, Home Department, File 495/1930 in L/P&J/6/1996. IOL.

65. RDDEC, p. 11.

66. In 1930 Gandhi led a widely publicized protest march to protest an increase in the salt tax. The protesters marched to the sea and urged Indians to manufacture salt naturally.

67. Bengal Local Government Reports: Fortnightly Report on the Political Situation for the First Half of April 1930, p. 36. L/P&J/12/13 (separate papers).

68. Ibid, p. 12.

69. Ibid.

70. Ibid, p. 13.

71. GOB Home Poll 501/26 sl. no. 17. WBSA.

72. The Fourteen Points (there were actually fifteen) proposed among other things that India should have a federal government, with the provinces retaining some powers; that separate electorates be maintained; that Muslims have one

third of the seats in the Central Legislature, and that no community be reduced to equal or minority status in any provincial legislature where they formed a majority in the province. Peter Hardy refers to this as the first constitutional acknowledgement by Hindus of their vulnerable position in Muslim majority provinces. Hardy, pp. 213–214.

73. GOB Home Poll 501/26 sl. no. 28. WBSA.

74. RDDEC, p. 23.

75. Ibid., p. 13.

76. Ibid., p. 24.

77. Copy of a letter District Officer No. 557 C from the District Magistrate Dacca to the Chief Secretary, Government of Bengal, June 18, 1930, in L/P&J/6/1996. IOL.

78. Ibid.

79. Ibid.

80. Copy of letter from the commissioner of the Dacca division to the Government of Bengal, Political Department, June 3, 1930, in L/P&J/6/1966. IOL.

81. Ibid.

82. RDDEC, p. 24.

83. Ibid.

84. Ibid.

85. Ibid.

86. "Long live the British Raj, long live the Nawab." RDDEC, p. 20.

87. Ibid., p. 38.

88. Ibid., p. 22.

89. Ibid., p. 39.

90. The constable was assaulted by Congress workers returning from a political meeting, and the Europeans complained about their cars being stoned and about being prevented from entering shops. Ibid., p. 12.

91. Ibid., p. 42.

92. Ibid., p. 23.

93. Local government report for the second half of May, 1931, L/P&J/12/25.

94. The Bais Panchayat had been a rival body to both the Anjuman and the District Association, but had all but disappeared after the two groups merged. RDDEC, p. 23.

95. Ibid.

96. Ibid.

97. Local government reports: Fortnightly report for the first half of June, 1930 (secret), L/P&J/12/13 (Separate Papers).

98. Local government reports for the second half of July, 1931 (confidential) L/P&J/12/25.

99. Ibid.

100. Local government reports for the second half of August, 1931 (confidential) L/P&J/12/25.

101. *Report on the Disturbances in Chittagong on August 30th, 1931 and following days* (Calcutta: Government of Bengal, 1931), p. 18, in L/P&J/7/220, ff. 163–183. IOL. Hereafter, RDC.

102. Ibid., p. 32.

103. Ibid., p. 5.

104. *Report of the Non-Official Enquiry Committee on Recent Disturbances in Chittagong (September 1931)*, p. 2, in P&J/5569/1931 in file P&J/4741/1931 in OIOC volume L/P&J/7/220. Hereafter, RNOECC.

105. Ibid., p. 2. On April 18, 1930, a radical group destroyed the Chittagong Armory and seized a quantity of weapons.

106. RDC, p. 8.

107. RDC and Confidential letter from A. H. Kempo, District Magistrate, Chittagong, to the Commissioner of Chittagong Division, September 1, 1931, in P&J/4760/1931 in file P&J/4741/1931 in OIOC volume L/P&J/7/220. IOL.

108. RDC, p. 19.

109. RNOECC, p. 4.

110. Ibid., p. 2.

111. Ibid., p. 7.

112. Local government reports for first half of September 1931 (confidential), L/P&J/12/25.

113. This referred to the scheduled tribes and castes, those (also known as "untouchables") designated on a schedule under British law (and later the Indian Constitution) as entitled to special consideration, including some quotas for educational and employment opportunities, in recognition of their historically disadvantaged status.

114. *Report of the Dacca Riots Enquiry Committee* (Calcutta: Government of Bengal, 1942), p. 27. Hereafter, RDREC.

115. Report on the political situation in Bengal for the first half of August 1938," GOB Home Poll, File 127/36, p. 1. WBSA.

116. RDREC, p. 2.

117. Ibid.

118. Ibid.

119. Ibid., p. 8.

120. Ibid.

121. Ibid., p. 5.

122. Ibid., p. 6.

123. Ibid., p. 54.

124. Ibid.

125. Ibid., p. 55.

126. A. D. Gordon, Inspector-General of Police, Bengal, *Report on the Police Administration in the Province of Bengal excluding Calcutta and its suburbs for the year 1941* (Calcutta: Bengal Government Press, 1942), p. 29. (Cambridge University Library–OP.1182.351.02(104)). Hereafter, Report on the Police Administration, 1941.

127. Ibid.

128. Ibid.

129. RDREC, p. 6.

130. Ibid., p. 7.

131. Ibid., p. 11.

132. Ibid.

5

The Muslim League's Struggle for Bengal

Until 1937, the party that came to be identified with the Pakistan movement had virtually no presence in Bengal. In that year, the Muslim League, in coalition with the Krishak Praja Party (KPP), formed the first provincial government under the reformed constitution of 1935.[1] The administration's record during that period was decisive in shaping the way issues and symbols would be used to create popular momentum for the Pakistan movement in Bengal. Having come to power largely because of its platform on radical agrarian reform, the KPP soon found itself in conflict with the League over which would become the voice for Muslim interests in Bengal. Divisions between the League and KPP over support for land reform were exacerbated by power struggles within the provincial League and between it and the national League. In both instances, the struggle for control of the Bengal Ministry was waged over winning peasant support and capturing the language of agrarian reform.

Ultimately, the decision to adopt more openly "communal" symbols marked the abandonment of a commitment to progressive land reform and the triumph of the faction of the League which identified more with the north Indian leadership of the All-India Muslim League than with Muslim leaders who had emerged out of the *praja* movement in east Bengal and those who articulated an identity based on less divisive aspects of Bengali culture. For these leaders, adopting a policy of genuine land reform in Bengal posed too great a threat to the League's support among landholders in north India. Thus, for the League to succeed in Bengal it had to link peasant interests with a communal identity and the call for a separate "homeland." As the *maulvis* had done after the first partition of Bengal in 1905, the League used symbols and language to evoke the suffering peasant, the "backward" minority, and the vulnerable Muslim threatened by a Hindu *raj* to consolidate its support among Bengal's Muslims.

During this period, the institution of the commission of inquiry as a means of identifying "communalism" was appropriated by all of the major contenders for power, particularly the Congress and the Muslim League.[2] Although there had been unofficial inquiries into incidents of violence from very early on, notably the Congress inquiry into the Kanpur violence of 1913 and the Unofficial Commission of Enquiry into the Calcutta "Riot" of 1918, these focused largely on the role of the British government and the force used to put down the disturbances.[3] Later inquiries which took place after the establishment of provincial governments sought to discredit not only the British authorities, but Congress and Muslim League provincial authorities and party officials. In Bengal, the 1941 communal outbreaks—in which Hindus were the principal victims—occurred on the watch of the Muslim League-KPP ministry, marking the first time that abuses by agents of the state were directly linked to a Muslim administration. Nearly all of the other provincial governments were Congress-led, and Muslim leaders, particularly but not exclusively those of the Muslim League, claimed Muslims as the "victims" of oppression by a "Hindu" *raj* in those provinces.

The principal incidents of communal violence during this period demonstrated the efforts by the League and other parties to use specifically Islamic symbols to assert their claim to represent Bengali Muslims. At the same time, the Congress in Bengal continued to lose ground to extremist Hindu organizations like the Hindu Mahasabha, an organization which relied on the use of symbols which evoked Hindu dominance. In the final years before partition, a power struggle nearly split the Muslim League in Bengal. At issue was the fundamental nature of the party's mass organization and its support for controversial issues like land reform. Contradictions within the Muslim League's leadership prevented it from mobilizing support around issues which, while they had support among the majority in Bengal, were bitterly opposed by the leadership of the All-India Muslim League. The continuing factionalism resulted in a shift in strategy for the League and other parties who claimed to represent Muslim interests in Bengal. The violence that came to dominate Bengali politics between 1946 and 1947 signalled not only the successful polarization of Hindu and Muslim communities, but the triumph of leaders who used these incidents of violence to stake their party's claim as the sole body capable of protecting not just Muslim or Hindu interests, but Muslim and Hindu lives.

The Search for a Muslim Party (reprise)

The Muslim League—the party credited with successfully mobilizing support for the creation of a separate state of Pakistan—had virtually no

organization in Bengal until 1936. Indeed, the party had little organization elsewhere in India. Throughout the country, the League was moribund, its place taken by parties representing various provincial interests.
League president Mohammad Ali Jinnah, frustrated by the Congress'
failure to address what he believed to be Muslim grievances, had re-
treated to England, and did not return until 1935. Although the League
continued to exist in name in Bengal, in the first half of the 1930s the
principal parties were the Praja party, later named the Krishak Praja
Party under Fazlul Huq's leadership, and Khwaja Nazimuddin's United
Muslim Party. It was not until 1937 that the League established branches
throughout the province.

The history of the Bengal Provincial Muslim League is one of repeated
schisms and attempts by rival groups to challenge the authority of the established League and set themselves up as the rightful representative
body of the Bengal Muslims. In 1917, loyalist Muslims criticized the
League for having abandoned the policies of the hereditary ruler of Bengal, the Nawab, and taken a pro-Congress stance:

> [T]he Bengal Moslems have always been opposed to the Congress, and they
> shun the Muslim League also, which is now wholly under the domination of
> the Congress. So long as the League worked on the lines approved by its
> founder, the late Nawab Salimulla, it enjoyed the support of Bengal
> Moslems. . . . The paper regrets that the Moslem League has wholly identi-
> fied itself with the Congress and has thus fallen from the object of present-
> ing the Government the rightful demands of the Muhammadan community
> for which it was created.[4]

With the launching of the Khilafat movement, and the combined Khi-
lafat/Non-cooperation campaign of 1919–1924, the Muslim League all
but disappeared from Bengal politics, its membership overtaken by these
more dynamic movements.

In the aftermath of the Non-cooperation and Khilafat campaigns, the
movement that won a significant following among Muslims in Bengal
was the *praja* (tenants) movement, which succeeded in forcing political
leaders to address peasant concerns. As noted in chapter three, this
movement paralleled the emergence of a class of prosperous Muslim
cultivators who had become involved in politics in east Bengal. The
growth of the *praja* movement was also a result of the increased awareness of the near-crisis conditions obtaining in rural Bengal because of
the increased pressure on the land and the tightening of rural credit.
Praja organizations were formed as early as 1914; by the late 1920s some
had province-wide organizations and wielded considerable clout. When
the League re-emerged after the collapse of the Khilafat Non-coopera-

tion campaigns, it was only one of a number of small Muslim parties vying with the Nawab for recognition from the British authorities. Following communal disturbances in east Bengal in 1926 and 1927, a split developed between the All-India Muslim League and the Bengal Provincial Muslim League (BPML), and within the BPML, over the issue of separate electorates. Members of the BPML sympathetic to the *praja* cause argued that Muslim landlords were taking advantage of separate electorates to side with Hindu landlords against the rights of tenants and *bargadars*. Arguing in favor of genuine land reform measures, these members of the BPML opposing separate electorates argued that "the Permanent Settlement is the greatest curse upon our tenants and it cannot be done away with if the masses of Bengal cannot be organised on a Non-Communal economic basis."[5]

By contrast, others, including Fazlul Huq, argued that the BPML had been taken over by Congress sympathizers and "so-called Nationalist Muslims."[6] Abandoning the BPML, Huq then attempted to launch a separate League.[7] At the same time, a split developed among the district branches of the BPML, driving senior Muslim League leaders to complain about "the deplorable split among the Mussalmans of Bengal," and the fact that one rival faction was bringing in *goondas* to break up meetings.[8] On July 24, 1932, the BPML petitioned the All-India Muslim League (AIML) on the grounds that separate electorates had failed to achieve their object, and in fact had proved detrimental, hampering "the necessary exertion for political progress and stunt the growth of a sense of common citizenship." The BPML argued that recent elections had returned Muslims in numbers less than their numerical strength in the province:

> The case of the Muslims of Bengal is altogether different from that of their co-religionists in other Provinces. In Bengal, an overwhelming majority of the community as well as of the whole population—about 86 per cent—come from the cultivating class. The interests of these tillers of the soil really constitute the interests of the community and the country. Unless proper arrangements are made for their adequate representation in the legislature, their interests, which are different from the interests of other sections of the population, cannot be furthered and safeguarded. In fact, the economic conditions of the masses cannot be improved until the Hindu and Muslim masses, who are at present divided by communal electorate, make common cause in a common electorate.[9]

The resolution of the BPML provoked a sharp response from the AIML. On December 12, the Council of the AIML called an urgent meeting to discuss among other things "the attitude taken by the Bengal and Madras Provincial[10] Muslim Leagues in passing resolutions, on impor-

tant questions of policy, against the decisions of the parent League." At
the meeting, the Madras and Bengal Leagues were asked to fall in line
with the AIML, to which the BPML responded that the proposals of the
AIML were "reactionary" and "altogether overlooking the interests of
the peasants and laborers who form an overwhelming majority of the
population of the Province." The BPML immediately withheld its sub-
scription fees to the AIML.[11] As the parties began to make plans for the
1937 elections, the BPML remained divided. In May 1936, the AIML
tried again to reorganize the BPML, and put the head of the Dacca District League organization, Khan Bahadur Syed Abdul Hafeez, in charge
of the effort.[12]

The All Bengal Praja Samiti was formed in 1929 and by 1931 was actively participating in union board, municipal, and legislative politics.[13]
Between 1930 and 1934, the *praja* leadership was dominated by prominent Muslim leaders based in Calcutta, most of whom had been active
Khilafatists, including Abdur Rahim, Musharraf Hossain, Akram Khan,
and Khan Bahadur Abdul Momen. The leadership of the party shifted to
east Bengal when Fazlul Huq became president of the party in 1935.[14] After that, the party came to be known as Krishak Praja Party.[15]

Capturing the Symbols of Agrarian Reform

Growing awareness of the agrarian crisis in Bengal resulted in the revi-
sion of the 1885 Tenancy Act.[16] Debate on the amended act, passed into
law in 1928, centered on three main concerns: the rights of sharecroppers,
the transferability of holdings, and the status of under-*raiyats* (those who
rented their land from *raiyats* with larger holdings). The first issue was
opposed by *jotedars* and other wealthier cultivators who feared that
changing the law would grant tenant status to sharecroppers. The 1928
bill recognized as tenants only those sharecroppers who paid a fixed
quantity of their produce as rent.[17] The bill also provided safeguards
against the eviction of under-*raiyats,* and gave the tenants the right of
transferring their holdings. These provisions were opposed by *zamindar*
organizations, including the east Bengal Landholders Association under
the presidency of Nawab Habibullah of Dacca.[18]

Debate on the bill within the Council followed communal lines. In the
vote on retaining the landlords' traditional transfer fees (*salami*)—a practice peasant-based groups had long sought to end—all the Hindu members, including Swarajists, voted in favor, whereas all but four Muslim
members, regardless of whether they were landlords, voted against.[19]
Nearly every amendment on behalf of tenant rights introduced by a
Muslim council member was defeated.[20] The Tenancy Act of 1928 as
passed retained the landlord's transfer fee and right of pre-emption, de-

nied safeguards against eviction to under-*raiyats*, and failed to give occupancy rights to produce-paying tenants. As a result, it provided the necessary impetus for the formation of a tenants' party and set the stage for a subsequent bill, the Bengal Tenancy Act of 1938.

In the interim, the standard of living for many cultivators continued to fall, particularly after 1929. The situation was further aggravated by the tightening of rural credit. Such conditions worsened in the mid-1930s. As the Land Revenue Commission noted, "the Bengal Agricultural Debtors Act was passed in 1935 with the object of scaling down the debts of cultivators and allowing them to repay their debts . . . ; but excellent as were the intentions of the Act, it has resulted in an even greater restriction of credit, and it would not be too much to say that at present rural credit is almost non-existent."[21]

In 1935, the British government passed the Government of India Act, providing for semi-autonomous provincial governments and expanding the franchise to include an additional 35 million voters, including six million women. The extension of the franchise to more of the rural population after the 1935 Government of India Act meant that a cultivator paying a minimum tax of six annas a year had influence.[22] In Bengal, agrarian issues dominated the campaign, as evidenced by the increased activity of Krishak Samitis, which had proliferated since the early 1930s and began carrying out agitations in favor of land reform legislation.

The 1936–37 Election Campaign

Land reform issues and the rhetoric of agrarian interests dominated the 1936–37 election campaigns for all parties. The Tenancy Amendment Bill provided the vehicle for both the Congress party and the KPP to try and attract mass support.[23] Other politicians also demonstrated their support for peasant interests. On February 21, 1936, an All-Bengal Peasants and Debtors conference was held in Pabna district, with H.S. Suhrawardy presiding.[24] At a *praja* conference in Hili in 1936, 3,000 attended and passed resolutions supporting the Agricultural Debtors Bill, requesting government to fix a minimum price for sugarcane, and pressing for abolition of landlords' fees and landlords' right to pre-empt. A government report noted that "the evidence is accumulating that the cultivating tenant classes are becoming more and more interested in their own economic condition, and are probing into the causes of their difficulties and seeking remedies."[25] The KPP took advantage of the political climate and campaigned principally on land issues, using public meetings and traveling from village to village to make its pitch at weekly *hats* and mosques during prayer.[26] In Noakhali, Maulvi Mohammad Fazlulla, a member of the Legislative Council, organized a Krishak Samiti, reportedly to further his own election prospects. The government reported on similar meetings with similar objectives in Rajshahi and Mymensingh: "There seems to be little doubt that the Krishak Samiti movement will be made use of by prospective candidates to the provincial Legislative Assembly for electioneering purposes, especially in Eastern and Northern Bengal where the movement is coloured by communal feeling against Hindu landlords and money-lenders."[27]

Whatever communal animosity the debate over land reform engendered, however, it did not inspire the Muslim parties to adopt a united front. The KPP's campaign platform called for the abolition of *zamindari* without compensation; this issue resulted in a breakdown of talks between Huq and Jinnah before the elections.[28] In the campaign, Huq was harshly critical of the Muslim League's landlord base. When League leaders convened a meeting on September 8, 1936, without consulting KPP leaders, including himself, Huq couched his attack in the language of peasant politics, reproaching the League for its "fresh and deliberate attempt to insult the Krishak Praja Party and to make them feel that as *Krishak* and *Praja* they must submit here as elsewhere to what the nawabs and *zamindars* may choose to decide on their behalf."[29]

League leaders, on the other hand, tried to use religious symbolism to discredit the KPP. In its official Bengali-language newspaper, *Azad*, the Bengal Provincial Muslim League responded, "[R]espectable Fazlul Huq is forgetting that his Krishak Praja Party is proceeding towards Karbala. Destruction is inevitable."[30] Khwaja Nazimuddin, a nephew of the Nawab and a leading figure in the Muslim League, criticized the KPP on the grounds that it was "not a purely Muslim organization" and had not sought the cooperation of those who really represent the community.[31] For his part, the Nawab, who opposed the reforms advocated by the KPP, formed the United Muslim Party (UMP) in May 1936.[32] Huq also criticized it as a *zamindar* party, and in August 1936, the UMP joined the Muslim League on the promise that Jinnah would nominate its representatives to the League Parliamentary Board. Only big landlords were nominated; "the rest of Jinnah's nominees were from the non-Bengali business sections of Calcutta."[33]

Congress was divided, with much of its *bhadrolok* base siding with the landlords' interests, as it had in 1928, a fact which "enhanced electioneering value from the point of view of anti-Congress Muslims . . . for abolition of landlords' fees and drastic curtailment of landlords' privileges generally."[34] A government report observed that "many supporters of Congress . . . actually [had] the interests of the landlords and the middle classes at heart."[35] For its part, the League made use of explicitly religious symbolism. In January, *Azad* published an editorial arguing that "as a Muslim is the property of Allah, so also his vote is the property of Allah.

It is the directive of Islam and Imam that the vote is not given against Allah and his followers."[36] During the campaign in Patuakhali, the League got the support of a fatwa issued by Shah Sufi Maulana Abu Bakr, the *pir* of Furfura: "*Maulanas* and *maulvies* from all over Bengal came down to Patuakhali to prevail upon the villagers not to go against Islam and to vote for Nazimuddin (the League candidate)."[37] Fazlul Huq's defeat of Khwaja Nazimuddin in the Patuakhali elections catapulted the KPP into a position as the dominant Muslim party in east Bengal,[38] but the KPP did not win an outright majority in the elections. After being rebuffed by the Congress party, Huq reached an agreement to form a coalition ministry with the Muslim League. The coalition government was headed by Fazlul Huq.

The KPP-Muslim League Ministry

Almost immediately after assuming office, the ministry came under pressure to distance itself from *praja* interests. Having come to power on a platform to represent peasant interests, the KPP found itself constrained by those within the Muslim League who opposed any sweeping reforms. In the first few months of its coalition with the Muslim League, the KPP backed away from its campaign promise to abolish *zamindari*. Instead, it proposed amendments to the tenancy act which were not as sweeping but more acceptable to the League's supporters.[39] In U.P., it attracted the support of landlords nervous about Congress' proposed tenancy legislation.[40] In fact, because of its Muslim League component, the *Modern Review* criticized Huq's cabinet as being no longer true to the interests of the *raiyats*.[41] Many of the cabinet members were landowners, prominent businessmen and the man Huq beat in the Patuakhali election, Khwaja Nazimuddin, the Nawab's nephew. In fact, Dacca was considered as something of a battleground for Huq and the Dacca Nawab family.[42]

No effort will be spared in attempting to create a split between the two wings of the Muslim coalition by detaching members of the Praja section with which the Chief Minister is more closely identified. I have good reason to believe that attempts were made by not too scrupulous Muslims at Dacca to give the Chief Minister the feeling that in a place so much under the influence of the Nawab family and the League party he was in the stronghold of his enemies.[43]

The tenancy amendment bill dominated the first year in office of the coalition government. The major provisions of the amendment were the abolition of landlords' fees for the transfer of land, abolition of the landlords' right of pre-emption when occupancy holdings were sold, reduction of the rate of interest on arrears of rent from 12.5 percent to 6.25 percent, suspension of rent enhancements for ten years for tenure-holders and *raiyats*, and making *abwabs* (illegal taxes) punishable by fine.[44] Landlords opposed the bill because it would deprive them of the advantage they obtained in the Act of 1928.[45]

Government officials also accused Congress of trying to undermine the ministry's support by claiming that its proposals were not radical enough, in order to buy time and win back support of some Muslim cultivators.[46]

> When the [Tenancy Amendment Bill] reached its final stages, the leader of the Congress Opposition condemned it on the spurious ground that it did not go far enough but was put in an awkward position when the Ministry arranged for a division to be called: the result was that the Congress could not vote for the Bill and dared not vote against it. . . . While the Congress Party in the Assembly, on the plea of attempting to benefit the actual tillers of the soil, supported extremist amendments to the Tenancy Bill in the hope of splitting the Ministry's support, the Congress-controlled press is clearly nervous about the Permanent Settlement and the interests of the Hindu middle classes.[47]

However, according to other interpretations, in the years between the two tenancy bills, Congress had come under pressure by a radical faction within it to move to the left on land issues, in part to attract greater Muslim support. This transformation was due in part to the growth of a Hindu urban middle class less dependent on income from the land that was gradually supplanting the *zamindars* as the dominant social group in west Bengal.[48]

The League also had to walk a fine line. If the council decided to reduce the transfer fee substantially for "genuine cultivators" while leaving it intact for rent-receiving tenants who had obtained the legal status of occupancy *raiyats*, then they would be attacked on one hand for not having gone far enough and on the other for going against the interests of many of their Muslim supporters who "while claiming to be tenants and possessing '*raiyati*' status are in fact rent-receivers and no less oppressive than the much-abused class of *zemindars* in their dealings with their under-tenant cultivators."[49] Ignoring the calls by communists and more radical members of Congress for more drastic reforms, the League newspaper, *Azad*, came out in support of the Act and condemned the "impudence and audacity of the *zamindars*, Europeans and Congressite rich businessmen" who opposed it.[50]

A year later *Azad* continued its attack linking Congress to anti-tenant interests. It editorialized that in 1928, "the non-cooperating Congress had cooperated with the bureaucrats and landlords to turn the oppression and outrages of the *zamindars* into permanent law."[51] It claimed that "at that time, the Muslim leaders and the representatives of the tenants had protested against this, but the protests and arguments were in vain. . . . It is a matter of joy that those injustices were ended on April 1, 1928"[52] when the Tenancy Act was passed. *Azad* condemned the proliferation of *krishak* and *praja samitis* (peasant and tenant organizations) as a conspiracy by "sweet-tongued" but malicious politicians to keep [the peasants] isolated and weak and prevent them from uniting under one name:

> It must be said that if the aim of all these samitis is the same—if the goal is only to do good to the *krishak-praja* society—then there would never be so many samitis under different names. . . . All the *krishak samitis* are really branches of the Congress except the All-Bengal Krishak-Praja Samiti headed by *maulvi* Fazlul Huq. . . . As it is not possible to defend peasants' rights by joining the Congress, that is why a peasant movement in Bengal was necessary. Because the Tenants' Act which favored the *zamindars* was passed in 1928 under the leadership of Mr. Subash Chandra Bose, that is why a strong peasant movement was launched in Bengal. . . . Some Muslims of Bengal have dissimulated in the name of the raiyats and tenants. They want to divide and isolate Muslim society using the excuse of the peasants. A reporter from Barisal wrote in yesterday's *Azad* about the nature of this class: 'For the last few months the local Congressites have been trying in many ways openly and secretly to persuade the uneducated Muslims to their party. . . . Society should be very careful about the activities of this "peasant sympathizer" class who are out to destroy Muslim cohesion.[53]

Although the act was far more limited in scope than the pre-election rhetoric, even the Nawab of Dacca observed that the political atmosphere of the entire country had been changed as a result.[54] *Praja* organizations stepped up their activities, and in May 1938, an All-India Krishak conference was convened at Comilla, attracting participants from Madras, Punjab, Gujarat, Bihar, Assam, and many Bengal districts.[55] By 1938, a "no-rent mentality" was in evidence throughout much of rural east Bengal. British authorities blamed Congress, which had developed a network of *krishak* organizations, for the development. Chatterjee argues that there was "little evidence to suggest that this was a centrally organised movement. . . . Certainly the central leadership of the Praja Party did not adopt any programme of this kind."[56] The leadership behind the campaign was more likely local *praja* leaders.[57] By 1938, the no-rent agitation reached such a state that governor and district officers complained to the Huq ministry and demanded action, including allowing for the forcible recovery of rent and the imposition of section 144 of the penal code, prohibiting public gatherings.[58] Other disturbances appeared to have the support of Muslim parties. In the Kishoreganj subdivision of Mymensingh, friction broke out over the levy of a tax on the sale of jute. Local merchants, under the leadership of a Muslim MLA, led the protests.[59] In order to counter Congress and Krishak Praja Party efforts to win peasant support through the *krishak samitis*, Muslim League members of the Legislative Assembly began setting up Muslim League branches at the district and *thana* levels.[60]

However, Huq's opportunistic decision to join the Muslim League in October 1937 without resigning the presidency of the KPP alienated many of his supporters,[61] including some members of the *Praja Samitis*. The allotment of four out of six ministerial posts to Muslim League members incensed many in the KPP "who had fought a fierce campaign against the *zamindars* only to see them elevated to a position where they could dilute any programme of agrarian reform."[62] In March 1938, Tamizuddin Khan, a member of the KPP and one of the strongest proponents of tenancy reform, deserted Huq's ministry coalition to form the Independent Praja Party.[63]

The Bengal Tenancy Amendment Act came on the heels of other bills which had directly benefitted the peasantry but were perceived by Hindu leaders as deliberate efforts by the KPP-Muslim League ministry to attack Hindu interests. The Agricultural Debtors Act of 1933, which established arbitration boards and a set a moratorium for debtors, and the Bengal Money-Lenders Act of 1932, which abolished compound interest, established fixed rates of interest and provided for repayment by installment, primarily affected Hindu businessmen and landlords who had money-lending operations on the side. Just as *Azad* had attempted to paint Congress' support for *krishak samitis* as opportunistic and ingenuous, the Hindu press attacked these legislative acts as thinly disguised initiatives to promote Muslim interests in the name of agrarian reform. While there is little doubt that the measures were pro-peasant, the ministry did not hesitate to take credit for the fact that they also disproportionately benefitted Muslims: the ministry's department of public information published two weeklies, one in English and the other in Bengali, which extolled the work the ministry was doing for the peasantry, while at the same time making a point of the fact that under previous ministries Muslims suffered.[64]

Two other legislative acts were seen as attempts to wrest from Hindu control Bengal's educational system and the administration of the city of Calcutta itself. Controversy over proposed bills on secondary education, Calcutta University and the Calcutta Municipality quickly took on communal overtones in the press. The secondary education act removed control of the high schools from Calcutta University and gave it to a board which was largely under government control. Of particular concern was the fact that the bill proposed statutory representation of Muslims on the board. The Muslim press supported it; the Hindu press called it "reactionary and retrograde."[65] The legislation was seen as inspiring similar moves at the local level: in Mymensingh, a resolution for reforming the constitution of the local board to reflect the proportion of Muslims and Hindus evoked strong opposition from Hindus.[66] The Calcutta Municipal (Amendment) Act of 1937 reintroduced separate electorates and provided for the appointment of officers of the Calcutta Corporation by the Public Service Commission, a move which was "naturally . . . regarded as a direct attack on Hindu interests."[67]

Capturing the Symbols of Victimization

The first elections held under the Government of India Act in 1937 brought Congress governments to power in seven provinces.[68] The Muslim League fared badly throughout India, winning less than a quarter of the reserved Muslim seats nationwide.[69] Only in Bengal did it form a government, in coalition with the Krishak Praja Party. For the next several years, the League's organization grew dramatically in Bengal, with League district offices opening throughout the province. Bengal's League leaders were also actively engaged in generating Muslim support in Assam. For its part, Congress never recovered from the schisms it underwent during the first Non-cooperation campaign and the subsequent defection of many of its top leaders to the Swarajists. Broomfield has described the post-1926 period for the *bhadrolok* politicians who dominated the Bengal Provincial Congress as one of "virtual paralysis" characterized by a progressive "disillusionment with constitutional methods" and "an overriding involvement with communal affairs."[70] As noted in chapter four, the defection of Subhas Chandra Bose from Congress in 1938 benefited the Mahasabha, as did the imprisonment of most of the senior Congress leadership during the Quit India movement in 1942.[71] But the disillusionment with Congress had begun a decade earlier and coincided with the constitutional reforms that had enlarged the franchise and generally benefitted Muslims. Every Bengal Ministry after 1927 was headed by a Muslim. Furthermore, because Hindu politicians, whether Congress or Swarajist, were associated with civil disobedience or other "obstructionist" policies, Muslim ministries generally attracted European nonofficial and official British support.[72] Not surprisingly, this added to the perception of government bias during communal disturbances. At the same time, Hindu opposition to the electoral reforms convinced many that both the Congress and Mahasabha were elitist and anti-democratic. In 1930, the provincial Hindu Sabha had argued against electoral reforms on the grounds that "[t]o further extend the franchise, much less to grant adult suffrage will have the effect of giving votes to men who have neither political consciousness, education, sense of civic responsibility nor any stake in the country."[73] With the establishment of provincial governments in 1937, the Congress and other parties had an opportunity for the first time to exploit a mechanism long used by the British Government to control its subjects through the investigation of incidents of "communal" rioting, among other things.[74] As the British had done, the Congress and the Muslim League used such inquiries as tools for constructing "communal" identities by painting the provincial authorities, party officials, and British officials as complicit in the oppression of the minority community.

Muslim League Commissions of Inquiry

In 1938, the Muslim League at the national level and in Bihar established two commissions of inquiry into Muslim grievances in Congress-ruled provinces. This followed complaints about the Congress' "mass contact" campaign of 1937–38 which had alienated Muslims in its overtly Hindu appeals, and, in particular, the adoption of cow-protection legislation and the promotion of the Hindi language over Urdu in Congress-led provincial governments. The principal reports of this kind, the Sharif and Pirpur reports, detailed many of these accounts.[75] Although the incidents referred to in the Sharif and Pirpur reports concerned U.P., Bihar, and other Congress-led provinces, in Bengal, Fazlul Huq made use of them to boost his own ministry and advance the Muslim position with the British government:

> It is evident that at the end of the war there is going to be a tremendous political advance in India and the present constitution will be very materially changed in the direction of an advance towards dominion status. When the time comes for such a change, it will be necessary for the Muslims to substantiate their claim for protection against the majority community. Unless we can prove to the satisfaction of all concerned that the Congress Governments have hitherto failed to deal justly with the minorities, it will not be of any avail when the time for the revision of the Constitution comes to make random charges without proof. . . . I can assure you that on the success or otherwise of my attempt to prove these charges will depend the entire future of the 99 millions of the Mussulmans of India.[76]

Citing such incidents in a press statement, subsequently published as a pamphlet in December 1939, Huq claimed that his decision to publish the accounts was prompted by criticism from Bengal Congress leaders who accused him of inventing stories of atrocities in order to discredit the

Congress administrations. Huq claimed that "[w]henever there was any communal trouble [the Bengal Congress party] blamed the Muslim League for it but they were ever careful not to condemn the conduct of the Hindus, Congressmen and Mahasabhites, of whose communal activities they themselves had proofs."[77]

The Huq pamphlet describes a familiar pattern in the incidents which sparked violence, many of which began with the "forcible prevention of cow-sacrifice," or the "insistence on the triumphant passage of noisy processions before mosques at prayer time."[78] He also accused the ministries of attempting to intimidate Muslims by "effect[ing] compromise" after the Muslims of a locality had been "oppressed," the terms of the compromise usually being that the Muslims either "voluntarily" undertook not to eat beef or perform cow-sacrifice or "apologised to their tormentors for some unknown offence." Huq also singled out the police under Congress ministries for "delaying arrests and searches" so that "although outrages against Muslims could not be denied, sufficient evidence could not generally be found to prosecute the culprits or to secure conviction."[79] The pamphlet also included a chronological list of "anti-Muslim" events in Bihar, U.P. and the Central Provinces, and Berar from 1937 through 1939.

What stands out in many of the incidents described is Huq's deliberate effort to link Congress officials, the police, and Hindu organizations to the alleged abuses. In most cases the culprits are identified simply as being "Hindus" or the "Hindu mob." However, in those cases, Huq blames police, judges, and other agents of the provincial government for failing to act. For example, after Hindus in Bihar were convicted of trespassing in a Muslim graveyard and assaulting a number of Muslims in September 1937, they were acquitted on appeal by a Hindu judge, S. P. Chatterji. Following the acquittal, supporters of the defendants took out a procession. Although, according to Huq, "the attention of the Bihar Ministry was drawn" to the incidents, it "gave no protection to the local Muslims."[80] After an outbreak of violence in Bhalapur in July 1938, several Muslim members of Congress in Bihar accused the Congress ministry's decision to overrule a district magistrate's prohibition on a procession which went "against previous custom."[81] In Tanda, U.P., police opened fire on a crowd of Muslims who were blocking a Hindu procession which did not have the "sanction of previous custom" to pass in front of a mosque. A judge was eventually appointed to conduct an inquiry, but Muslims, protesting that evidence had been suppressed, boycotted it.[82] In addition, Congress' mass contact campaign provoked Muslim protests over the singing of Bande Mataram,[83] and the use of the "Sri" and the lotus—both Hindu symbols—as part of the crest of Calcutta University.[84] The Calcutta Muslim League worked through its branches throughout the city to counter attempts by the Congress party to win over Muslims, and organized Muslim students to launch a campaign against Calcutta University. The entire Muslim student body boycotted the university on Foundation Day and organized a black flag demonstration instead.[85]

The Muslim League and its supporters in the press kept alive the controversy over the symbols. At an All-Bengal Moslem Conference held in Berhampore in November 1937, resolutions were passed stressing the need for a Muslim League organization in every village. At the meeting, the Huq ministry was congratulated on the recent Bill amending the Tenancy Act, and, again, the Calcutta University crest and singing of Bande Mataram were condemned as unacceptable to Muslims.[86] *Azad* attacked the Congress on the use of these symbols in an editorial, condemning the crest as "an idolatrous emblem . . . hostile to Islam" and complaining that because Muslims were demanding "another, secular symbol . . . our Hindu leaders are calling us communal."[87] When a Hindu member of the assembly pointed out that Mohammad Ghuri, who established the Delhi sultanate in 1186 A.D., had ordered coins imprinted with the word "Sri" and with other "Hindu" symbols, and that Sher Shah, who seized Delhi in 1538, had signed his name with "Sri," *Azad* retorted:

> Mohammad Ghuri and Sher Shah were not very well educated persons. It is not improbable that they were not well-informed about Islamic ideals and culture. . . . Is there any necessity to go so far as to use the example of Sher Shah or Mohammad Ghuri? At present there are many Hindu-minded Muslims who observe Hindu religious practices out of ignorance of Islam. . . . But it would be absolutely wrong to interpret that as the Islamic ideal.[88]

The battle over symbols and the anti-Congress campaign boosted support for the League nationally, particularly in the Muslim minority provinces.[89] Publicity about the incidents further damaged Congress' reputation among Muslims in Bengal. When Subas Chandra Bose visited Brahmanbaria in 1938, local Muslims threw stones. Similar protests greeted him in Noakhali.[90] Huq went so far as to threaten retaliation against Hindus in Bengal for alleged injustices to Muslims in U.P.[91] Congress leaders countered the charges with their own selection of atrocities committed against Hindus, and accused the Muslim League of instigating the attacks.

As noted above, the Huq ministry was accused of pursuing policies designed to insure that Hindus would lose influence in the political affairs of the province and to undermine their influence in such traditional strongholds as the Calcutta Municipality and Calcutta University. The ministry was also accused of blatant favoritism when it supported an increase in reservations for Muslims in government service. More damaging, however, were the charges that the ministry had interfered on a number of occasions to protect Muslims in criminal and communal rioting cases. The outbreak of "communal" violence in Dacca in 1941 was an embarrassment to the Muslim League-KPP ministry, as it provided ammunition to Hindu leaders to counter Muslim League charges that Muslims had been oppressed by a "Hindu" *raj* in other provinces. During the riots, the KPP-ML ministry was accused of interfering with the police. During the outbreaks of violence in rural areas which followed, witnesses testified that Muslim mobs shouted *"Allah-o-Akbar"* ("God is great") and *"Pakistan-ki-jai"* ("Long live Pakistan"). The official investigation concluded that the timing and general choreography of the looting implied a prearranged plan, and that "the attack was the result of some organisation and not merely a sporadic outburst."[92] The mobs were reportedly led by "three or four men dressed in khaki or black shirts and shorts, armed with swords and carrying petrol tins and syringes." Some "had note-books or papers which they consulted before giving orders to loot and burn."[93] The mobs also reportedly engaged in forcible conversions.[94] Local officials were accused of complicity, including several MLAs and the president of the union Board, Maulvi Ambarali Khondkar.[95] The Muslim League claimed that the perpetrators were all Hindus "dressed as Muslims" and that the incident had been invented to discredit the ministry.[96]

Even before the disturbance in Dacca, ministry officials had stepped in to protect prominent Muslim leaders from prosecution in incidents of communal violence or intimidation. In one case in 1940, trouble had broken out in Murappa, a village in Dacca district, over a building that some Muslims claimed was a mosque which was situated on the property of a Hindu. The local *maulvi* was accused of starting an agitation, and police at the site were attacked and opened fire. Orders were given for the *maulvi*'s arrest, but as soon as he was detained, the government ordered him released and the trial was adjourned indefinitely. In a similar case involving persons accused of involvement in communal disturbances in Kulti in March 1941, the trial was again adjourned indefinitely on the orders of the government. According to the official inquiry into the Dacca disturbance, the climate of impunity had left many with the impression that "their co-religionists in the government would protect them from the legal results of criminal actions committed in communal disorders."[97] Muslims involved in Dacca riots claimed they were given one week's immunity; according to the official report, "[t]he illiterate and fanatical persons by whom these crimes were committed were more easily persuaded to believe in such immunity" because of the Murappa case.[98]

The Fight for Control of the
Bengal Provincial Muslim League

In the last years before partition, the Muslim League consolidated its hold in Bengal by insuring that no other Muslim party could be considered as representative of "Muslim" interests. This concern was driven in part by apprehension about the influence of Congress Muslims, but the League's chief worry was about the divisions within its own ranks, represented first by Fazlul Huq and his Praja party associates, and later by the secretary of the Bengal Provincial Muslim League, Abul Hashim. Having successfully identified with *praja* interests in the KPP-Muslim League ministry, the League in these later years returned to the symbols of Muslims as a threatened community and argued that only a united party speaking with one voice could guarantee the Muslims' security.

But the All-India Muslim League leadership's authoritarian approach to crushing dissent at the provincial level continued to feed discord. An early casualty was the first Huq ministry. When, in 1940, the Muslim League Working Committee ordered party members not to serve on district War Committees, Huq refused to obey. He resigned from the League in July 1941. In his resignation letter to Muslim League secretary Liaqat Ali Khan, Huq protested that the All-India Muslim League was behaving undemocratically and arrogating to itself powers that belonged to the provinces:

> I protest emphatically against the manner in which Bengal and Punjab Muslim interests are being impelled by Muslim leaders of the minority provinces. . . . At present I feel that Bengal does not count much in the counsels of political leaders outside the province though we constitute more than one-third the total Muslim population of India. . . . As a mark of protest against the arbitrary use of powers vested in the President I resign from membership of the Working Committee and Council of the All-India Muslim League. I cannot usefully continue to be a member of a body which shows scant courtesy to provincial leaders. . . . [R]ecent events have brought home to me that the principles of democracy and autonomy in the All-India Muslim League are being subordinated to arbitrary wishes of a single individual who seeks to rule as omnipotent authority even over the destiny of 33 millions in Bengal who occupy key positions in Indian Muslim politics.[99]

In reply, Liaqat Ali Khan issued a press statement questioning Huq's presumption "to speak for thirty-three million Bengali Muslims" and claimed that "Muslim Bengal is solidly behind the All-India Muslim League. . . . Every true well-wisher of the Muslim community realises that Muslims throughout India must stand solidly united if they are to survive."[100]

By December 1941, Huq had cobbled together a second ministry which included members of Sarat Bose's Forward Bloc,[101] former KPP members, scheduled caste leaders and Shyam Prasad Mukherjee, the head of the Bengal Hindu Mahasabha, under the name of the Progressive Coalition Assembly Party. Huq again became chief minister. The new ministry was promptly attacked by *Azad*,[102] and Jinnah cabled Huq, accusing him of "treachery" and of "intriguing with [the] Opposition"[103] to "break Muslim League and Muslim solidarity in Bengal."[104] Other League leaders, including H.S. Suhrawardy and Khwaja Nazimuddin, traveled around Bengal, accusing Huq of betraying Islam.[105] The second Huq ministry fell in March 1943, and a Muslim League ministry came to power under Suhrawardy.

The power struggle between Huq and Jinnah had brought to the surface fundamental questions about the autonomy of provincial League leaders and the authoritarian nature of the League's organization.[106] It was no accident that this challenge to the AIML's leadership emerged just as the Bengal Provincial Muslim League was, for the first time, building a genuinely mass-based organization in the districts due to the efforts of its provincial secretary, Abul Hashim. Hashim, who by his own account had relatives who were leaders or workers in every party except the Hindu Mahasabha, had been president of the Burdwan district Muslim League when the KPP-Muslim League ministry was formed in 1937. When he became secretary in 1943, the League had virtually no organization in the districts:

> The Dacca District Muslim League was, in fact, a prisoner within the four walls of the Ahsan Manzel, the family headquarters of the Nawab family of Dacca. To be more correct, the Bengal Provincial Muslim League was in the pocket of the Khwajas of Ahsan Manzel. Nine members of the Dacca Nawab family were members of the Bengal Provincial Legislative Assembly. . . . the Nawab family enjoyed a unique prestige in East Bengal. . . . the office in Calcutta was in a state of complete disorganization. There was no treasury— Khwajas collected funds in the name of the League and used them as they liked. There were no district offices in Bengal.[107]

From the outset, Hashim's organizational strategy was at odds with that of League leaders whose loyalty lay with the Nawab and Muslim landed interests. Hashim's efforts were directed toward working with local peasant organizations, the *krishak samitis*, to expand the League's organization. He also sought assistance from Communist Party leaders about how to expand the League's organization.[108] Under his leadership, the Dacca district

Muslim League offices and local *krishak samiti* cooperated in campaigns against local landlords. These moves were opposed by the Khwajas (the Nawab's family), who avoided the *krishak* groups, relying instead on links with the *maulvi*s and *madrasah* teachers to extend their influence.[109] Hashim's efforts to democratize the League angered many of the League's most powerful leaders who had "a lurking fear in their mind that if these [district] organizations were democratized and strengthened, their leadership . . . might be eliminated."[110] When Hashim organized the first ever district level election for the Dacca League, the Nawab family candidate lost by a landslide.[111] In addition, Hashim's continuing appeal to economic reform to attract peasant support worried League leaders who knew that such promises did not have the support of All-India League leaders.[112]

The communal violence which characterized the last months before partition, or which, to use Pandey's phrasing "constituted Partition,"[113] was replete with examples of both Hindu and Muslim leaders claiming— often justifiably—victimization at the hands of members of the "other" community. The League's call for a general *hartal* in support of Pakistan on a day designated as "Direct Action Day" in Calcutta resulted in the single worst incident of "communal" violence in pre-partition India. The "Great Calcutta Killing" left hundreds dead, and leaders from all of the parties played some part in the bloodshed. Congress and the Mahasabha were accused of using the violence to force the dismissal of the League Ministry; League leaders of deliberately arranging for violent clashes as a demonstration of their intention to "win Pakistan by force."[114] More Muslims lost their lives than Hindus, and on September 7, 1946, a meeting of local *maulvi*s of Noakhali under the leadership of Maulana Ghulam Sarwar declared that Muslims should get revenge for the Calcutta killing. Riots in Noakhali and Comilla, in which Hindus were the principal victims, followed.[115]

The battle for control of the Bengal Muslim League was a fight for the symbols that would attract the support of Bengal's predominantly Muslim peasantry. This meant that for the League to succeed against other more obvious representatives of peasant interests, like the KPP, it had to adopt the rhetoric, if not the substance, of agrarian reform. The struggle that dominated Muslim politics in Bengal during this period was one fundamental to the representation of Bengali Muslim identity. In 1937, the KPP, the first party in Bengal to represent the interests of Muslim peasants and tenants, formed a coalition government with the party that cast itself as the sole representative of Muslims as Muslims. Although fundamentally opposed to radical agrarian reform, League leaders recognized the need to win peasant support. By the early 1940s, the Muslim League had usurped the KPP and absorbed its membership, leaving it free to base its appeals on communal, rather than class, issues.

Having captured much of the membership of the KPP on the strength of the first coalition government and the alienation of KPP members from Huq's second ministry,[116] the Bengal Provincial Muslim League no longer needed to engage in the rhetoric of agrarian reform. Instead, League leaders who were wary of Hashim's intention to create a mass-based organization again framed their appeals in terms of a Muslim solidarity, the security of which was threatened by any kind of dissent. Their concern now was to insure that the League spoke with one voice and that Bengali Muslims perceived their security as being dependent on a single Muslim homeland. The symbols they used drew on images of Bengal's Muslims as victims, suffering as their co-religionists elsewhere in India had under "Hindu" provincial administrations. By using incidents of violence to stake their party's claim as the sole body capable of protecting Muslim interests, League leaders succeeded, however temporarily, in winning support among Bengali Muslims for the idea of Pakistan.

Notes

1. For a detailed account of Muslim League politics generally, see Ayesha Jalal, *The Sole Spokesman: Jinnah, the Muslim League and the Demand for Pakistan* (Cambridge: Cambridge University Press, 1985).

2. For more on this, see Vinay Lal, "Committees of Inquiry and Discourses of 'Law and Order' in Twentieth-Century British India" (University of Chicago: Doctoral Dissertation, 1992).

3. During the negotiations between Gandhi and the viceroy, Lord Irwin, in 1931, Subhas Bose and others demanded official inquiries into police atrocities which included the killing of over one hundred civilians. Gandhi's agreement to withdraw the demand outraged Bose and many others of the "radical" wing. Stanley Wolpert, *A New History of India* (New York: Oxford University Press, 1982), p. 318.

4. *Moslem Hitaishi*, cited in "Home Rule Agitation in India," GOB 219/1917, s. 1–2.

5. Abdul Hakim, MLC, to Secretary, AIML. Papers of the BPML, Vol. 38, p. 27, Archives of the Freedom Movement (AFM), University of Karachi.

6. Amiruddin Ahmad to Mohammad Yakub, 29 August 1932. Papers of the BPML, Vol. 38, p. 33. AFM.

7. Shahid Soherwardy to Mohammad Yakub, 14 June 1932. Papers of the BPML, Vol. 38, pp. 10–13. AFM.

8. Papers of the BPML, Vol. 37, pp. 55–58, 74–77. AFM.

9. Bengal Presidency Muslim League, "Its Opinion Regarding Electorates." Bengal 1:6. The Correspondence of Qaid-i-Azam Mr. M. A. Jinnah, Shamsul Huq Collection, Qaid-i-Azam Academy, Karachi, Pakistan (QAA).

10. There is little consistency in the documents surveyed on calling the BPML the Bengal Provincial Muslim League or the Bengal Presidency Muslim League. The present author has attempted to use the full name when so cited by the original text.

11. Shamsul Hasan Collection, Bengal 1:13–1:18, QAA.

12. Khan Bahadur Abdul Hafeez to Secretary, AIML, 4 May 1936. Papers of the BPML, Vol. 38, p. 39, AFM.

13. Chatterjee, 1984, p. 141.

14. Jatindranath De, "The History of the Krishak Praja Party of Bengal, 1929–1947: A Study of Changes in Class and Inter-Community Relations in the Agrarian Sector of Bengal," Unpublished Ph.D. dissertation, University of Delhi, 1977, p. 92, cited in Chatterjee, 1984, p. 141.

15. Ibid.

16. Partha Chatterjee's *The Land Question* focuses on the making of the 1928 Tenancy Act and its impact on the agrarian economy.

17. Chatterjee, 1984, pp. 1–3.

18. Ibid., p. 4.

19. Sen, p. 63.

20. Chatterjee, 1984, p. 85.

21. *Land Revenue Commission of Bengal*, vol. 1, p. 76.

22. Shila Sen, pp. 20–21.

23. Anderson to Linlithgow, Governor's fortnightly report: "Review of political events in Bengal for the first half of June 1937" (Confidential) L/P&J/5/141.

24. Governor's fortnightly report for the second half of February 1936, File 127/36, p. 1.

25. "Report on the political situation in Bengal for the first half of March, 1936," F. 127/36, pp. 1–2.

26. Sen, p. 85.

27. "Report on the political situation in Bengal for the first half of May 1936," F. 127/36, p. 2.

28. Chatterjee, 1984, p. 168.

29. *Star of India*, September 1936, cited in Sen, p. 77.

30. *Azad*, January 16, 1937, cited in Sen, p. 84. Karbala was the plain on which Husein, who was the son of Ali, the fourth Caliph of Islam and Mohammad's son-in-law, was killed.

31. *Statesman*, June 16, 1936, cited in Sen, p. 75.

32. Sen, pp. 74–75.

33. Ibid., pp. 76–77.

34. Anderson to Linlithgow, Governor's fortnightly report: "Review of political events in Bengal for the first half of June 1937" (Confidential) L/P&J/5/141.

35. Ibid.

36. *Azad*, January 9, 1937.

37. *Azad*, January 17, 1937; *Ananda Bazar Patrika*, January 10, 1937. In some places the divisions were not so much ideological as personal. The Dacca Commissioner observed that "[i]n Bakarganj district . . . there is no clear demarcation between Praja Party and Muslim League candidates. It is more a matter of persons than of policies." The Chittagong commissioner similarly remarked that the personal element predominated and that there was talk of a local amalgamation of the Praja and the United Moslem Party. Report on the political situation for the second half of November 1936. File 127/36, p. 2. WBSA.

38. Chatterjee, 1984, p. 167.

39. Ibid., p. 168.

40. Hardy, p. 227.

41. "Editor's note," *Modern Review*, April 1937, p. 488.

42. Governor's fortnightly report: "Review of events in Bengal for the first half of November 1937." L/P&J/5/141.

43. Anderson to Linlithgow, Governor's fortnightly report: "Review of political events in Bengal for the first half of July 1937" (Confidential) L/P&J/5/141.

44. Government of Bengal, "A Resume of the Bengal Government's Activities since April 1937," in L/P&J/5/143.

45. "A brief summary of political events in Bengal, 1938," p. 7. Government of India (Home Department) Political File 66/40/1940.

46. Ibid.

47. Ibid.

48. See Chatterjee, 1984, pp. 172–182.

49. Anderson to Linlithgow, Governor's fortnightly report: "Review of political events in Bengal for the first half of June 1937" (Confidential) L/P&J/5/141.

50. "*Praja-Swato Ain* (The Tenancy Act)" (editorial), *Azad*, May 7, 1938.

51. "*Praja-Swato Ain* (The Tenancy Act)" (editorial), *Azad*, April 5, 1938.

52. Ibid.

53. "Praja-Doeder Swarup (The True Nature of Compassion for the Tenants)" (editorial), *Azad*, May 6, 1938.

54. Governor's fortnightly report: "Review of events in Bengal for the first half of August 1938." L/P&J/5/143.

55. "A Brief Summary of Events in Bengal, 1938," GOI Home Dept. Pol. File 66/40/1940, p. 7.

56. Chatterjee, 1984, p. 166.

57. Ibid.

58. Ibid., pp. 166–167.

59. Governor's fortnightly report for the second fortnight in October 1938, L/P&J//5/143.

60. Shila Sen, p. 123. See also GOI Home Political File 66/40 of 1940.

61. Shila Sen, p. 119, n. 57.

62. Ian Talbot, *Provincial Politics and the Pakistan Movement* (Karachi: Oxford University Press, 1988), p. 64.

63. Shila Sen, p. 119.

64. Ibid., p. 109.

65. Governor's fortnightly report: "Review of events in Bengal for the second half of November 1937" (confidential), December 6, 1937. L/P&J/5/141.

66. Governor's fortnightly report: "Review of events in Bengal for the first half of December 1937" (confidential), December 6, 1937. L/P&J/5/141.

67. Governor's fortnightly report: "Review of events in Bengal for the second half of November 1937," (confidential), December 6, 1937. L/P&J/5/141.

68. The Congress governments were in Bihar, Bombay, the Central Provinces, Madras, the Northwest Frontier, Orissa, and U.P. In a separate election held in 1938, a Congress government came to power in Assam.

69. The Government of India Act had retained separate electorates for Muslims.

70. Broomfield, p. 283.

71. The "Quit India" campaign was launched in August 1942. The British authorities considered the campaign an act of treason during wartime. Efforts to repress it resulted in the arrest of tens of thousands of Congress leaders; hundreds of protesters were injured or killed during the campaign when police opened fire on marches.

72. Broomfield, p. 285.

73. Statement for All-Parties Meeting, March 31, 1930, in Tej Bahadur Sapru papers, National Library of India, Calcutta, cited in Broomfield, p. 289.

74. For more on the significance of such commissions as an instrument of control, see Lal.

75. *Report of the Enquiry Committee appointed by the Council of the All-India Muslim League to inquire into Muslim grievances in Congress Provinces, 1938,* and *Report of the Enquiry Committee appointed by the Working Committee of the Bihar Provincial Muslim League to enquire into some grievances of Muslims in Bihar, 1939.* See Hardy, p. 228. Hereafter ML Inquiry Committee reports.

76. Letter from Fazlul Huq, November 4, 1939, in the AFM, vol. 39, p. 41.

77. *Muslim Sufferings Under Congress Rule* (Being a Reprint of a Statement Issued to the Press by the Hon'ble Mr. A. K. Fazlul Huq, Premier of Bengal), December 1939, p. 2. AFM.

78. Ibid.

79. Ibid., p. 3.

80. Ibid.

81. Ibid., p. 6.

82. Ibid., p. 15.

83. In 1937 the All-India Congress Committee decided that only the first two verses of the song should be sung at nationalist functions in order not to offend Muslims. Bengali Congress party members defied the ruling, which they felt was an insult to the song's Bengali author, Bankim Chandra Chatterjee. See Broomfield, p. 307.

84. Governor's fortnightly report: "Review of events in Bengal for the second half of October 1937." L/P&J/5/141.

85. *Annual Report on Police Administration of Calcutta and Suburbs for 1937,* by L.H. Colson, Commissioner of Police, Calcutta (Bengal Government Press, 1938).

86. Governor's fortnightly report: "Review of events in Bengal for the second half of November 1937." L/P&J/5/141.

87. "'Sri, 'o 'Padma' ('Sri' and 'Lotus')" (editorial), *Azad,* 15 Bhadra, 1344 (1937).

88. Ibid.

89. ML Inquiry Committee reports. See Hardy, p. 228.

90. "A brief summary of the political situation in Bengal, 1938," GOI Home Pol. F. 66/40 1940, p. 13.

91. Governor's fortnightly report for the second half of October 1937 (confidential), L/P&J/5/141.

92. Ibid., p. 34.

93. RDREC, p. 34.

94. Ibid.

95. Ibid, pp. 36–38.

96. Ibid.

97. Ibid., p. 30.

98. Ibid., pp. 53–54.

99. "Miscellaneous reports on Muslim League," telegram from governor-general to secretary of state summarizing Huq's letter to Liaqat Ali Khan, File No. 17/4/41, GOI Home Dept Poll (I) .

100. Summary of Liaqat Ali Khan's press statement in reply to Huq's letter, in ibid., 16 September 1941, p. 62.

101. The Forward Bloc party, founded by Bose in 1939, was committed to "revolutionary struggle." It was banned in 1940.

102. "Extract from fortnightly report on political situation in Bengal for the second half of August 1941, rec'd from CID, Calcutta," in File No. 17/4/41, GOI Home Dept. Poll (I)., p. 63.

103. "Summary of Jinnah's telegram to Huq," in ibid., December 9, 1941, p. 75.

104. Telegram from Governor-General to Secretary of State, 7 December 1941, summarizing most of the text of a telegram sent by Jinnah to Fazlul Huq on December 6 and subsequently released to the press, in ibid., p. 77.

105. Talbot, p. 67.

106. Broomfield notes that similar frustrations with the All-India Congress Committee drove many Bengal Congress members to leave the organization after 1940. See Broomfield, pp. 307–308.

107. Abul Hashim, *In Retrospection* (Dacca: Nowroze Kitabistan, 1974), pp. 36–38.

108. Ibid., p. 40.

109. Ibid., p. 87.

110. "Review of the Muslim League Organization in Bengal" submitted by secretary, Bengal Provincial Muslim League to secretary, All-India Muslim League, 30 July 1944, Shamsul Hasan Collection (Karachi), Bengal 1:42, as cited in Talbot, p. 71.

111. Talbot, p. 70.

112. Ibid., p. 68.

113. Pandey, 1994, p. 189.

114. *India Annual Review*, July-December 1946, p. 183, as cited in S. Das, p. 178.

115. Hashim, pp. 119–120.

116. According to Jatindranth De, "By 1943 the bulk of the Muslim jotdar base shifted to the Muslim league, leading to a mass exodus of members from the [Krishak Praja] Party . . . " See Jatindranath De, p. 6, as cited in Chatterjee, 1984, p. 170.

Conclusion

The term "communalism" has a peculiarly South Asian derivation, although it is used to describe a phenomenon that is certainly not limited to South Asia in its application.[1] Even in this task, however, the word "communalism" generally does a poor job. As part of a vocabulary that historians, area specialists, and political scientists apply to various manifestations of identity politics, religious revival, and outright bigotry, the resort to the word "communalism" causes more problems than its use as an explanation of events or beliefs solves.

Those who have examined the political history of the use of the term "communalism" note that for most colonial writers, the word described what they saw as a characteristically South Asian perversion of nationalism, a phenomenon that buttressed the colonial belief that South Asians were as incapable of conceiving of themselves as a nation as they were of evolving and sustaining the institutions of a modern nation-state. Nationalist writers, on the other hand, naturally rejected the racist implications of this definition of communalism, but nevertheless adopted its corollary: for them, communalism is the opposite of nationalism, a corruption for which the uneducated and backward masses, and the unscrupulous leaders who used them, were responsible. For both unrepentant colonialists and fervent nationalists, communalism was a "given," an inherent characteristic of the colonized peoples of South Asia and a problem to be solved through education, democracy, industrialization—in short, modernity.[2] This interpretation of communalism persists in popular beliefs about "ethnic" violence elsewhere in the world.[3]

Symbols, Elections, and Violence: A 1990 Parallel

To anyone familiar with the kind of "communal" violence that has racked South Asia since independence, it is painfully obvious that violence of this kind is not a primordial aspect of the character of the people of this region. As Brass argues, the persistence of communalism in India is tied to the competing ideologies of secularism and Hindu nationalism, both of which require the threat of Hindu-Muslim violence to justify their call for a strong state.

> Secularism has been an ideology of a strong centralized state that has defined itself in such a way as to place the Indian state not at a remove from religion, communalism, and Hindu-Muslim issues, but at the center of them. While proclaiming the irrelevance of religion and community to citizenship, the national leadership has consistently defined India as a country containing two large religious groups that will tear each other apart if the state is not strong enough to prevent it. . . . [Hindu nationalism] is a form of secular ideology of state exaltation that says, *contra* the existing secular ideology, that India cannot define itself as a society containing two antagonistic religions, but as a society with one culture, a Hindu culture, in which all must partake if they want to be true citizens.[4]

In this view, politicians of both stripes pursue policies and electoral strategies that feed rather than minimize communal tensions, and engage in the rhetoric of victimization when it suits their purposes to do so.

A quick survey of the more notorious communal outbreaks in India in the last twenty years amply testifies to the fact that what is commonly described as a communal riot is more often than not an event that is well-planned, with the participants armed, targets selected, and rumors planted, and with the government absent, ineffectual, or openly complicit. The same is true for the decades of "communal" riots that prepared the ground for the ultimate confrontation of partition. Because it is not possible to recreate the exact historical circumstances of these pre-partition riots, some examples from the 1990s should shed some light on how and why riots are organized. The two incidents discussed below occurred in late 1990 during a period of heightened tension surrounding the Hindu nationalist Bharatiya Janata Party's (BJP) campaign to raze the Babri Masjid, a sixteenth-century mosque in the town of Ayodhya, U.P., and build a temple to the Hindu god Ram in its place. While those issues provided the national context for the riots that took place in a number of cities in India,[5] the two discussions below demonstrate that local politics were key to determining whether and how violence would result.

In her analysis of the 1990 riots in Bijnor, U.P.,[6] Amrita Basu concentrates on the role of the state in giving legitimacy to caste and community politics. Her emphasis is less on the state at the national level and more on power struggles over elections and offices at the local level. Residents of Bijnor traced the origins of the 1990 riot to a municipal council election several years earlier in which a Muslim, Zafar Khan, had been elected chair. In their efforts to dislodge him, a group of council members representing three militant Hindu organizations—the Shiv Sena, Bajrang Dal and Vishva Hindu Parishad (VHP)[7]—accused Khan of using his office to grant preferential treatment to Muslims, specifically by renting land to Muslims rather than to Hindus who, they claimed, wanted to build a *dharamsala* (a religious facility). In fact, no such group had petitioned Khan to rent the land.

On August 25, 1990, a group made up of members of the BJP, VHP, Bajrang Dal, and Shiv Sena trespassed on the land and announced their plans to construct a temple on the site. A clash was avoided at that time, but it was followed by two other BJP/VHP-organized confrontations which culminated in a riot. On October 5, barricades that had been put up to block the entry of Ram devotees carrying torches from Ayodhya were torn down, in defiance of a government order against letting the devotees proceed through the town. On October 30, the VHP organized a "victory" procession to celebrate what was believed to be the triumphant capture of the mosque at Ayodhya.[8] The processionists headed into the Muslim part of town and began shouting inflammatory slogans. The street fighting that ensued was quickly followed by a systematic attack on Muslims by the Provincial Armed Constabulary (PAC), a state police force with a reputation for brutality, particularly against Muslims. During the attacks the PAC was accompanied by local Hindu residents; one observer told Basu that "[a]t that stage, Hindu organizations were no longer necessary" because the state was taking up their part.[9] Official accounts put the number killed at eighty-seven; unofficial accounts vary from 198 to 300, the majority of them Muslims.[10] The riot achieved its objective. Zafar Khan was removed from the council and other Muslim leaders who had been prominent before the riot dropped out of politics.

> Another mark of the 'success' of the 1990 riot was that it effectively removed Muslims from Bijnor's political landscape. . . . In electoral terms too, the riot had worked. The BJP candidate won with overwhelming support in the parliamentary elections from the Bijnor constituency in 1991. . . . Similarly, all seven BJP candidates from Bijnor won the legislative assembly elections in 1991. . . . Several observers commented that while the riot prompted a large Hindu turnout. . . it had the opposite effect on Muslims, who stayed away from the polls out of fear.[11]

One BJP activist told Basu, "We have found that after a riot, Muslims remain silent for the next eight years."[12]

Javeed Alam's examination of the 1990 riots in Hyderabad provide further evidence of the part local political contests play in communal violence.[13] In December 1990, the city of Hyderabad in the state of Andhra Pradesh experienced serious riots that left over 150 people dead and hundreds wounded. But, like Bijnor, the violence that wracked Hyderabad for five days had much more to do with a local power struggle than with the rights of those defending either temple or mosque. According to Javeed Alam, the riots occurred at a time when the BJP was struggling to

win a sufficient number of seats in the Hyderabad Municipal Corporation to counter the Muslim *Majlis-e-Ittehad-ul-Muslimeen* (United Muslim
Council), which had largely controlled the city's politics since 1985.[14] At
the same time, dissidents within the Congress Party were eager to bring
about the dismissal of the Chief Minister, Chenna Reddy, by paralyzing
the administration once the riots began. One of the key leaders behind
this riot was a Congress politician, Sudhir Kumar, who had briefly de-
fected to the BJP and then rejoined Congress. Kumar was a member of
the Kapu community, which is considered among the Other Backward
Castes (OBCs), a voting bloc on which Congress had traditionally relied.
Alam notes that whenever communal tensions rise, "Congress has to
protect the Kapus and allow their activities in order to retain their support for electoral purposes."[15]

As a consequence of the Hyderabad riot, Muslim identity politics became tied to a new sense of vulnerability. Muslims in the city came more
and more to see themselves as the victims of discrimination and physical
intimidation.[16]

The growth of communal organizations parallels the decline in the
state's ability or willingness to provide for and protect those classes or
communities.[17] Communal riots, which have now become endemic to
Hyderabad, began with an outbreak in 1979 sparked by the expansion of
nouveau riche Muslims, with money repatriated from relatives working in
the Gulf, into areas of the city dominated by Hindu traders.[18] In the aftermath of the riot, in which Muslims lost considerable property, the Majlis-
e-Ittehad-ul-Muslimeen called on Muslims to rely on themselves and not
the state for protection. It collected donations for relief and provided affected families with better homes than they had lost, and businesses with
start-up money and security guards. As a result, the Majlis' popularity
soared and over the next several years, its percentage of the vote climbed
steadily until it gained control of the Municipal Corporation and a plu-
rality of the vote in the 1989 Assembly elections. After the 1990 riots, it
was again involved in relief work. In fact, its role in rehabilitation had become so well established that many Muslims no longer sought relief
funds from the government.[19] "Ask any of the victims as to why they do
not avail of the rehabilitation assistance of the government, and the common refrain one hears is: 'It is a waste of time, sir. They won't give it to
us. It is all meant for Hindus.'"[20]

Accusations of bias on the part of the police and other government
agents are commonplace in instances of communal violence. Indeed, as
the role of the PAC in Bijnor made clear, the charges have been found to
be true in many cases. "Publicizing police failures at the center or state
level has become a way of incriminating one's political opponents. . . .
[I]n national politics, the police have acquired a reputation as the prime

instrument of a lawless state and of state violence."[21] Indeed, it can generally be assumed that police will intervene on behalf of whichever party
has the support of powerful politicians or is likely to pay more.[22] The
Majlis, for its part, had its own strongmen to call upon who, despite their
criminal reputations, or because of them, commanded popular support
among many poor Muslims. But while both Congress and the Majlis
made use of criminal networks well-known to police and politicians on
both sides, the riots represented less a law and order problem than a
"strategy to close the space for other kinds of politics."[23] Part of this strategy is the establishment of what Brass calls an "institutionalized riot system" of which criminal networks form a part, together with political, religious and cultural organizations that make it a point to keep their
religious community aware of any potentially "communal" incident that
takes place, and to foment a riot if by doing so they can embarrass a political opponent or otherwise gain political advantage.[24] As these 1990 examples show, many of the patterns established in the pre-partition years
have contined well into the post-independence period.

Was Bengal Unique?

While Bengal featured prominently among provinces with a history of
serious communal violence in the years before partition, it has featured
among the states with a lower incidence of such violence since then. This
is not to say there have been no incidents of communal violence in the
state since partition, but that, compared to U.P., Bihar, or Gujarat, the incidents have been fewer and less intense. The partitioning of the province
of Bengal, with all of Muslim-majority east Bengal going to Pakistan, dramatically altered the balance of power between the two communities. It
also fundamentally altered the economies of both Bengals, as the western
half was stripped of its agricultural heartland, and the east of its access to
the port of Calcutta and the factories and mills of the more industrialized
west. In the state of West Bengal, the ultimate dominance of leftist political parties and the rise of radical land reform movements focused political leaders away from Hindu-Muslim competition and back to agrarian
issues and other economic concerns.[25]

The communal violence that racked Bengal in the pre-partition years
did not differ markedly from the clashes that took place in U.P. and elsewhere in north India. Indeed, as noted earlier, Muslim leaders made a deliberate effort to link common concerns and symbols such as music before mosques. What was different was the effort made to make Bengali
Muslims, who otherwise differed in many respects from their north Indian co-religionists, see that their interests were the same as those of
other Muslims throughout north India. And where they were not, in the

area of land reform, for example, the rhetoric of solidarity and vulnerability had to substitute for more tangible political and economic gains.
That solidarity was short-lived, however. As Pakistan's new leaders increasingly engaged in the rhetoric of national unity, they employed the
same devices used by their predecessors fifty years before them. Claiming that the Bengali language was not "Muslim" enough, and fearing dissent in the new state, they sought to impose Urdu as the official state
language in East Pakistan. The move sparked widespread protests,
and within a few years of partition, Bengalis in East Pakistan were mobilizing support around a new set of symbols: their threatened language
and culture.

The Logic of Violence

Communalism, as examined here, is not a "given" political identity but
a tool, a deliberate strategy employed to secure political advantage. It is
thus neither an inherent characteristic of peoples or groups, nor is it simply a construct used by colonial or formerly colonial powers to describe
the colonized (or formerly colonized). Instead, the phenomenon of communalism may be defined as the use of violence to distinguish groups
on the basis of religious or "ethnic" identity. As Stanley Tambiah argues,
"[t]he structuring role of this collective agonistic violence may reach a
point at which it actually becomes efficacious in the construction, pro-
duction, maintenance, and reproduction of ethnic identity and solidarity
itself."[26] What is particularly important about this application of the
term is the emphasis on the element of violence as itself constitutive of
identity. The representation and routinization of violence has become "a
regularized mode of enacting mass politics,"[27] and as such, plays a critical role in crystallizing popular constructions of identity and forging
group solidarity.

In this analysis of communal violence I have set out to do three things:
to demonstrate by examples from pre-partition Bengal that the motives
behind much of what has been described as communal violence are political; that violence is consciously chosen as a tool to discredit political rivals and challenge established authority; and that violence is used as a
symbol to identify one's own community as the "victim" and another as
the "aggressor." By giving objective differences symbolic meaning, political actors compete with one another to "construct" a political identity
that will override other, potentially competing claims on the loyalty of
members of that community. The particular components of an "ethnic"
identity, such as language, religious or sectarian affiliation, are variable;
they may bring together members of a group so defined only so long as
there is a discernible advantage in such unity. Communal identity and

communal violence are not products of historical inevitability but rather functions of political choices.

The state plays a significant role in the process of forging communal identities by defining the arenas in which groups will compete, the categories by which groups will be ordered, and the leaders who will be recognized to represent the interests of their communities. In Bengal, the colonial authorities identified a particular group of *ashraf* Muslims associated with the Nawab of Dacca as "natural leaders,"[28] and turned to them as representatives of an imagined Bengali Muslim community, despite the fact that these leaders had, at best, limited contact with most of that community.

Acts of state create opportunities for competition between groups. The act of boundary-drawing that resulted in the first partition of Bengal in 1905 provided the framework in which Bengali Muslims could begin to think differently about themselves. The partition not only divided Muslim and Hindu leaders on a question of policy, but provided the impetus for the promotion of a new kind of popular leader and a new form of political action. It provided the occasion for political organizers to reformulate Bengali Muslim political identity. The violence that followed made both Hindu and Muslim leaders aware of the dangers and advantages of using religious symbols to sway popular opinion for or against government policies. In 1905 the interests of the established elite—designated "natural" leaders by the colonial authorities—and those of religious reformers with a popular base in the countryside coincided. Within a decade of the annulment of partition, a new class of upwardly mobile rural leaders who claimed a more self-consciously "Muslim" identity were in a position to challenge these "natural" leaders and colonial policy, and frame political debate in terms of both religious identity and tenant interests.

Muslim leaders who carved a political role for themselves out of the religious associations—the *anjumans*—that they organized attempted to prove themselves as more representative of Muslim interests by the distance they could put between themselves and nationalist Muslims and the Congress party. Some of the time, this meant supporting British policies. At other times it meant challenging British recognition of the traditional authority of other Muslim leaders. Techniques of political mobilization used during the Khilafat and Non-cooperation movements legitimized the use of religious symbols and created a political role for rural leaders and religious leaders who had an interest in promoting a more exclusivist image of the Bengali Muslim community. Over time, the symbols increasingly merged the sufferings of the Muslims and their need for the security of a "homeland" with the language of agrarian reform.

The renegotiation of the status order among Muslims was framed in terms of competition with Hindus because acts of state, such as the partition of 1905, the government of India acts of 1919 and 1935, and the Communal Award of 1932, gave Muslim and Hindu leaders an incentive to make use of symbols and issues which appealed to a constituency defined by the colonial framework on the basis of religious affiliation. British authorities gave these contested symbols a validity they would not otherwise have had by granting legitimacy to leaders whom they believed most likely to uphold "law and order." For Muslims, this meant that symbols which evoked exploitation by Hindus and the need to protect an "endangered" Muslim population would resonate among the newly enfranchised cultivators of east Bengal.

Bringing together the right symbols to attract Muslim votes was not a straightforward task, however, as there were significant differences between Bengali Muslim leaders of the Praja party and those of the Muslim League on issues related to tenancy legislation. The ultimate success of one faction of the Muslim League in emerging—temporarily—as the single Muslim party in Bengal was due in part to the fact that it successfully brought together the language of agrarian reform and the symbols of a threatened Muslim community to attract mass support.

One of the principal causes of the "communal" riots that punctuated this period were these power struggles among various Muslim parties. Thus, much of what is depicted as "communal" conflict in Bengal reflects a reordering of power not between Hindu and Muslim leaders, but among various groups within their own communities. The violence that resulted was aimed at challenging existing custom through organizing public displays, or protests against them. As the study of popular culture has shown, public ceremony and collective ritual function to legitimize authority and shape political identities.[29] Rival Muslim leaders deliberately highlighted differences between Hindus and Muslims and sought to undermine other leaders who called for accommodation. They made use of religious symbols which emphasized those differences, such as music before mosques, and defied customary conventions governing processions and other public events. Processions became a demonstration of the dominance of one community, its sanction by state or moral authority, and its potential for taking power through violent force.

There is ample evidence that many of the riots were planned events: both official and non-official reports identify important political figures among the perpetrators; the stockpiling of weaponry and distribution of inflammatory material is described in detail. I examined a number of riots: As targets of attack, or recruiters of the perpetrators, and as creators of the myths in their roles as regular witnesses before government commissions of inquiry, the representatives of these organizations used the violence to redefine relations between the two communities and to construct a politically self-conscious Bengali Muslim community. Riots were not spontaneous protests against the established order. Rather, popular religious leaders, peasant activists, and other "subaltern" leaders engaged in mobilizing support around symbols that evoked a more exclusionary Muslim identity, and linked that identity to land reform issues which had appeal for the vast majority of Bengal's Muslim cultivators and tenants. A decade later, agitations around these same issues provided a base for the Muslim League's rise to power in the province.

I have used the evidence of contemporary riots to show that such incidents are planned and executed for specific political objectives. The incidents of communal violence examined here represented a challenge to the status order. These were planned attacks, orchestrated by actors who stood to gain by using occasions of public ceremony to assert the rights of communities they claimed to represent. These actors—be they the *maulvis* in anti-*swadeshi* clashes, or new political groups defying the Nawab or attempting to discredit nationalist Muslims—picked a fight over public space with Hindu leaders in order to set themselves apart from leaders who had "compromised" on those rights. As the violence became routinized, the same choreography was repeated in subsequent riots, setting a pattern that was reiterated in disturbances over the next twenty years.

Official accounts also provide important insights into the colonial construction of communalism. In particular, the official inquiries "explained" violent outbreaks in terms of "historic" antagonisms which only the British presence could contain. Even the choice of terminology is revealing: Government reports on the Non-cooperation and Khilafat campaigns described the agitations surrounding school boycotts as "riots."[30] The political parties also constructed their own versions of such narratives to explain riots in terms favorable to their own interests and portray their constituency as victimized. Portrayed in the official accounts as unfortunate but inevitable events, the major riots of 1918–1926 tell a very different story from that recorded in the "communal riot narratives" of British officials. These incidents represent efforts by a leadership with a popular base in rural east Bengal to challenge the moral authority of established leaders—those considered the "legitimate" leaders of the Muslims by the British. The new leaders made use of public arenas to expose the failure of traditional leaders and the British government to protect Muslim interests.

The subalternist school has provided an important corrective to the elitist assumptions upon which much of traditional South Asian history has been based. However, in their efforts to credit the subaltern masses with a rationality denied them in colonialist accounts, some subalternist writers have overstated the contrast between organized and unorganized (i.e. elite-mass) arenas of politics. This dichotomy leaves no place for intermediary structures of authority that had a popular base and yet linked their activities to the "organized" world of elections and council politics. An example of this was the role played by itinerant *maulvis*, one group of political actors who were not of the traditional elite but who did mobilize Bengali Muslims around political symbols. Legitimized by their claim to moral authority at a popular level and the support of a class of socially mobile peasants with increased political status, the *maulvis* and the religious organizations, the *anjumans*, linked peasant concerns with a self-consciously Muslim identity.

The subalternists also have difficulty with "instrumentalist" politics that presume that elites manipulate mass responses to political symbols. The argument that political actors plan and carry out acts of communal violence challenges certain assumptions common to colonialist, nationalist and subaltern "constructions" of communal violence. Though they differ in their conclusions about the motivations behind communal violence, all three share a common flaw in attributing either irrationality or an idealized class consciousness to those who participate in acts of violence. In addition, all three fail to adequately account for the role of the state in promoting and perpetrating communal violence.

This is not to say that no incident of "subaltern" violence is spontaneous, or that there is not an element of spontaneity in crowd violence. Many of the incidents that most concern the subalterns involve peasant uprisings and other acts of resistance against colonial exploitation. And certainly within incidents of "communal" violence there may be acts of violence motivated by personal or economic considerations. But as Amrita Basu has observed, an approach which attempts to understand identity construction only "from below," that is, apart from the influence of formal state and political institutions, underestimates the importance of local state institutions in creating opportunities and reasons for groups to forge separate political agendas. The state, in this analysis, includes not only those mechanisms operating at the national level, but more importantly the local institutions, including the police, which are likely to be under the control of other elements of civil society including political parties.[31] The 1926 elections provided the context for increased conflict as rival Muslim leaders exploited opportunities for communal tension to discredit one another and bolster their own standing. Political changes created conditions for competition between the Congress, the Swarajists, and the various Muslim parties. For much of this time, however, the political cleavages that divided these groups were not "communal," that is, Hindu-Muslim. Throughout this period, the Muslim leadership in Bengal was riven with internal feuds. The possibility of constructing a separate political culture depended on changing popular perceptions about what a Bengali Muslim should be. The years between 1926 and 1941 opened up new opportunities for Muslim leaders in Bengal to position themselves as leaders of a community which was self-consciously Muslim. This generation of Muslim leaders represented a constituency with its roots in rural east Bengal which was newly conscious of its "Muslim" identity and which had seen the benefits of that identity in status and power. The "communal" violence of the 1920s and 1930s reflected the renegotiation of political power within the Muslim leadership. Muslim leaders seeking to challenge those identified by the British as the "natural" and legitimate representatives of the Muslim community used public spaces to assert their own claims to represent Bengali Muslims and interpret tradition.

In the final years before partition, the Bengal Muslim League splintered into rival factions in the province, each claiming to represent the interests of Bengali Muslims but promoting very different policies. The formation of the Muslim League-Krishak Praja party coalition government in Bengal in 1937 was critical in determining what symbols would be used to generate popular support for the Pakistan movement in Bengal. The struggle for control of the Bengal Ministry was waged over winning peasant support and capturing the language and symbols of agrarian reform.

For the League, the use of aggressively Muslim symbols in the last years before partition paralleled the party's abdication of any commitment to land reform and reflected the ambivalence of Jinnah and other national Muslim League leaders about building a mass-based organization in Bengal. Rather than challenge the Muslim League by taking up the agrarian cause, the Bengal Congress' *bhadrolok* leadership instead mirrored the League by identifying itself with "Hindu" interests. In the aftermath of the last violent episodes of communal violence, the League could successfully frame its appeal to Bengal Muslims on the vision of a Muslim homeland where Muslims could be safe. By creating out of the violence symbols that cut across class and other divisions, League leaders succeeded in mobilizing support among Bengali Muslims for the movement for a separate state of Pakistan, but their success in that effort was fleeting. Their failure to reconcile more fundamental issues that divided Bengali Muslim society meant that they failed to construct a political identity that could continue to provide a logic for union in the years that followed.

Notes

1. See Human Rights Watch, *Playing the Communal 'Card'* (New York: Human Rights Watch, 1995).

2. Gyanendra Pandey summarizes this line of thought in the introduction to *The Construction of Communalism in North India,* pp. 6–7.

3. Pandey argues that the term "communalism" is never applied to similar conflicts in Europe, such as the one in Northern Ireland. However, since the genocidal conflict in the former Yugoslavia broke out in 1991, similar analyses emphasizing "ancient hatreds" between Serbs and Bosnian Muslims and between Serbs and Croats have surfaced, and the term "communalism" has been used to describe ethnic conflicts in other countries. See ibid.

4. Brass, 1997, p. 283.

5. In October and December 1990 there were violent outbreaks in a number of cities, including Ahmedabad, Allahabad, Baroda, Bijnor, and Hyderabad.

6. Basu, pp. 2,605–2,621. The details of the incident come from this account.

7. Shiv Sena means army of Shiva; the Vishnu Hindu Parishad is the World Hindu Council; Bajrang Dal is the VHP's youth wing.

8. Rumors had circulated that the *kar sevaks* (volunteer workers) had taken possession of the mosque and had begun to demolish it. In fact, that did not take place until two years later. The Babri Masjid was destroyed by *kar sevaks* on December 6, 1992.

9. Basu, p. 2,617.

10. Ibid., p. 2,620, n. 1.

11. Ibid., pp. 2,620; 2,621, n. 10.

12. Ibid., p. 2,620.

13. Javeed Alam, "The Changing Grounds of Communal Mobilization: The Majlis-E-Ittehad-Ul-Muslimeen and the Muslims of Hyderabad," in Gyanendra Pandey, ed., *Hindus and Others: The Question of Identity in India Today* (New Delhi: Viking Penguin, Ltd., 1993), pp. 146–76.

14. The Majlis was founded in 1927 as an organization dedicated to uniting Muslims in the princely state of Hyderabad and protecting their interests. Its military wing was responsible for attacks on Hindus in 1946–47 until independent India incorporated the princely state into the federal union in a brutal police action. Ibid., p. 149.

15. Ibid., p. 153.

16. Alam notes that in his travels around India, Muslims would frequently ask him, "Are there riots in your area? Are Muslims safe there?" Ibid., p. 172.

17. Alam, pp. 161–162.

18. Hyderabad had suffered a number of communal disturbances in the prepartition period.

19. Alam, pp. 155–157.

20. Ibid., p. 157.

21. Rudolph, Lloyd I., and Susanne Hoeber Rudolph, *In Pursuit of Lakshmi: The Political Economy of the Indian State* (Chicago: University of Chicago Press, 1987), pp. 93–94.

22. Paul Brass describes the "characteristic mode" of local police as "implicated directly in local conflicts, open to bribery, capable of looting and harassing innocent persons and of vicious retaliatory actions against those who are not so innocent, and a potential danger to the exercise of state and national power when they cannot be controlled effectively at the local level and cannot be used to re-

strain and conceal potentially embarrassing situations rather than creating them." Brass, 1997, p. 203.

23. Alam, p. 150.

24. Brass, 1997, p. 284.

25. Ibid., p. 39.

26. Stanley Tambiah, *Leveling Crowds: Ethnonationalist Conflicts and Collective Violence in South Asia* (Berkeley, CA: University of California Press, 1996), p. 223.

27. Ibid., p. 323.

28. Sandria Freitag has used this term to describe the British policy of identifying "those exercising power through personal, patron-client relationships, whether operating through residential, occupational, caste, ritual, or extended kinship networks" as their intermediaries. See Freitag, 1989a, p. 57.

29. See in particular Freitag, 1989a.

30. "History of the Non-cooperation Movement and Khilafat Movement in Bengal," 3.c. F. 395/24, p. 5 (9). WBSA.

31. Basu, p. 2,619.

Glossary of
Selected Terms

abwabs   illegal taxes
achkan   Turkish-style hat
Allah o Akbar   "God is great"
anjuman   society, associations
ashraf   those who trace their lineage to the Prophet Mohammed, or his
   companions; in India the term is used to refer to the Muslim elite

bargadars   sharecroppers
bahas   religious debates
Bande Mataram   Hail to the Mother, referring to the Hindu goddess
bhadrolok   respectable people; the Hindu elite
bhakti   devotional religious movement
burqa   cape-like garment covering the body from head to toe; worn by
   women in very conservative Muslim societies
bustees   slums

dacoits   bandits
dalan   bathing place attached to a mosque
dar-ul-harb   zone of war
Dalit   "untouchable"; member of the lowest castes
desi   indigenous
dharma   religion, moral code
dhoti   a wrapped and tucked lower body garment worn by Bengali
   Hindu men
dobhasi   literally, two languages: the mixture of Persian or Urdu and Bengali spoken by some Bengali Muslims in the late 1800s and early 1900s

farz   obligatory duties of Islam
fatwa   formal legal opinion issued by a qualified religious authority, pl.
   fatawa
fez   hat

goondas criminals
gurudwara Sikh temple

hajj the annual pilgrimage to Mecca
hartal strike or boycott
Hindutva Hindu rule

'*Id* two Muslim holy days commemorating the end of Ramadan
  and Abraham's offer to sacrifice his son Isaac, 'Id-ul-Azha and
  'Id-ul-fitr
'*idgah* open field or park where 'id prayers are held

jihad a war carried out against unbelievers
jolahas weavers
jotedar landholder below a *zamindar*
jumna community

kabuliyat deed of property
Kali Hindu goddess of a frequently fierce demeanor
khalifa successor, particularly the successors to the Prophet
khanqah Sufi hospice
khatians settlement papers
Khilafat Persian rendering of caliphate; the institution of the caliph of
  Islam
ki-jaya or *ki jai* victory
korbani cow sacrifice
krishak peasant
krishak samitis peasant organizations

lathi truncheon made of bamboo
lathikhel martial arts practice involving *lathis*
lungi cloth worn around the lower part of the body

madrasah college of religious studies
mahajan money lender
maulana title given to religious leaders
maulvi learned man
mofussil Muslim leaders in rural areas
mohalla neighborhood or quarter
mohalla sardars neighborhood leaders
momin faithful
Muharram first month of the Islamic year when the death of Hosain is
  commemorated
mutavalli managers of Mosques

para   neighborhood
patta   lease
patwari   schoolmaster
pir   Sufi mystic or saint
piratta   rent-free land dedicated to a pir
praja   tenant
pucca   well-made, solid; a paved road instead of a dirt one
puja   religious worship or festival
puthi   Muslim Bengali religious tracts

raiyat   peasant
raj   rule, government

salami   landlord's transfer fees
samitis   groups
Shivaji   Maharashtrian leader 1627–1680 who fought the Mughals
sharafatnama   certificate of respectability
shuddhi   reconversion   (from Islam to Hinduism)
swadeshi   indigenous, self-made
sunnyasi   Hindu mendicant who has renounced the world

tabligh   proselytization (Muslim)
tariqah   Sufi spiritual path
Tariqah-i Muhammadiya   Nineteenth century Muslim reform movement
thana   police precinct
topi   a kind of hat

Vaisnav   relating to the Hindu god Vishnu

waqf   an endowment or trust held for religious purposes (Islam)

zamindar   substantial landholder in post-colonial and colonial India

Bibliography

Printed Books

Ahmad, Aziz. *Studies in Islamic Culture in the Indian Environment*. Oxford: Oxford University Press, 1969.

Ahmed, Imtiaz, ed. *Caste and Social Stratification Among the Muslims*. Delhi: Manohar Book Service, 1973.

Ahmed, Rafiuddin. *The Bengal Muslims 1871–1906: A Quest for Identity*. Delhi: Oxford University Press, 1981.

Ahmed, Sufia. *Muslim Community in Bengal 1884–1912*. Dacca: Oxford University Press, 1974.

Akzin, Benjamin. *State and Nation*. London: Hutchinson University Library, 1964.

Anisuzzaman, ed. *Muslim Banglar Samayik Patra, 1831–1930*. Dacca, 1968.

Brass, Paul. *Ethnicity and Nationalism: Theory and Comparison*. New Delhi: Sage Publications, 1991.

———. *Theft of an Idol: Text and Context in the Representation of Collective Violence*. Princeton, NJ: Princeton University Press, 1997.

———. *Language, Religion and Politics in North India*. Oxford: Oxford University Press, 1974.

Bose, Sugata. *Agrarian Bengal: Economy, Social Structure and Politics, 1919–1947*. Cambridge: Cambridge University Press, 1986.

Broomfield, J. H. *Elite Conflict in a Plural Society: Twentieth Century Bengal*. Berkeley: University of California Press, 1968.

Chatterjee, Bankim Chandra. *Anandamath*. Translated from Bengali by Aurobindo and B. Ghosh. Calcutta, 1906.

Chatterjee, Partha. *Bengal 1920–1947: The Land Question*. Calcutta: K. P. Bagchi, 1984.

———. *Nationalist Thought and the Colonial World: A Derivative Discourse?* London: Zed Books, 1986.

Cohn, Bernard S. *An Anthropologist among the Historians and Other Essays*. Delhi: Oxford University Press, 1987.

Das, Suranjan. *Communal Riots in Bengal 1905–1947*. Delhi: Oxford University Press, 1991.

Das, Veena, ed. *Mirrors of Violence: Communities, Riots and Survivors in South Asia*. Delhi: Oxford University Press, 1992.

Das Gupta, Shashibhushan. *Obscure Religious Cults*, 2nd ed. Calcutta: K. L. Mukhopadhyaya, 1962.

Deutsch, Karl M. *Nationalism and Social Communication: An Inquiry into the Foundations of Nationality*, 2nd ed. Cambridge, MA: Massachusetts Institute of Technology Press, 1966.

De Vos, George, and Lola Romanucci-Ross, eds. *Ethnic Identity, Cultural Continuities and Change*. Palo Alto, CA: Mayfield Publishing Co., 1975.

Eaton, Richard M. *The Rise of Islam and the Bengal Frontier*. Berkeley: University of California Press, 1993.

Engineer, Asghar Ali, ed. *Communal Riots in Post-Independence India*. New Delhi: Sangam Books, 1984.

Freitag, Sandria B. *Collective Action and Community: Public Arenas and the Emergence of Communalism in North India*. Berkeley: University of California Press, 1989 (cited as 1989a).

———, ed. *Culture and Power in Banaras: Community, Performance and Environment, 1800–1980*. Berkeley: University of California Press, 1989 (cited as 1989b).

Gandhi, Mohandas. *Collected Works of Mahatma Gandhi*. Delhi: Publications Division, Ministry of Information and Broadcasting, Government of India, 1958.

Gilmartin, David. *Empire and Islam*. Berkeley: University of California Press, 1988.

Gordon, Leonard A. *Bengal: The Nationalist Movement 1876–1940*. New York: Columbia University Press, 1974.

Paul R. Greenough. *Prosperity and Misery in Modern Bengal: The Famine of 1943–44*. New York: Oxford University Press, 1982.

Guha, Ranajit and Gayatri Chakravorty Spivak, eds. *Selected Subaltern Studies*. Oxford: Oxford University Press, 1988.

Guha, Ranajit, ed. *Subaltern Studies I: Writings on South Asian History and Society*. Delhi: Oxford University Press, 1982.

———, ed. *Subaltern Studies II: Writings on South Asian History and Society*. Delhi: Oxford University Press, 1983.

———, ed. *Subaltern Studies III: Writings on South Asian History and Society*. Delhi: Oxford University Press, 1984.

———, ed. *Subaltern Studies IV: Writings on South Asian History and Society*. Delhi: Oxford University Press, 1985.

———, ed. *Subaltern Studies V: Writings on South Asian History and Society*. Delhi: Oxford University Press, 1987.

———, ed. *Subaltern Studies VI: Writings on South Asian History and Society*. Delhi: Oxford University Press, 1989.

Hardy, Peter. *The Muslims of British India*. Cambridge: Cambridge University Press, 1972.

Hashim, Abul. *In Retrospection*. Dacca: Nowroze Kitabistan, 1974.

Hobsbawm, Eric J. *Primitive Rebels: Studies in Archaic Forms of Social Movement in the 19th and 20th Centuries*. New York: Manchester University Press, 1967.

Hobsbawm, Eric J. and Terence Ranger, eds. *The Invention of Tradition*. Cambridge: Cambridge University Press, 1983.

Hodgson, Marshall G.S. *The Venture of Islam: Conscience and History in a World Civilization: The Gunpowder Empires and Modern Times*, Vol. 3. Chicago: The University of Chicago Press, 1974.

Huque, Azizul. *The Man Behind the Plough*. Dhaka: Bangladesh Books International Ltd., 1939.

Human Rights Watch. *Playing the Communal 'Card.'* New York: Human Rights Watch, 1995.

Hunter, W. W. *The Indian Musulmans: Are They Bound in Conscience to Rebel Against the Queen?* Calcutta: Government of Bengal, 1871.

Islam, Mustafa Nurul. *Bengali Muslim Public Opinion as Reflected in the Bengali Press 1901–1930.* Dhaka: Bangla Akademi, 1973.

Jahan, Rounaq. *Pakistan: Failure in National Integration.* New York: Columbia University Press, 1971.

Jalal, Ayesha. *The Sole Spokesman: Jinnah, the Muslim League and the Demand for Pakistan.* Cambridge: Cambridge University Press, 1985.

Karim, Abdul. *A Social History of the Muslims of Bengal, Down to A.D. 1538.* Dhaka, 1959.

Khan, Muin-ud-din Ahmed. *History of the Fara'idi Movement in Bengal, 1818–1906.* Karachi: Pakistan Historical Society, 1965.

Lelyveld, David. *Aligarh's First Generation: Muslim Solidarity in British India.* Princeton: Princeton University Press, 1978.

McPherson, Kenneth. *The Muslim Microcosm: Calcutta, 1918 to 1935.* Wiesbaden: Franz Steiner, 1974.

Metcalf, Barbara. *Islamic Revival in British India: Deoband, 1860–1900.* Princeton: Princeton University Press, 1982.

Minault, Gail. *The Khilafat Movement: Religious Symbolism and Political Mobilization in India.* Delhi: Oxford University Press, 1982.

Mookerjee, Radharamon. *Occupancy Right: Its History and Incident.* Calcutta: Calcutta University Press, 1919.

Neal, Frank. *Sectarian Violence: The Liverpool Experience, 1819–1914, An Aspect of Anglo-Irish History.* Manchester: Manchester University Press, 1988.

Pandey, Gyanendra. *The Construction of Communalism in Colonial North India.* Delhi: Oxford University Press, 1990.

———, ed. *Hindus and Others: The Question of Identity in India Today.* New Delhi: Viking Penguin Ltd., 1993.

Philips, C. H., ed. *Patron and Society in India.* London: George Allen and Unwin, 1963.

Ray, Rajat Kanta. *Social Conflict and Political Unrest in Bengal 1875–1927.* Delhi: Oxford University Press, 1984.

Robinson, Francis. *Separatism Among Indian Muslims: The Politics of the United Provinces' Muslims, 1860–1923.* Cambridge: Cambridge University Press, 1974.

Rudé, George. *The Crowd in History.* New York: Wiley, 1959.

Rudolph, Lloyd I. and Susanne Hoeber Rudolph. *In Pursuit of Lakshmi: The Political Economy of the Indian State.* Chicago: University of Chicago Press, 1987.

Said, Edward. *Orientalism.* New York: Random House, 1978.

Sarkar, Jadunath. *History of Aurangzeb.* London, 1920.

Sarkar, Sumit. *The Swadeshi Movement in Bengal: 1903–1908.* New Delhi: People's Publishing House, 1973.

Sarkar, Tanika. *Bengal 1928–1934: The Politics of Protest.* Delhi: Oxford University Press, 1987.

Sen, Shila. *Muslim Politics in Bengal, 1937–47.* Delhi: Impex, 1976.

Stevenson, John. *Public Disturbances in England, 1700–1832.* London: Longman, 1979.

Talbot, Ian. *Provincial Politics and the Pakistan Movement*. Karachi: Oxford University Press, 1988.

Tambiah, Stanley. *Leveling Crowds: Ethnonationalist Conflicts and Collective Violence in South Asia*. Berkeley: University of California Press, 1996.

Wise, James. *Notes on the Races, Castes and Tribes of Eastern Bengal*. London: 1883.

Wolpert, Stanley. *A New History of India*. Oxford: Oxford University Press, 1979.

Yinger, J. Milton. *Ethnicity: Source of Strength? Source of Conflict?* Albany, NY: State University of New York Press, 1994.

Zaidi, A. M., ed. *Evolution of Muslim Political Thought in India*, Vol. 2. New Delhi, 1975.

Articles

Alam, Javeed. "The Changing Grounds of Communal Mobilization: The Majlis-E-Ittehad-Ul-Muslimeen and the Muslims of Hyderabad." In Gyanendra Pandey, ed., *Hindus and Others, The Question of Identity in India Today*. New Delhi: Viking Penguin Ltd., 1993.

Basu, Amrita. "When Local Riots are not Merely Local: Bringing the State Back In, Bijnor 1988–1992." *Economic and Political Weekly*, Vol. 29, No. 40, October 1, 1994.

Bertocci, Peter. "Models of Solidarity; Structures of Power: The Politics of Community in Rural Bangladesh." In Myron Aronoff, ed., *Political Anthropology Yearbook I: Ideology and Interest: The Dialectics of Politics*. New Brunswick: Transaction Books, 1980.

Chakravarty, Dipesh. "Communal Riots and Labour: Bengal's Jute Mill-Hands in the 1890's." *Past and Present*, No. 91 (May 1981).

Chatterjee, Partha. "Agrarian Relations and Communalism in Bengal." In Ranajit Guha, ed., *Subaltern Studies I: Writings on South Asian History and Society*. Delhi: Oxford University Press, 1982.

Dimock, Edward C., Jr. "Hinduism and Islam in Medieval Bengal." In Rachel Van M. Baumer, ed., *Aspects of Bengali History and Society*. Hawaii: University of Hawaii Press, 1975.

Engineer, Asghar Ali. "Communal Violence and Role of Police." *Economic and Political Weekly*, Vol. 29, No. 15 (April 9, 1994).

Freitag, Sandria B. "State and Community: Symbolic Popular Protest in Banaras's Public Arena." In Sandria B. Freitag, ed., *Culture and Power in Banaras: Community, Performance and Environment, 1800–1980*. Berkeley: University of California Press, 1989.

Gossman, Patricia A. "Poets and Politics: Some Reflections on the Language Movement in East Pakistan." In Ray Langsten, ed., *Research on Bengal: Proceedings of the 1981 Bengal Studies Conference*. East Lansing, MI: Asian Studies Center, Michigan State University, 1983.

Kaplan, Robert D. "The Coming Anarchy." *Atlantic Monthly*, Vol. 273, No. 2 (February 1994).

Mathew, George. "Politicization of Religion: Conversion to Islam in Tamil Nadu," Parts 1 and 2. *Economic and Political Weekly*, June 19 and 26, 1982.

McLane, John R. "The 1905 Partition and the New Communalism." In Alexander Lipski, ed., *Bengal: East and West*. East Lansing, MI: Asian Studies Center, Michigan State University, 1969.

Pandey, Gyanendra. "In Defence of the Fragment: Writing About Hindu-Muslim Riots in India Today." *Representations*, No. 37 (Winter 1992).

Sarkar, Sumit. "The Conditions and Nature of Subaltern Militancy: Bengal from Swadeshi to Non-Cooperation, c. 1905–22." In Ranajit Guha, ed., *Subaltern Studies III: Writings on South Asian History and Society*. Delhi: Oxford University Press, 1984.

Sen Gupta, K. K. "The Agrarian Leage of Pabna, 1873." *Indian Economic and Social History Review*, Vol. 7, No. 2 (1970).

Shah, Ghyanshyam. "Identity, Communal Consciousness and Politics." *Economic and Political Weekly*, Vol. 29, No. 19 (May 7, 1994).

Southard, Barbara. "The Political Strategy of Aurobindo Ghosh: The Utilization of Hindu Religious Symbolism and the Problem of Political Mobilization in Bengal." *Modern Asian Studies*, Vol. 14, No. 3 (1980).

Russell, Ralph. "Strands of Muslim Identity in South Asia." *Journal of Asian Studies*, Vol. 35, No. 1 (November 1975).

Unpublished Papers

Freitag, Sandria B. "Religious Rites and Riots: From Community Identity to Communalism in North India, 1870–1940." Unpublished PhD. Dissertation. Berkeley: Department of History, University of California, 1980.

Lal, Vinay. "Committees of Inquiry and Discourses of 'Law and Order' in Twentieth-Century British India." University of Chicago: Doctoral Dissertation, 1992.

Rudolph, Susanne Hoeber. "Now You See Them, Now You Don't; Historicizing the Salience of Religious Categories." Paper presented at conference on "Religious Forces in the New World Disorder" at the University of California at Santa Barbara, February 23, 1995.

Government Documents

Political Records and Files:

Archives of the Freedom Movement, University of Karachi, Karachi, Pakistan

Bangla Akademi, Dhaka, Bangladesh

India Office Library (British Museum and Library, London)

National Archives of Bangladesh, Bangladesh Secretariat, Dhaka, Bangladesh

National Archives of India (NAI), New Delhi

Nehru Memorial Museum and Library, New Delhi

Qaid-e Azam Academy, Karachi, Pakistan

West Bengal State Archives, Calcutta

Published Reports

Bell, F. O. *Final Report on the Survey and Settlement Operations in the District of Dinajpur, 1934–1940*. Alipore: Bengal Government Press, 1941.

Calcutta University Commission 1917–1918 Report, Vol. 1. Government of India, 1920.

Census of India, 1911, Vol. 5: Bengal, Bihar and Orissa, and Sikkim, Part 1. Calcutta, 1913.

Colson, L. H., Commissioner of Police, *Annual Report on Police Administration of Calcutta and Suburbs for 1937*. Calcutta: Bengal Government Press, 1938.

Gordon, A. D., Inspector-General of Police, *Report on the Police Administration in the Province of Bengal excluding Calcutta and its suburbs for the year 1941*. Calcutta: Bengal Government Press, 1942.

Report of the Land Revenue Commission. Government of Bengal, 1940.

Report of the Dacca Riots Enquiry Committee. Calcutta: Government of Bengal, 1942.

Report of the Non-Official Commission on the Calcutta Disturbances, 1918. Calcutta: Bangiya Jana Sabha, 1919.

Report on the Administration of Bengal, 1921–22. Calcutta: Bengal Secretariat Press, 1923.

Report on Bengal and Assam: Papers relating to the Reconstitution of the Provinces of. Simla: Government Central Printing Office, 1906.

Report on the Calcutta Riots of April 1926, First Phase—2nd to 15th April. Calcutta: Bengal Government Press, 1926.

Report of the Working of the Reformed Constitution. Government of Bengal, 1927.

Report on the Calcutta Riots of July 1926, 11th to 25th July. Calcutta: Bengal Government Press, 1926.

Report of the Dacca Disturbances Enquiry Committee. Government of Bengal, 1930.

Sachse, F. A. *Final Report on the Survey and Settlement Operations in the District of Mymensingh, 1908–1919*. Calcutta: Bengal Secretariat Book Depot, 1920.

Newspapers Consulted (selected issues)

Amrita Bazar Patrika
Azad
Bengalee
Dhaka Prokash
Indian Quarterly Register
Moslem Chronicle
Modern Review
Mussulman

Ephemera

Mia, Adeb Ali. *Polli-Dosa*. Panatipara, Rangpur: Abed Ali Mia, 1925, at National Library of India, Calcutta.

Index

Abwabs, 32, 144
Ahmed, Rafiuddin, 27
Alam, Javeed, 162
Ali, Mohammad, 55, 63
Ali, Shaukat, 55, 63
Ali, Syed Amir, 27
Anjumans, 28–29, 32, 40, 49, 51, 53, 67, 89, 92, 166
Arya Samaj, 32, 70, 76, 78–79, 86
Ashraf Muslims, 21, 22, 40, 41, 65, 166
Assam, 35. *See also* Eastern Bengal and Assam, province of
Ayodhya, 1, 2, 161
Azad
    attacks on A. K. Fazlul Huq, 153
    supporting agrarian reform, 144–145
    use of religious rhetoric, 142
Azad, Abul Kalam, 55, 80

Babri Masjid, 2
"Backwardness"
    of Bengali Muslims, 25–26, 27, 35
    of Indian Muslims, 25–26
    exploited during Non-cooperation campaign, 64
Bande Mataram, 37, 87, 107, 116, 117, 122
    as issue at Calcutta University, 150
Bangladesh, 5
Barelwi, Sayyid Ahmad, 24
Basu, Amrita, 84, 161
Bayly, C. A., 50
Bengal
    partition of, in 1905, 4, 34, 40, 41

repeal of 1905 partition, in 1911, 4, 40–42, 49, 51
    See also Eastern Bengal and Assam, province of
Bengali language, 5, 165
Bengali Muslim leadership
    fragmentation of, 129
    power struggle within, 103, 105–106, 109–110, 167–168
Bengali Muslims, efforts to become "more Muslim," 26–27, 69
Bengal Provincial Muslim League, 41
    fight for control over, 152–155
    internal divisions in, 139
    split with All-India Muslim League, 139–140
Bhadrolok, 34–35, 63, 64, 66, 142, 147, 170
Bhakti movement, 23
Bharatiya Janata Party (BJP), 161–163
Bombay, riots of January 1993, 13
Bose, Sarat 127, 153
Bose, Subhas Chandra, 127, 147, 150
Brass, Paul, 6, 25, 160, 164
Broomfield, J. H., 78, 147

Calcutta
    "riot" of 1918, 8, 53, 54, 56–63, 73, 91
    "riots" of 1926, 8, 75–86, 91
Calcutta Municipal (Amendment) Act, as election issue, 147
Calcutta University
    crest of, as target of Muslim protest, 150
    as election issue, 146–147

Census, identifying Muslim names in,
     26–27
Central Muslim Party, 113
Central National Muhammadan
     Association, 27
Chatterjee, Bankim Chandra, 37
Chatterjee, Partha, 32, 88, 89, 90, 108
Chauri Chaura, 63, 71
Commissions of inquiry
     by the Congress Party, 119, 123, 124
     as means of identifying
          communalism, 137
     Muslim League, 148–151
     official, 62
Congress Party, x, 5, 7, 67, 70, 93, 105,
     115–117, 120
     attracting Muslim leaders, 117, 118,
          166
     Bengal Provincial Congress
          Committee, 127, 131
     blamed for abuses against Muslims,
          148–149
     civil disobedience campaign and,
          120–122, 147
     elections of 1937 and, 142–146, 147
Cow protection. See Korbani
Criminals, role in communal violence,
     13, 79, 84
Curzon, Lord, 34

Dacca
     "riot" of 1926, 105, 106–114
     "riot" of 1930, 117–124
     "riot" of 1941, 125–128, 151
Das, C. R., 54, 70–71
Das, Veena, 13
Deoband School, 89
Dhaka. See Dacca
District Moslem Association, 110–112,
     122

Eastern Bengal and Assam, province
     of, 19. See also Bengal
Education, Muslims and, 24–28, 66–67,
     73
Elections of 1937, agrarian issues and,
     142–143

Engineer, Asghar Ali, 9–10
Ethnic identity, 2, 6
     as a political construction, 1, 2, 3, 6
     primordialist analysis of, 1, 6

Fara'idi movement, 21, 23–24, 26, 88
Farangi Mahal, 59
Forward Bloc Party, 127, 153
Freitag, Sandria B., 10, 13, 59, 74, 109

Gandhi, Indira, ix
Gandhi, Mohandas, 6, 12, 51, 70, 71
     calls off Non-cooperation campaign,
          63
Gilmartin, David, 4, 23, 77
Government of India Act of 1919, 52,
     53, 167
Government of India Act of 1935, 125,
     167
"Great Calcutta Killing," 154
Guha, Ranajit, 12

Hashim, Abul, 152
     disputes with Muslim League
          leadership, 153–154
     efforts to build mass-based Muslim
          League, 153
Hindu Mahasabha, 70, 76, 78, 79, 90,
     110, 115, 119, 122, 127, 137, 150,
     153, 154
Hindu-Muslim Pact, 51, 54, 70–71, 84
Hindutva, 13
Hobsbawm, Eric J., 10, 75
Hunter, W. W., 24–25, 27–28
Huq, A. K. Fazlul, 61, 62, 65, 68, 70, 71,
     113, 130, 138
     accused of bias during communal
          riots, 151
     attacks Congress Party, 149
     and Bengal Provincial Muslim
          League, 139
     criticized by Azad, 142
     heads ministry, 148
     resigns from Muslim League, 152

Independence Day disturbance,
     115–117, 118, 130

Independent Muslim Party, 113
Indian National Congress, 34–36. *See also* Congress Party
Israel, minority consciousness in, 18(n32)

Jami'at-i ulama-i Hind, 63, 72, 76
Janmastami celebration, 105, 106, 108–109, 114, 117, 130
Jinnah, Mohammad Ali, 138, 142
    conflict with A.K. Fazlul Huq, 153
Jotedars, 31, 32, 33, 36, 39, 66, 67, 68, 69, 112

Kanpur mosque affair, 55, 59–60, 91
Kaplan, Robert D., 2
Kashmir, 17(n29)
Khan, Liaqat Ali, 152
Khan, Maulana Akram, 63, 65, 68
Khilafat movement, 6, 42, 52–53, 54, 63–66, 68, 72, 75, 89, 92, 93, 138, 166, 168
Korbani (cow sacrifice), 32–33, 38, 74
Krishak Praja Party, x, 67, 71, 131, 138, 140, 146
    coalition with Muslim League, 136, 143–147, 151, 170
    elections of 1937, 141–142
    loses membership to Muslim League, 154–155

Liverpool, processions in, 105

Malaviya, Pandit Madan Mohan, 70, 84
Marwaris, 61, 62, 79
Maulvis, 21, 32, 38–40, 42, 65, 88–89, 113–114, 136, 168
Mir, Titu, 24
Miyan, Dudu, 23, 24
Montague-Chelmsford Reforms, 68
Mughals, 21, 22
Music before mosques, 74–75
    Calcutta "riots" of 1926 and, 75–76, 82–83

Dacca "riots" of 1926 and, 106–114, 115
    Pabna "riots" of 1926 and, 87, 90
Muslim League, x, 5–6, 40, 41, 63, 71, 77, 85, 167
    coalition with Krishak Praja Party, 136, 143–147, 170
    commissions of inquiry. *See* Commissions of inquiry, Muslim League
    Direct Action Day, 154
    elections of 1937, 142, 147
    fight for control of the Bengal Provincial Muslim League, 152–155
    founding of, 35
    Fourteen Points, 118
    growth of, in Bengal, 147, 167

Nawab. *See* Salimulla, Nawab of Dacca
Nazimuddin, Khwaja, 142, 153
Nehru, Jawaharlal, 12
Non-Cooperation movement, 52, 54, 63–66, 67, 68, 75, 77, 92, 138, 166, 168
    effect of, on Congress Party in Bengal, 147

Pabna
    disturbances of 1870s in, 30
    disturbances of 1926 in, 86, 91–92
Pabna Agrarian League, 30
Pakistan, 155, 165, 170
Pandey, Gyanendra, 2, 11, 25, 33, 74, 77
Permanent Settlement of 1793, 29, 68, 144
Pirs, 4, 22
Police, bias among, 38, 85, 124, 128
Praja movement, 66–70, 131, 138
    All-Bengal Praja Samiti, 140
    and elections of 1937, 141–147
Processions, significance of, 104, 117, 126
Progressive Coalition Assembly Party, 153

Provincial Muhammadan Association, 111–112
Punjab, conflict in, 4, 17(n29)
Puthis, 39–40, 41

Rahim, Abdur, 58, 62, 77, 78, 82–86
Ray, Rajat, 31, 78
Rent Act of 1859, 31
Robinson, Francis, 25
Rude, George, 10
Rumor, role of in communal violence, 84, 86–87
Rwanda, 1, 2

Salimulla, Nawab of Dacca, 35–37, 42, 51, 54–56, 71–72, 93, 105, 108, 110–112, 117–118
    challenge to his authority, 122–123, 139
    as "natural" leader of the Muslims, 120, 166
Sarkar, Sumit, 32, 36, 39, 40
Sen, Paritosh, 108
Sen, Shila, 85
Shah, Ghanshyam, 89
Shariatullah, Haji, 22, 23
Shiv Sena, 13
Shivaji procession, 105, 114–115, 118
Sikh massacre of 1984, ix, 10
Singh, Ranjit, 24
Spivak, Gayatri Chakravorty, 84
Sri Lanka, minorities in, 18(n32)
Subaltern school, 3, 4, 6, 7, 50, 84, 168–169
Suhrawardy, Hussein, 58, 62, 78–80, 82, 84, 86, 113
    as head of ministry, 153
Swadeshi movement
    during anti-parition agitation 1905–1911, 20–21, 36, 38–41, 53, 62, 63, 65, 73, 85, 87, 89
    as part of Non-cooperation movement, 63
Swaraj Party, 51, 52, 67, 70–71, 75, 77, 113, 131, 140, 147

Tambiah, Stanley, 165
Tantric Buddhism, 21
Tariqah-i-Muhammadiyah, 24
Tenancy Act of 1859, 29–30, 66
Tenancy Act of 1885, 30–31, 66, 73
    revision of, in 1928, 140–141, 143–145, 146
    revision of, in 1938, 141
Turkey
    early influence on Bengal, 21
    focus of Indian Muslims' concern, 28, 55–59

United Muslim Party, 138, 142
Urdu, 5
    controversy over Congress Party's support for Hindi, 148
Uttar Pradesh, Muslims of, 3, 25

Vaisnava sects in Bengal, 21
Violence
    as attack on status order, 105, 167
    colonialist discourse on, 10–11, 49, 104, 123, 168
    as defining communalism, 165
    insurgent *versus* "communal," 12
    routinization of, 130, 165
    used to discredit Congress Party, 123
    used to discredit "nationalist" Muslims in Bengal, 105

Wahhabis, 24, 58, 88

Yinger, J. Milton, 2
Yugoslavia (former), 1